INTENSIVE PSYCHOTHERAPY

of the

BORDERLINE PATIENT

COMMENTARY

"With the erudition and clinical sensitivity that characterizes his earlier work on the subject of psychotherapy, Chessick has now turned to the broad topic of narcissistic disorders. He has undertaken the ambitious task of integrating what is currently known about narcissistic psychopathology, in relation to both the analyzable narcissistic personality disorders and the so-called borderline patient.

"Chessick allows his readers to follow his hard-won understanding and treatment approach along with his sincere attempt at making sense of the widely disparate theories and technical precepts offered in the literature. He boldly strives to incorporate the views of Balint, Klein, Kernberg, Gedo, Goldberg, Kohut, Giovacchini, and others, astutely selecting the issues relevant to such an endeavor.

"The usefulness of Chessick's contribution lies in the fact that he illuminates his formulations with clinical vignettes and raises the central and still unanswered questions. This permits the reader to make his own evaluation of the various theories and techniques, guided by the fine, synthesizing mind of the author."

Paul Ornstein, M.D.

INTENSIVE
PSYCHOTHERAPY
of the
BORDERLINE PATIENT

RICHARD D. CHESSICK, M.D.

JASON ARONSON INC.
Northvale, New Jersey
London

Chessick, Richard D   1931-
    Intensive psychotherapy of the borderline patient.

    Bibliography: 10 p.
    Includes index.
    1. Pseudoneurotic schizophrenia. 2. Narcissism. 3. Psychotherapy.
I. Title. [DNLM: 1. Psychotherapy. WM420 C524i]
RC514.C47   616.8'5   76-22867
ISBN 0-87668-254-9

New Printing 1987

Manufactured in the United States of America

THIS BOOK IS DEDICATED
TO MY MOTHER

We are still underestimating the pathogenicity, but also the character-building, the personality-integrative role of preverbal levels of development; and we are underestimating in particular the importance of ego and superego precursors—and especially their capacity for creating hard-to-decipher proclivities to intrapsychic conflicts!

Margaret Mahler
Symbiosis and Individuation

Contents

PART IV:

PSYCHOTHERAPY—GENERAL APPROACH

PART V:

PSYCHOTHERAPY—SPECIAL PROBLEMS

PART VI:

METAPSYCHIATRY

Part I
HISTORICAL AND CLINICAL DESCRIPTION

CHAPTER 1

Introduction to the Concept

The concept of the borderline patient is poorly understood and vague, and it is almost lost in a semantic morass these days. Some psychiatrists wish to entirely discard the term—"borderline" of what? However, semantic disputes will not make the concept go away, and the present book is dedicated to improvement of our understanding and treatment of the borderline patient. It is written from the point of view of the psychotherapist; the clinician who treats patients day in and day out over the years and who wishes to understand the application of various theoretical conceptions about the borderline patient to the office practice of psychoanalytically informed psychotherapy.

The best overall review article (Gunderson and Singer 1975), which attempts to identify areas of agreement in the literature, reviews eighty-seven references—many of which on careful examination contradict each other. This overview paper enumerates a number of features most authors believe seem to characterize borderline patients. These features are

1. The presence of intense affect, "usually of a strongly hostile or depressed nature"
2. A history of impulsive behavior of all sorts
3. Fairly good social adaptiveness (at least apparently)
4. Brief psychotic experiences, which are likely to have a paranoid quality

5. Bizarre, dereistic, illogical or primitive responses on unstructured
    psychological tests such as the Rorschach, but not on more
    structured tests such as the WAIS. (Characteristically, their
    interpersonal relationships "vacillate between transient superfi-
    cial relationships and intense, dependent relationships that are
    marred by devaluation, manipulation, and demandingness.")

The borderline patient represents a frequently encountered type of
patient, posing special problems for the psychotherapist and the
general physician and a thorny challenge to those interested in the
etiology and nosology of mental illness (Mack 1975). Painful lack of
agreement about the concept has been known for some time. A serious
attempt was made by Grinker and his co-workers (Grinker et al., 1968)
using meticulous methodology, to try to better delineate the borderline
patient: "It matters little whether we call the borderline syndrome a
disease, an arrest of development, an emotional disturbance or a type
of behavioral deviance. Likewise it is restrictive to view the borderline
from a single frame of reference such as the biological, medical,
psychological or social. The borderline, like health and illness, is a
system in process occurring in time: developing, progressing and
regressing as a focus of a large biopsychosocial field."

I think that we have to stay with this rather profound conclusion also
in the light of current knowledge on the subject. Therefore, I have to
warn the reader that if he is hoping from this book to get *the* answers
about the diagnosis, dynamics and treatment of the borderline patient,
he will be bitterly disappointed. The current state of our knowledge on
the subject does *not* permit a resolution of the wide disagreement.

The best one can do at this time is to delineate the areas of general
agreement and indicate where there are unresolvable differences.
Summoning our patience, we then must look further at the clinical
material in the true tradition of psychoanalytically oriented psychotherapy and hope eventually, by further and further study and
accumulation of clinical experience, to resolve the disagreements. As
Freud wrote (1914), "I was not subject to influence from any quarter;
there was nothing to hustle me. I learnt to restrain speculative
tendencies and to follow the unforgotten advice of my master,
Charcot: to look at the same things again and again until they
themselves begin to speak."

The reader will discover fundamental and unresolvable differences of opinion as to the foundations of psychic development, and although we can discard a number of theories of basic development as being too flamboyant or too "far out" or contrary to common sense or reading like science fiction, there still is a fundamental disagreement in the literature from at least two basic points of view. This disagreement is not resolvable and leads to entirely different theories of the development and treatment of the borderline patient.

Although the term "borderline" appears from time to time in psychiatric writing, major credit for delineating this concept and making it clinically respectable goes to Stern. In three papers (Stern 1938, 1945, 1948), the first as early as 1938, he painted the clinical and psychodynamic picture in broad outline and discussed special problems in the treatment. Using the definitions of Freud in his famous paper "On Narcissism," Stern regarded narcissism as the basic underlying character component of these patients, leading to the development of an individual with certain typical personality features. These in Stern's terms are: (1) psychic bleeding—the patient goes down in a heap at each occurrence of stress in his life; (2) inordinate hypersensitivity—the patient is constantly insulted and injured by trifling remarks; (3) rigidity; (4) "negative therapeutic reaction"—a response of depression and anger to any interpretation, which is experienced as an injury to a patient's self esteem; (5) feelings of inferiority and lack of self-assurance; (6) a tendency toward masochism and wound licking—that is, toward self-pity and chronic depression; (7) a strange "pseudo-equanimity," or outward calm, which may be present, although not always, in spite of the inward chaos; (8) a tendency to use projection, especially with people in authority, and corresponding peculiarities in reality testing.

The study of the narcissistic neuroses, considered by Freud to be among the most difficult to approach, has come into the foreground in psychoanalytical research in the past fifteen years, together with an increased interest in ego function and research in the borderline psychoses and psychotic illnesses. Stern's (1938) first paper is entitled "Psychoanalytic Investigation of and Therapy in a Borderline Group of Neuroses" and is a very important study, giving a clinical description as well as an attempt at a therapeutic approach to what he calls the narcissistic character neuroses. According to Stern, the narcissistic neuroses are closely related to borderline psychoses and are in general unaffected by therapeutic methods successful with the classical psychoneuroses. It is on the basis of narcissism, he writes, that the entire clinical picture is built.

These patients suffer in the psychic field what Levy termed "affect hunger," and according to Stern this group never develops the sense of security from being loved that is the birthright of every child. Stern emphasized the borderline patient's "flatness of affect," in contrast to Gunderson's description mentioned above.

According to Stern, the patient cannot identify himself with the analyst except through illusion. That is, the patient never identifies himself with the analyst, but only with his conception of him through a process of projection of his own "ego ideal." It is this psychic figure which talks to the patient. Therefore, if the patient is told, for instance, that what he has just said indicates some suppressed hostility from childhood to an older brother or father, the patient literally collapses through fear of punishment by virtue of this having been discovered.

In further describing the transference difficulties, Stern adds that these patients very often react to a given interpretation with "chagrin, guilt, fear of punishment, and dread of not being approved." All the patient's energies are directed toward being approved and a real awareness or ego integration of his own behavior does not take place. Stern states, "Actually, the investigation of the transference phenomena informs us that as far as people go, these patients still live in a world of their own childhood—so that getting well and being adult are attained through wishing to be able to do what grown-ups do, and this they dare not risk. In the imagination it is easy enough and even while in the analysis, but independently the anxiety is too great."

Stern summarizes by saying that a certain vagueness in the paper is unavoidable because the material this group offered for study ran so clearly in two directions: the psychotic and the psychoneurotic. He insists that much more time and investigation are necessary to evaluate the rather obscure phenomena these patients present.

In 1945 Stern published an extension to his first paper entitled "Psychoanalytic Therapy in the Borderline Neuroses." This paper dealt with a technical change in therapeutic approach, namely, having the patient sit facing the analyst during the interviews rather than lie on the couch. Stern emphasizes the importance of the patience and *love capacity of the analyst* in affording the patient a corrective experience of his childhood environment, which conspicuously lacked libidinous giving. I remind the reader that this was thirty years ago.

Stern regarded the entire problem as a developmental injury caused by the lack of spontaneous affection from the mother. Such patients were described—as indeed they are described today, and correctly so—as traumatized preoedipal children suffering from a profound affect-hunger. I thing Greenson's (1958) "screen patients" also fall in this category.

The second author to make an important contribution to the subject was Deutsch (1965), who described the "as-if" personality, which represents a subclass of the borderline patient group. In general the as-if personality is an extreme caricature of Riesman's (1955) "other-directed" personality. Although he appears outwardly amiable, he has no identity of his own and is not capable of forming any genuine emotional attachment to people or moral principles. While there is a poverty of object relationships and again the central issue seems to revolve around narcissism, no obvious defect in reality testing is present; in fact, he may become a very successful politician or administrator.

The subject of the borderline patient gained tremendous current prominence with the introduction of new terms by well-known and highly respected authors. The first of these was "pseudo-neurotic schizophrenia," introduced and investigated by Hoch and his co-workers (Hoch 1949, 1959, 1962). Patients suffering from this disorder are characterized by "pananxiety"—they are made anxious by everything conceivable—and "panneuroses"—they present all varieties of neurotic symptoms, shifting back and forth over our nosological classifications. They may at times show clear-cut psychotic manifestations and even psychotic episodes, but these do not last and the patients as a rule do not deteriorate into chronic schizophrenic psychoses. Hoch vigorously opposed including pseudoneurotic schizophrenic patients among borderline patients; he considered them a variety of paranoid or catatonic schizophrenics.

However, clinical experience and common usage have tended to include pseudoneurotic patients among borderline patients, because their pananxiety and panneuroses make it impossible to classify them as either neurotic or psychotic and, more importantly, because these conditions do not deteriorate into schizophrenia—indicating a certain remarkable stability to the condition. The previously described narcissism and poverty of object relations of as-if or borderline patients are typically present in pseudoneurotic patients.

It is very important not to confuse the concept of borderline patient with such cases as "ambulatory schizophrenia" or "latent schizophrenia," generally designating schizophrenic patients who are not so sick as to require hospitalization. Thus, ambulatory or latent schizophrenics show the typical symptoms of schizophrenia, except to a less obvious degree; careful clinical examination may be necessary to pick up the typical schizophrenic syndrome, and a diagnosis then can be accurately established.

In many ways the evidence from clinical work militates *against* including the borderline personality disorder on the genetic spectrum that has been called "the schizoid spectrum" by a number of authors. Thus, if there is a genetic or polygenetic diathesis to the schizophrenic spectrum, it is different than any such diathesis involved in the development of the borderline personality disorder, and indeed there is currently no evidence that genetic factors are involved in the latter at all.

Knight (Knight 1953, 1962a, 1962b) gave impetus to the serious psychoanalytic investigation of borderline cases by discussing them in terms of variable impairment of ego function. This provided a partial theoretical explanation for the confusion in the nosology, although his use of the term *borderline schizophrenias* again tended to blur the distinction—which is a very important one—between borderline patients and ambulatory schizophrenia patients. Knight explains that in the borderline patient "the ego is laboring badly." The superficial clinical picture of the variety of neurotic symptoms and so on represents a holding operation in a forward position; the major portion of the ego has regressed far behind this forward position in varying degrees of disorder. The great danger to the clinician is to misunderstand these forward holding positions as constituting the illness and to attempt to treat them, whereas they actually represent the healthiest part of the patient's ego function.

Not only may the borderline patient show a variety of neurotic symptoms, but he may show a variety of delinquent or acting-out or "pseudopsychopathic" symptoms, involving him in all kinds of difficulties with society. This would be logically expected if the condition represented the impairment of ego function. Such patients, for example, may involve themselves in all sorts of delinquent activity at various times in their lives, but it is unusual to find them engaged in any kind of brutal crimes.

In our era the most typical of these patients appear in the general physician's office due to the syndrome of "periodic hyperingestion" (Chessick 1969). To the despair of their physicians and the panic of their families, these patients may consume large quantities of substances or combinations of substances including opiates, barbiturates, marihuana, meprobamate and other tranquillizers, nicotine, mescaline, alcohol, amphetamines and other psychic energizers and food. At other times there may be complete or almost complete abstention.

Various physical and psychic symptoms may periodically become intense; these include aches and pains, gnawing and weird abdominal sensations, insomnia (sometimes very severe), anxiety attacks, epileptiform seizures, tics and twitchings and, of course, the symptoms of depression. Such symptoms are sometimes followed by an explosion of hyperingestion in which the patient is functionally partly or completely paralyzed and concentrates all his energy on a compulsive stuffing in of various substances while other activities are neglected. Substances hyperingested may vary from episode to episode and the diagnosis of alcoholism or addiction may be mistakenly made at this point. However, although the patient may shift back and forth, he is on the whole able to function reasonably effectively in society and he does not deteriorate.

The clinical delineation of the borderline patient (Chessick 1975) then should include the following characteristic features:

1. Any variety of neurotic or quasi-psychotic, psychosomatic and sociopathic symptoms in any combination or degree of severity may be part of the initial presenting complaint. Either a bizarre combination of such symptoms cuts across the standard nosology or the relative preponderance of any symptom group is constantly changing or shifting. Thus at least two and preferably three diagnostic interviews at least a week apart are mandatory in establishing the diagnosis, in addition to a careful history taking including details of all symptoms and their vicissitudes.

2. Vagueness of complaint or even a bland, amazingly smooth or socially successful personality may be encountered. Careful investigation in such cases reveals a well-hidden poverty of genuine emotional relationships behind an attractive and personable social facade. Thus the patient may present either a very chaotic or stormy series of relationships with a variety of people or a bland and superficial but relatively stable set of relationships. In both cases a lack of deep emotional investment in any other person may be carefully consciously or unconsciously concealed.

3. The capacity for reality testing and the ability to function in work and social situations is not seriously impaired, although the degree of functioning may vary from time to time. On the whole, these patients are able to maintain themselves, raise families and otherwise fit into society. They do not present as drifters, chronic hospital or long-term prison cases, totally antisocial personalities or chronic addicts. On the other hand, they have often *tried* everything and may present a variety of sexual deviations, but they are not functionally paralyzed by these or by their neurotic symptoms or anxieties for very long periods of time.

4. These patients do not deteriorate. The borderline patient suffers from a relatively stable and enduring condition. He may endure what appear to be transient psychotic episodes either for no apparent reason or as a result of stress, alcohol, drugs, improper psychotherapy and so on, but he does not remain psychotic for long. He snaps out of it and often he learns what will snap him out of it and administers a self-remedy. At times this remedy may simply consist of dropping out of an improper psychotherapy; at other times it involves all varieties of ritual or bizarre behavior. Sometimes his marital partner or friends know about this and apply self-remedies for him—they consider this just his "hang-up."

When the borderline patient is in one of his panneurotic, pananxious, hyperingestive or psychopathic states, he causes tremendous alarm in those around him and appears to be in a terrible condition. At the same time he may frustrate all efforts to "help" at that point, or if "helped" he may show a surprising lack of gratitude. Borderline patients who suffer from various transient episodes soon acquire a reputation in the family and are often rejected by physicians as "crocks" or bad patients. They stimulate many unconscious and not so unconscious maneuvers by both family and physicians to get rid of them, for example, by sending them to a sanitarium "for a rest".

A number of sociological authors have emphasized the major change in presenting symptomatology found in the office of the psychotherapist over the recent years. Nowadays, the presenting statements deal with vague complaints of maladjustments and discontent—in short, they sound more like the borderline patient and less like the classical neuroses described by Freud. The lack of identity in these patients is linked by sociologists to the collapse of institutional absolutes and values, allegedly leading to a sense of futility, emptiness and longing. This problem is so serious in our time that it deserves careful delineation, the purpose of the next chapter.

CHAPTER 2

Etiology

What are the factors in our rapidly changing Western society which may spawn or facilitate the development of the borderline? First of all, it is important to keep in mind that the complaints of the borderline patient often resemble a caricature or exaggeration of the complaints and behavior of the so-called normal people in our current society. In fact, many "as-if" and other borderline patients are quite successful in the superficial social and business world. This is in marked contrast to the latent or ambulatory schizophrenic, whose complaints are consistently more bizarre and who is usually an unsuccessful person by society's standards of success.

Why is this a more difficult time to raise children than other times? One way to look at this question is to look at other times. Mirabeau wrote, "The civilization of a people is to be found in the softening of manners, in growing urbanity, in politer relations and in the spreading of knowledge in such ways that decency and seemliness are practiced until they transcend specific and detailed laws. ... Civilization does nothing for a society unless it is able to give form and substance to virtue. The concept of humanity is conceived in the bosom of societies out of these ingredients." What we are currently immersed in is the *opposite* of civilization, and, in spite of how hard individual parents may try, their children are caught up in the current whirlwind of barbarism. This provides a counterforce from which only the very strongest adolescents can emerge unscathed. Here are some briefly described features of modern western culture that interfere with maternal functioning and child development:

1. The breakup everywhere of family and family authority, traditions and values, so that adolescents now more than ever are more influenced by their peers—and usually the most malevolent of their peers—than by their family.

2. The presence of a stable family, of a permanent and peaceful marriage, is no longer even accepted universally as desirable. In actual experience the adolescent from such a household discovers he is in a dwindling minority; if there is no fighting, no divorce, no smoking and drinking in the house, the adolescent almost feels a bit deprived and must seek or create his own "excitement."

3. In this era of "future shock" (Toffler, 1970) there is NO sense of the future! Perhaps it can be argued that the aimless hippie drifting of the flower child is a form of preparation for a dark uncertain age with no future, with atomic warfare impending, subject to unpredictable shortages, economics disasters and what else?

4. The destructive effect of the loss of grandparents and ancillary family members such as uncles and aunts and so on living in close proximity and playing a significant and in older times often therapeutic role. The same can be said for the loss of religious values and religious figures and traditions and the constant moving of homes with subsequent breakups of old friendships and the necessity to keep new ones superficial in the anticipation of moving again.

In discussing schizophrenia, Arieti (1974) points out that in between the first edition of his book (1955), and the second edition (1974), we have witnessed in the United States a marked increase in cases of schizophrenia occurring in adolescence and early adulthood from the age of thirteen to the age of twenty-three. He writes, "We must assume that the present cultural climate in the United States facilitates the occurrence at an early age of that conceptual attack to the self that brings about resonance and unification with primary process experience." He also stresses Riesman's (1955) discussion of the "other-directed" culture. The models for youth are their peers, their contemporaries, not the older generation or the heroes of the past. As one borderline patient told me, "George Washington, Thomas Jefferson, those memorials in Washington are now obselete." The conceived ideals are considered less distant and expected to be more quickly attained, and consequently the despair of the self occurs earlier in life.

5. Affluence—our children usually have no personal experience of deprivation or really hard times, which makes it impossible for them to really imagine what hard times are like and does not motivate them to provide against deprivation.

6. Parents today live without values and without restrictions on their own abuses of drugs, tobacco and alcohol. All these are instantly and easily available; how can we expect the child to deny himself when adults who "should know better" do not and even spend a fortune in advertising to urge people to take all kinds of chemicals for every possible discomfort?

7. Insecurity and unsureness of parents as to how to raise children and what to do. This is a relatively new phenomenon in history, fostered by amateur psychology, which abounds everywhere with promises of instant solutions and instant relief for everything—and every advice contradicts every advice. Most destructive is the *inconsistency* of mothering based on this confusion.

8. An age of high mobility and fast transportation; jet planes, motorcycles and so on, with an emphasis on speed. Mobility for the sake of mobility becomes a symbol of independence and masculinity; only Ferdinand, the queer bull, sits under the trees and smells the flowers. "Even" girls run away and hitchhike if they are "with it."

9. Television: fast on-the-spot communication of sensational and exciting "news," the bloodier the better, and to fill in the time between newscasts, the "shows" which make up all sorts of violence and sexual sensation to keep the viewer watching. Dedicated to only one purpose—to get the viewer to watch the commercial—there is no level to which television will not descend and no end in sight to the decadence. Thus our children are bombarded from the earliest time of life with primitive sensations, and this is their concept of reality. What child today has the experience of Bertrand Russell (Russell 1967) as he describes it in his *Autobiography*—long quiet afternoons in his grandparents' large library, with nothing to do but read and think?

10. The general decline of social values and the quality of life in general, with corruption in fashion from the White House down. To quote Nef (1967): "Evil can be as contagious as virtue. To the fast multiplication of people and things, the mechanization and automa-

tion, the hurry and crowding which art has had increasingly to absorb or contend with during the last hundred and fifty years, has been added the peculiar fascination of doing wrong as an end in itself, at a time when the word "wrong" has lost its meaning and gratuitous acts of violence have acquired prestige."

It is clear from this brief description that the potential effect of society in forming the borderline patient is both *direct*, in lethal impact on the emerging personality of the child and adolescent, and *indirect*, by serious interference with the mother's capacity to respond to her infant due to a lack of her own sense of calm and security in the maternal environment. The mothers of borderline patients have been described as intelligent and overfeeding and as mothers who were able to hide their anxieties and the emotional impoverishment of their personalities behind pseudogiving. This is combined with a stern and almost cruel often unverbalized demand that the child live up to their expectations. This combination of overfeeding and pseudogiving accompanied by the hidden stream of demands produces in the child's mind a chaos that Leuba (1949) has labelled "deception," leading ultimately to severe defects in ego development.

Based on the work of Marie Bonaparte, Leuba, the French psychoanalyst, introduced a new concept in the study of narcissism, namely the phobia of penetration, which means the fear of each living cell and each living being of being penetrated and destroyed. This is rather romantic but is interesting and useful clinically. He visualized in this broader concept, which he called, "biological narcissism," an elementary fear and threat to the integrity of the body, "the fear of the cut-up body," and believed that all manifestations of this fear are identical with the concept that Odier (1956) called "primary phobias." Just as one recognizes in all men the biological bisexual polarity, these primary phobias are common to all beings and represent biological narcissism.

The primary phobias embrace all phobic reactions of early infancy—for example, the anxiety responses of a nursling to an unexpected noise, a bright shining light unfamiliar to the baby's eyes or even a simple change in the dress of the nurse. Summarizing briefly, these are elementary fears due to changes in the accustomed environment and are experienced in the dim light of the ego function of an infant as a terrifying unknown danger. Upon this elementary core

Leuba (1949) believed is added, without the infant's being able to establish any limit whatsoever, the concept of the fear of penetration.

Turning to clinical material, Leuba quoted many cases of an early dream of resistance to psychotherapy. Because of deep-seated primary phobias and their weak ego structure, these cases either pretend to get well or break up treatment after a few hours.

Secondary narcissism, according to Leuba, is a regressive phenomenon and it is *a defense against the recurrence of deception,* the fear of the feeling of abandonment arising from early, mostly preoedipal childhood experiences. The point of departure for narcissistic regression is a feeling of frustration. In order to soften and despoil the armor of narcissism, treatment for Leuba, consists first in affording a corrective experience of being loved in spite of the deeply repressed aggressions engendered by the fear of abandonment. This permits the person of the therapist to be afforded a reinvestment in original libidinal drives that were so frustrated by the deceiving objects of infancy.

Odier (1956) made an early contribution to the understanding of these patients with his concept of the "neuroses of abandonment." He sees the anxiety of these patients as directly proportional to the amount of insecurity in early childhood, producing regression to the prelogical stage of infantile thinking. He describes this magic thinking in detail as involving either (a) objectification of fear—"Whatever threatens me is wicked, whatever protects me is good;" (b) objectification of anger— toward animistic malevolent objects as chosen; and (c) identification with the aggressor. The "objectification" is the magical defense— placing the anxiety and fear and anger outside of the psyche onto external objects, as in phobias, or onto fantasy objects, as in nightmares or religion. In a much later publication (Chessick 1972b) I have described in detail the process of externalization and existential anguish presented by the borderline patient. The description is based on the loose concepts of Odier.

In the neuroses of abandonment, the anxiety is objectified onto a human being instead of a cosmic image or a transitional object—a human being who is then given the power of creating or abolishing abandonment, insecurity and helplessness. This individual is seen as all-powerful, sometimes benevolent and sometimes malevolent. In this situation, the oscillation between love and hate, security and insecurity, dependency and paranoia, and the rapid transitions from euphoria to depression, all as a function of minor provocations or reassurances from the chosen object, lead to the typical picture of the borderline patient and the all-too-common phenomena described as narcissistic object relations.

These concepts of *deception* and *fear of penetration* are absolutely vital to an understanding of and empathic feeling for the borderline patient!

Modell's (1968) book *Object Love and Reality* is one of the important monographs on the borderline patient and must be read carefully. He bases his thinking on Winnicott's concept of good enough mothering, which I have also used repeatedly in my books on psychotherapy (Chessick 1969, 1971c, 1974b). He points out that autonomous structures will be impaired if there is an absence of empathy in the maternal environment, and the central theme of his whole monograph is that the acceptance of painful reality rests upon the same ego structures that permit the acceptance of the separateness of objects. Thus the ego structure whose development permits the acceptance of painful reality is identical to the psychic structure whose development enables one to love maturely. He writes: "In both instances the signposts that indicate whether or not such a successful historical development has been traversed is the sense of identity. If one is fortunate enough to have received "good enough mothering" in the first and second years of life, the core of a positive sense of identity will have been formed. This core permits the partial relinquishment of instinctual demands upon the object and in turn permits the partial acceptance of the separateness of objects. It is this process upon which reality testing hinges."

I strongly recommend that you review carefully Modell's monograph, because it is a very fundamental starting point in reaching a deeper knowledge of the borderline patient. Earlier, Modell (1963) stressed the importance of a core of positive sense of identity, "a sense of beloved self," which develops in infancy as a response to adequate mothering. Without this sense of inner sustainment (Saul 1970), thinking remains magical and object relations remain primitive.

Ferenczi (1950) wrote a major paper in 1913 on the stages in the development of the sense of reality. He delineated a series of phases that the individual goes through, named a period of unconditional omnipotence, a period of magical hallucinatory omnipotence, a period of omnipotence by the help of magic gestures, an animistic period, and a period of magic thoughts and magic words. In all of these narcissism is characteristic, as is the domination of the pleasure principle. There must take place the replacement, Ferenczi points out, to which we are compelled by experience, of the childhood megalomania by the recognition of the power of natural forces. This is the essence of the development of the nature ego and leads to what Ferenczi calls the stage of objectification, the ascendency of the reality principle. Thus the first five stages persist only in fairy tales and mythology under normal conditions.

This is developed further in an important paper by Murray (1964). He describes the deep narcissistic sense of entitlement that pervades the thinking of borderline patients which of course indicates that the patient has not reached the stage of objectification. He explains that the most important battle in the cure of these deep seated character neuroses, as he calls them, lies in *transforming the narcissism,* that is, transforming neurotic attitudes based upon persistent early narcissism into the adequate, appropriate and mature ego-ideal orientations of adult life. He explains that the patient lives in "the narcissistic world of omnipotence with its unlimited power of magical thinking and unlimited entitlement to the lust and destructions of pregenital excitements." If this is not given up, then the patient's life will be critically limited, circumscribed and indefinite. Therapeutic achievments are only passing in this situation. This paper, in my opinion, presages what we will discuss in great detail later, described by Kohut (1966) as transformations of narcissism, and therefore is of historical importance as well as clinical usefulness.

It is necessary to quote one more author in bringing the historical review of psychodynamic descriptions of the development of borderline patients to the place where we can consider contemporary work. Gitelson (1973) wrote in 1958 on ego distortion, which he considered fundamental in these kinds of disorders. He suggested that the cases of ego distortion represent a way of life, a method of adaptation demanded by peculiar or particular deviations in the internal and external environment. The interplay of the various factors cause what he calls inadequacy, hypertrophy and/or atrophy of ego functions as such and produces an apparent imbalance in the picture of the total ego. He explained that such patients have encountered unusual stress in their relation to their original objects—centrally the mother—and the consequences are seen in pregenital disturbances in the economy of the libido and aggression, in defective superego development and in compensatory internal and external adaptative and adjustive accommodations of ego function.

Gitelson feels that these syndromes should be thought of as narcissistic personality disorders. Already at this point it should be clear that anyone who is going to understand the borderline patient will have to have a thorough understanding of the vicissitudes of narcissism and of psychoanalytic ego psychology, because these patients represent in many ways the most subtle and complex malfunctions and maldevelopments of psychic structure of any patients that we deal with.

Kernberg (1967, 1968), for example, stresses the borderline patient's lack of anxiety tolerance, lack of impulse control and lack of sublimatory channels, and he contends that oral aggression poses a crucial role in the psychodynamics. There is a premature development of Oedipal conflicts as an attempt to escape from oral rage, with a subsequent condensation of pregenital and genital conflicts. In other words, there is fundamentally a "pathology of internalized object relationships" and an "intensification and pathological fixation of splitting processes" in the ego functions of these patients.

Even the descriptive difficulties in any discussion of the borderline patient get more and more confusing as one reads more and more of the literature. For example, take the so-called "good" or "bad" hysteric (Lazare 1971). The true "good" hysterical character is the person who is supposed to have quick and intuitive resonance with others, be a sexually exhibitionistic, competitive, buoyant and energetic, ambitious, histrionic individual with a strong sense of guilt who does well in his work. Such a person is not promiscuous, although he is not able to make a major sexual investment in others and he often is involved with an unavailable partner. He shows a predominance of Oedipal conflicts, retains significant ties with old parents and is relatively well integrated in ego and superego functions. This is contrasted in the literature to the borderline hysteric or the "bad" hysteric or the hysterical personality, which is manifested by low self-esteem, a sense of helplessness, whining and contrariness, inconsistent and irresponsible work habits, rapid shifts between intensive negative and positive feelings, sexual promiscuity, drifting relationships, a poor tolerance of frustration stress and the predominance of infantile oral conflicts. His mental life is characterized by polymorphous perverse fantasies and few conflict-free areas, and there is emphasis on the defense of splitting—that is to say, there is an incapacity for synthesizing good and bad introjects and identifications. We will have a lot more to say about the latter problem further on.

This represents a very confusing situation in the literature, and there is a lot of argument, as, for example, in the panel report by Rangell (1955), where much of the panel ended up in a discussion of whether borderline states exist at all. Some very highly respected people, such as Gregory Zilboorg, insisted that there is no such thing. At any rate, it was admitted in this panel that we are not sufficiently expert to judge *by any one measure* the psychological status of a borderline case, except at least to some extent intuitively and impressionistically.

CHAPTER 3

State of the Ego

The group reported by Rangell (1955) felt that such concepts as ego weakness tell us little. For example, an ego may be strong in one capacity and weak in another. It may have a great capacity for integration while remaining weak in regard to certain cultural realities, and so on. This group feels, to quote Rangell, "The essential pathology is in the ego functions, with regression and primitivization of these. The primary process invades the secondary, and there is difficulty in separating a judging ego from the experiencing ego. The implication of this for treatment is that it becomes necessary to tell such a patient not only, 'you are reacting as if I were your father', but also to add, 'and I am not your father', thus helping him acquire a judging ego." I think this is an important clinical pearl.

The issue of the ego state in the borderline condition has been reviewed by numerous authors, and it sometimes becomes rather mystical. For example, Cary (1972) insists that he can differentiate the borderline condition by what he calls a structural-dynamic viewpoint. He claims that the borderline structurally represents an arrest of early development when ego and object tended to be fused. From the structural-dynamic viewpoint, according to Cary, there is basically a fear "of the loss of a unified ego sense" and a fear of a loss of relations with others, leading "to an alternating struggle between the wish for fusion of ego with object and the opposing wish for separation of ego from object." This is a rather complicated way of describing a very common phenomenon that we encounter in the borderline patient having to do with the sense of self and the traditional need-fear dilemma.

What do we really mean when we speak of ego weakness or ego defect in the borderline personality disorder? The answer to these questions as they emerge from clinical experience in the treatment of borderline patients throws considerable light on the increasingly complex notion of the ego and its functioning. Knowledge gathered about the operations of the ego for the treatment of such patients is applicable to the treatment and understanding of *all* patients, just as in the old days information about derivatives of id processes as they appeared in raw form in the productions of schizophrenic patients was useful in investigating the unconscious of all types of patients regardless of the intactness of their defensive structures.

The whole concept of the psychoanalytic assessment of ego weakness is a very difficult one. For example, according to Zucker (1963), in such assessment a number of personality areas tend to get overlooked but are very important in detecting ego weakness:

1. The disturbance in screening activities with a reduction of sensitivity to external stimulation as overcompensation for inadequate boundaries between outer and inner reality

This is an interesting clinical point. For example, people with ego weakness at times simply do not "hear" what you are saying. They ask you to repeat yourself or they get confused in directions if they are going somewhere on a train or the bus. They don't notice the external stimuli they should be noticing and there seems to be a higher threshold at times for stimuli to register.

2. The fusion of different realms of cognitive experience
3. The tendency to multiple identifications
4. The phenomenon of the fluctuating body image [This in my experience is especially noticeable in borderline adolescents.]
5. The problem in segregating the consequential from the inconsequential [This is a good one to look for clinically.]
6. The extension of the ego field into other fields or entities

Some of these items may not be entirely clear so I will go into them a little more. In talking about the fusion of different realms of cognitive experiences, I think Zucker is talking essentially about microscopic difficulties in keeping associations orderly and not contaminating each other. He gives as an example the following statement of a patient: "The subway seemed to develop a terrific speed today—that is why I myself like to do things in a hurry." He sees this kind of logic as based on the person's inability to remain within a single frame of reference.

According to Zucker, extension of the ego field to other fields or entities is a peculiarity which shows up most distinctly in testing behavior but also can be observed clinically. He explains that the description pertains to the type of subject who in a varying degree encounters problems in keeping apart his inner reality from outer realities. For example, a patient may say he is afraid to die because he is convinced that with his death the world may come to an end too, or he may have difficulty in distinguishing between his daydreams and reality.

This is all on a microscopic level and it is similar to Knight's (1962) description of the borderline schizophrenic mentioned earlier. How do we distinguish ego weakness in the borderline patient from the borderline schizophrenic or ambulatory schizophrenic? Let us begin with DeWald (1964) on the subject of ego strength and ego weakness. Generally an individual who is capable of maintaining various activities, work and other relationships, in spite of his disturbances, and capable of meeting and dealing with the vicissitudes of his life can be said to have some ego strength and will successfully deal with the stresses of insight therapy. DeWald points out, "The more an individual has had a general pattern of persistent effort in a goal-directed fashion, and of success in the various ventures that he has undertaken, the more likely will he be to sustain his effort during the course of the treatment, and ultimately to achieve some measure of success".

At the other end of the spectrum, of course, the person whose life pattern has been one of repeated failures, ineffectual adaptations and major disturbances and disruptions will repeat these ego patterns in the therapeutic situation, and the patient may even be incapable of using what insight he gets to effectively modify his previous patterns of disturbance by virtue of his "inadequate overall ego capacity."

In addition to this, from clinical study it is apparent that certain specific ego functions have very important impact. Obviously, the patient who is able to make significant investments in other people will do better in psychotherapy. The capacity of the patient to make a sustained object relation over years of time is very important. By virtue of rigid defenses, some individuals are simply unaware of their inner emotional impulses, conflicts and reactions and insist on focusing everything on external, current, realistic events. Such patients will have great difficulty in uncovering psychotherapy; at the other extreme, patients who are morbidly introspective—to the point of excessive continuous rumination with so much internal awareness that they exclude reality in real life circumstances—are people with serious ego weaknesses who will have problems in psychotherapy.

There are certain specific defense mechanisms which when used extensively suggest ego weakness and poor prognosis in uncovering psychotherapy. DeWald mentions reliance on projection, massive denial, major withdrawal and so on. Especially difficult is the acting-out patient who deals with his psychic conflicts primarily that way; the prognosis is even worse if acting out is combined with projection. At least average intelligence is required in uncovering psychotherapy, although I would not say that a poor intelligence is quite the same kind of ego function as the others under discussion for purposes of evaluating whether a person is borderline or not. The capacity to tolerate anxiety and frustration while working toward a long-term goal is an important measure of ego strength or weakness as is the willingness to postpone immediate gratification in the hope of achievement of long-range goals.

To conceive of ego weakness simply as consisting of a rather frail ego barrier which, when assaulted by id derivatives, is unable to prevent them from breaking through and flooding the ego appears in the light of modern clinical experience to be superficial and insufficient. Today we conceive of the ego as an overall structure in which substructures determine specific functions as well as being determined by each other. Thus ego weakness should be conceptualized not simply as absence or weaknesses in such structures but as replacement of higher-level by lower-level ego structures. For example, Kernberg (1975a) explains, a typical feature of ego weakness in borderline patients is "... evidenced by the 'lower' defensive organization of the ego in which the mechanism of splitting and other related defenses are used, in contrast to the defensive organization of the ego around the 'higher' mechanisms of regression and other related defenses in the neuroses."

Typically the ego function in borderline patients is characterized by splitting in which internalized object relationships are split into good and bad and there is an emphasis on introjections and projections with externalization.

This view of Kernberg's is considerably more tricky than appears on the surface. Kernberg (1973) emphasizes *levels* of internalized object relationships. These are: "(1) a basic primitive level characterized by multiple self—and multiple object—representations, corresponding to primitive fantasy formations linked with primitive impulse derivatives; and (2) a higher level of internalized object-relationships, characterized by sophisticated, integrated self-images and by sophisticated, integrated object-images linked with higher levels of affect-dispositions." All of these higher-level object relationships reflect the early childhood experiences and conflicts between the individual and his parental figures and siblings.

In addition to this, the differentiation of the transference in the borderline patient from that of the transference in the neurotic patient is that the transference neurosis in the neurotic patient is "a more realistic, dyadic, Oedipal-triangular, or sibling relationship," while in the borderline patient, "primitive object-relationships are activated with multiple self-images and multiple object-images representing the deepest layers of the mind." Now most authors are agreed on the phenomena described here, but they are not in agreement on the *explanation* of these phenomena. The primitive multiple object relationships are of a fantastic nature and do not directly reflect actual past interaction with the parents as do the higher-level transference reactions in the neurotic. Rather, according to Kernberg, they reflect early fantasy structures, that is, fantastic relationships to inner objects which are normally submerged within the structure of more realistic transference dispositions in the context of an integrated strong ego and superego. Actually, even underneath what appears to be fragility in these patients there are often extremely rigid, primitive and pathological ego structures; anyone who has attempted psychotherapy with such patients can attest to this!

Sadow (1969) proposed a schema that utilizes the central role of the ego as the axis of a continuum along which are located the psychoses, borderline states, transference neuroses and conflict-free capacities. He presents a classification of the emotional disorders based predominantly on a view of the patient's ego functioning, thinking of the ego as "a relatively fixed group of functions within the personality, composed of both conscious and unconscious parts, and comprising a variety of attributes and skills which vary in composition and degree from individual to individual."

This ego axis represents the ego in a sequential line of development from earliest infancy to full maturity. Movement along this axis is depicted as a regressive shift or a progressive shift. Thus the successful interpretation of and working through of a neurotic conflict would result in a movement toward the conflict-free zone of ego functioning. Ego depletion, whether based on illness, fatigue, neurotic conflict, object loss or so on, would be depicted by a movement in a regressive direction. Obviously, the entire range of psychopathology can be superimposed on the axis, with very regressed psychotics at one end and healthy sublimated personalities with lots of conflict-free ego function at the other end.

In investigating the position of borderline patients on this ego axis, one of the most important clinical facts that emerges is the capacity of these patients to have a tremendous range and flexibility of movement along the ego axis. It is clear that in any evaluation of a patient's ego we must study the ego operations not only to discern higher or lower levels of predominating defensive processes, but also to discern the ego's capacity for motility back and forth on the ego axis—motility in which an oscillation occurs from nonstructuralized regressive organizations at one end to conflict-free functioning on the other. A great many therapists have been fooled into a pessimistic or hopeless decision about the prognosis for the treatment of a borderline patient because they observed the patient during a period when he was temporarily residing in the regressed area of the ego axis. Thus many borderline patients can sometimes function quite well and at the same time in other situations or during certain other periods appear to be psychotic and even hopeless.

The borderline patient can also fool us because under the regressive pull of drives and defenses, certain autonomous ego functions may become what Lowenstein (1972) calls "reinstinctualized" so as to act in the service of resistance. The specific medium through which we observe the mental apparatus is the autonomous ego of the patient. The interactions and conflicts in which we are interested take place not only between ego, id and superego, but also within the ego itself. Hartmann (1950) made the famous extension of the concept of conflicts from the well-known conflicts between drives and defenses to conflicts within the ego itself. Hartmann distinguished between the *intrasystemic* conflicts within the ego itself and the more traditional *intersystemic* conflicts.

Autonomous ego functions which become reinstinctualized appear on the surface to remain autonomous unless the therapist is extremely careful in his evaluation. For example, the use of fancy psychoanalytic terminology by a professional patient in therapy such as a social worker, psychologist or psychiatrist can fool the therapist into thinking that an autonomous function is being utilized in which the patient is observing and understanding himself in a very scientific manner—whereas actually there has been a reinstinctualization of speech in the service of resistance.

On the same subject of intrasystemic conflicts, it is important to note that typically in borderline patients mutually incompatible character traits may alternate as an indication of the extent to which conflicting identifications have been integrated into the character structure and tolerated by the ego or superego. Of course, a close correspondence exists between the levels of structural organization of the ego and of the superego, since related vicissitudes of internal object relationships determine both ego and superego pathology, and of course, borderline patients show frequent irregularities in superego development. Though frequently superego formation in borderline patients is superficially surprisingly good, the characteristic of alternating between subservience to conflicting ego ideals is a typical sign that underneath an apparently smooth superego functioning is a lack of consistency and integration within the personality.

Thus in the clinical evaluation of the patient—any patient—the concept of the ego state of the patient must be very carefully examined and assessed (1) from the point of view of the predominance of higher- or lower-level (primitive or less primitive) sets of ego operations; (2) in terms of the capacity for mobility along an ego axis in which, for example, the ego of the borderline patient shows a remarkable capacity to shift back and forth from very regressed states to autonomous ego function; (3) from the point of view of the patient's capacity for autonomous ego functioning, which is a necessity for any uncovering psychotherapy (this must be carefully distinguished from reinstinctual-ized situations in which the ego functioning is apparently autonomous but actually in the service of resistance); and (4) for the relative presence or absence of intrasystemic conflicts leading to what Erikson has called identity diffusion.

I am often asked about the value of psychological testing in borderline patients. There have been a number of comments on this in the literature, but there is no clear-cut pattern of psychological test results established as related to the diagnosis or detection of the borderline condition. According to Pfeiffer (1974), the value of psychological testing lies in delineating the area of current concern, conflict or symptomatology rather than in establishing the specific diagnosis of a borderline state. He suggests, for instance, that the MMPI and various kinds of depression or anxiety scales are distinctly useful in establishing the existence and severity of "target symptoma-tology," as he calls it, and similarly, he suggests the Rorschach and TAT to identify areas of concern or conflict.

More traditionally, the Rorschach test has been used to provide a measure of the patient's adequacy of reality testing in a descriptive sense. The traditional description in the literature is that borderline patients on unstructured tests such as the Rorschach show worse performance than the neurotics do, but on sturctured tests, like the MMPI, they do as well as neurotics. No characteristic or reliable descriptions of borderline psychological test results exist in the literature at the present time.

Therefore, the diagnosis of the borderline condition or borderline patient has to remain essentially a clinical diagnosis on the basis of careful clinical evaluation of the patient. Pfeiffer (1974) quotes Vaillant, who attempted to make a kind of classification for the defenses used as they are observed clinically. Level I is described as the "narcissistic" (which is not the proper term); what Vaillant called the narcissistic defenses include delusional projection, psychotic denial, distortion or depersonalization and so on. Level II defenses include projection, denial through fantasy, hypochondriasis, passive aggres-sive behavior and acting out. Level III defenses, called "neurotic," involve intellectualization, rationalization, repression, displacement, reaction formation and counterphobic and dissociative reactions. Finally, the so-called "mature" or Level IV defenses are altruism, sublimation, humor, suppression, avoidance, anticipation and conscious control. This classification, it should be noted, mixes several levels of discourse and is metapsychologically unsound.

At any rate, it is the fluid use of the variety of defense mechanisms which characterizes the borderline patient. Thus, the patient clinically shifts back and forth with great mobility among all these levels of defenses, so the therapist has to evaluate clinically not only the specific defenses the patient uses and how they are different at different times, but also the ease with which the patient shifts back and forth between these defenses and defense levels. This is essentially a clinical skill and must be based on a careful set of diagnostic interviews.

CHAPTER 4

Typical Borderline Complaints

For the past twenty years I have been frequently confronted in my office practice in psychotherapy with a rather typical patient as indicated by the following case vignettes. The first patient is a thirty-five-year-old woman who has reached a certain degree of executive success in a well-known corporation. She is respected by those around her. Her efficiency and industry are often without peer and she is responsible for the production of a number of items, with large sums of money hinging on her executive decisions. Yet she seeks therapy because, although she functions so well, she has vague complaints of restlessness, dissatisfaction and of being "alive but not alive." Her marriage has failed. Her husband has turned from her to some perversion, which surprised her entirely. Her later relationships with men have been characterized by mere sexual promiscuity, by utter lack of emotional attachment. Again and again she has started out to form a relationship with this man or that and again and again it has deteriorated into mere technical sexual prowess.

The patient's life consists essentially of two phases of existence which alternate with each other. Either she is crying herself into a state of exhaustion and then enjoys the relatively quiescent feeling after such catharsis or she is getting somebody to hold her, for which she is trading sexual relations. The holding provides a magical sensation that everything will be all right. She remembers as a child being in bed with her sister and insisting "I held on" by putting an arm around her sister in spite of her sister's repeated protests. Only while she was holding on in this manner could she go to sleep. There was nothing sexually arousing about this and no sexual play of any sort took place in this situation.

Here is a similar vignette: A twenty-seven-year-old nun has spent the last six years in a convent. She reports that she went about all her duties in exemplary fashion and with continual praise from her superiors. She was thought of as a pious dedicated, hard-working, reliable and mature woman. She followed all the rules correctly. There was never any serious problem.

At the same time the patient felt continuously that she was dead. She went through the motions of living always with a strange, almost indescribable feeling that she was not alive. This went on and on, and it seemed to the patient that it would always go on. She never consciously worried about it. She felt that somehow this was her perpetual fate, the background of her existence.

One of her superiors began to seduce her. She was attractive and young and this superior, who had a history of homosexual acting out, began to encourage the patient to come to her room and caress her. The patient refused to do any active caressing but did allow herself to be caressed, and a series of clandestine evening meetings began to take place in which the patient and the superior would climb into bed and the superior would hold the patient close and caress her breasts. In spite of increased and impassionate urgings and pressures from her partner, the patient never allowed this to progress to anything further.

This stirred up a tremendous conflict in the patient because she felt that what she was doing was really not in her best interest, although the superior kept describing the procedure as "therapeutic" for her, and indeed, the patient noted with surprise and astonishement that while she was being caressed and held, the feeling of being dead would go away! Finally the patient went to a higher superior and told the whole story. To her surprise she was asked to leave the convent and nothing was done about her seducer, who appears to have made a large financial contribution to the order.

The sudden experience of being held and caressed caused an explosion inside the patient. She did not become psychotic, but she could no longer accept as her fate the perpetual feeling of being dead. This is in interesting contrast to the schizophrenic patient, who might at this point develop a homosexual panic. She began to realize she was missing something that she could have and she began to strive for it. This was her chief reason for coming into therapy: "I feel dead all the time. I know I don't have to feel dead and I want to do something about it."

What were these women looking for? What was wrong? They were not overtly psychotic, and they were not neurotic as far as traditional diagnostic categories are concerned, but clearly they were severely disturbed individuals with deeply abnormal interpersonal relations. Their histories also contained serious transient psychosomatic disorders.

Hollender (1970; Hollender et al. 1969, 1970) has written three papers on the need to be held in women. He reports that for some women in his series, the need or wish to be held was so compelling that it resembled an addiction. Body contact commonly provides feelings of being loved, protected and comforted: "The need or wish for it is affected by depression, anxiety, and anger . . . both direct and indirect means are used to obtain the holding and the cuddling desired. Sexual enticement and seduction are common indirect means." But it is not really clear at all what being held does for these patients or what is really wrong. In repeated cases such patients (male and female) have begged significant others (and sometimes also me) even simply to hold their hand, because they insisted that without the tactile stimulation they just do not feel alive. It is not a sexual desire and it does not seem to be directly related primarily to infantile wishes for tactile pleasure— alhough certainly this is a component of it. There seems to be an additional component in which some sort of profound sensation of deadness can only be neutralized by the physical touching presence of another human being and not by anything else, according to the patient, including talk, psychotherapy or interpretations of any kind.

After a few cases of this sort, I began inquiring more carefully into my patients' habits regarding tactile contact and I found to my surprise that quite a number of patients with predominantly existential complaints (such as difficulty in finding meaning in life, vague restlessness and discontent, a sense of boredom or what Sartre would call nausea and so forth) often displayed in one or another way an extraordinary need to be held or for tactile contact—even with a transitional object—which could not be replaced by anything else.

(To anticipate myself, in later discussion I wish to insert the serious warning that for the therapist to *provide* such tactile stimulation under any guise whatsoever is very destructive for both the patient and the patient's therapy, and nothing that I am saying should be interpreted as implying that this is *ever* useful in the treatment of any patient in psychotherapy.)

Perhaps the most popular and well-known problem presented by borderline patients in office psychotherapy today is that of so-called existential anxiety. Here is an example: A. P. was a handsome twenty-nine-year-old man who began therapy in a state of almost psychotic collapse. Until 1962 he had been a brilliant and promising graduate student at a major university working for his Ph.D. He was the favorite of the department and even took over a professor's course while the professor was away on a tour.

As the time for finishing his Ph.D. approached, A. P. began to feel overwhelmed with the feeling that life made no sense, that it was absurd, that everyone and everything was a fake, and that all people were soon to die anyway. Suddenly one day in the middle of teaching a class he simply walked out of the classroom, packed his suitcase and left school. Not long afterward he got married and worked as a salesman.

During the marriage he had spells of silent withdrawal and depression during which he seemed almost catatonic. He was unable to concentrate or do anything during these spells. At other times he would have fits of uncontrollable rage and would break the dishes and kick out the paneling on the door. Needless to say, the marriage did not last and a divorce was obtained. In desperation he sought out psychotherapy, although he had few financial means. I saw him essentially as a charity case through a community agency; complete physical examination by several physicians revealed that he was without organic disease.

Even in the diagnostic interviews he displayed the same oscillation of moods described above. In addition, a flood of bizarre dreams and fantasies plagued him, along with homosexual preoccupations. His history showed many attempts to escape the dreary boredom and nothingness that he felt by travelling from city to city. He wrote to me, "I don't think you have any idea of the desparation I find myself in. Only to "split" (go somewhere else) is to give in to the ever present hope that somewhere life may be better. I don't know how much longer that might be the case, and when I realize that life is no better anywhere than here, then—I am *begging* you to show me something to make it worthwhile."

This sense of deadness, emptiness, nausea, anxiety, dread and lack of meaning in a dreamlike life is perhaps the most dramatic and common presenting symptomatology of the borderline patient, and it is often presented in an artistic or very articulate manner with very appropriate affect.

The immediate impact of this on the therapist is to call forth the notion of relationship. Clearly the relationship between the therapist and the patient has the most obvious and important dramatic influence on these kinds of complaints, and everyone knows this. But it usually does not have a lasting influence nor does it lead to any kind of basic changes in the patient. In fact, the whole question of how you bring about change in psychotherapy remains an exceedingly debatable one today.

To be more specific, three major debates are going on in our field on this subject, and these debates tend to be stirred up every time a discussion of a treatment of a borderline personality disorder takes place. In the first debate, one side argues that certain factors are crucial and common to all forms of intensive long-term psychotherapy, whereas the other argues that forms of intensive long-term psychotherapy can be distinguished on the basis of which factors are crucial to their success. In the second debate one side argues that the emotional interaction, the "real object relationship" or "the unconscious interaction between patient and doctor" is crucial in all forms of intensive long-term psychotherapy regardless of the rituals or theory or school that is employed. The other side maintains (a) that there are some forms of intensive long-term psychotherapy, for example supportive psychotherapy, where the emotional interaction is crucial, but (b) there are other forms where it is minor and "insight" is the crucial factor in success.

In the third debate one side maintains that there is no basic distinction between psychoanalysis and psychoanalytically oriented psychotherapy, as they are both forms of intensive long-term psychotherapy with common crucial factors. The other side argues that there is a distinction between the "pure gold" of psychoanalysis and the "copper" of direct suggestion as follows: In psychoanalysis "insight" through interpretation of the transference neuroses is crucial, whereas in "suggestion"—all other psychotherapy—there is merely "education" or "inspiration", etc.

In the most modern form of this debate, one side maintains that an existential encounter of some sort with the patient is vital to success in the psychotherapy or psychoanalysis, whereas the other side maintains that *only* if the patient can form a workable transference neurosis and undergo a careful and meticulous analysis of this transference neurosis can there be a major and lasting change in the personality of the patient and his disorder.

These issues will repeatedly come up in this book, and the reader who is hoping for a solution or an answer to them is going to be disappointed. There simply is no agreement on the issues raised in these debates, and I will adopt a middle position, which will be implicit in the various descriptions of the disagreements about the psychodynamics and psychotherapy of the borderline patient that will appear here. As I indicated at the beginning of the book, there is no set answer to some of these questions about the borderline patient and the reader will have to pick and choose and test clinically as he sees fit.

A great reward from the psychotherapy of the borderline patient is that it forces us to reexamine carefully and constantly every aspect of the psychotherapy process as well as every aspect of ourselves. No other type of patient so persistently, lucidly, and dramatically challenges our personalities and also our therapeutic procedures and convictions. The borderline patient provides a continual test of our capacity for empathy, of our frustration tolerance, and of how well analyzed we are and how well our infantile narcissism has been integrated into our adult personality structure. These patients sharply spotlight confusions or inconsistencies in our convictions about psychotherapeutic process and offer a unique opportunity for intellectual, professional and personal expansion.

Part II
METAPSYCHOLOGY

CHAPTER 5

Basic Metapsychology

The metapsychological characterization of the borderline patient is unclear and controversial. There is no doubt that Freud's paper "On Narcissism" in 1914 represents the starting point. In this paper he discusses how the ego invests both the objects and the self with libido, and he mentions, "Narcissism in the libidinal aspect of egoism." (Egoism is defined here as self-regard or selfishness.) This is carried further in his papers on "Economic Problems of Masochism" (1924) and "Mourning and Melancholia" (1917). In the latter he describes how the representation of the lost object is invested with libido formerly invested in the object. Thus the individual loves the memory traces instead of the lost object and in this case the ego has been invested with libido.

Even on basic definitions and word usage there are profound differences of opinion in the literature. As an example, see the review by Pruyser (1974), who discusses the concept of splitting as it is used in psychoanalysis and psychiatry. In forty-six pages he reviews this term—which is too slippery and too hard and probably should not be used at all—as it is used in a different way by almost every famous writer in psychiatry, writers such as Bleuler, Freud, Fairbairn, Hartmann, Guntrip, Jacobson, Jung and others. Terminological confusion is rampant in our field, so I feel it necessary to call attention to certain basic definitions.

There is enormous debate about the concept of the ego. The "English school" of object relations theory, especially Fairbairn and Guntrip, reject Freud's basic ideas of the ego. Instead Fairbairn (1952) postulates that at birth there is a "pristine," unitary, whole human psyche with ego potential that immediately begins to grow into a developing self, a "person-ego." There is no impersonal id; all is ego, and if the infant experiences absolutely good object relations, development could proceed as a stable, unified, steadily early-enriched growth of the pristine ego. Thus, for Fairbairn libido becomes the energy of the primary life drive of the ego, and energy and structure are not as separated as in Freud's conception of the id and ego. I mention the Fairbairn or Guntrip approach primarily to reject it, because it is clear that if one accepts this terminology then one must totally reject the entire metapsychology of Freud, which I choose not to do. In addition to this, the Fairbairn-Guntrip approach contains tremendous terminological confusion which in no way can be resolved by simply further study but has within it a worse inherent inconsistency than the standard metapsychology.

The commonly accepted concept of the ego as presented by Freud (1923) and refined by Hartmann and many others finds the ego as a substructure of personality defined by its functions. More specifically, these days we may think of four basic sets of apparatus that define the ego functions. First, of course, are all the defensive functions of the ego made famous by Freud and Anna Freud.

Hartmann (1950) introduced the "conflict-free sphere" of the ego. This contains the primary autonomous functions, such as memory, judgment, thought and reality testing, and the secondary autonomous functions.

These secondary autonomous functions, such as orderliness, are defined as functions which at one time were drive-connected or in the service of defense against unacceptable impulses but now during the course of epigenesis have developed a usefulness of their own in adaptation and therefore become part of the conflict-free sphere of the ego. Thus through a "change of function," (Hartmann 1950) what started in a situation of conflict may secondarily become part of the nonconflictual sphere and "come to serve different functions, like adjustment, organization, and so on."

Furthermore, beside defensive functions, primary autonomous functions and secondary autonomous functions, there are in the ego what we call *microinternalizations*. These microinternalizations are adaptative techniques and regulative techniques which the infant and child learns by observing the parents and significant others around him. Gradually in optimal circumstances he takes on these techniques of adaptation in an ego-syntonic way, so these become a part of the individual's concept of himself and a smooth part of ego functioning.

To further illustrate what is meant by these microinternalizations, we can contrast them with *macrointernalizations,* sometimes known as introjects. Introjects are "foreign bodies" within the ego. They are due to intense incorporation, which takes place when there is a phase-inappropriate disappointment or the loss of a significant individual in the person's life. These macrointernalizations, or introjects, have in a sense a psychic life of their own within the ego that carries on a dialogue with the individual, speaking to him and influencing his life. Schafer (1968) presents a detailed discussion of introjects.

Finally, within the ego we find self-representations and object representations, which will be discussed in detail later. The important point to be made on this subject with respect to the ego is that original and early self-representations and object representations gradually become attuned to reality and modified by reality under optimal conditions and so become smoothly diffused in the functioning ego systems. Thus when the self-representations and object representations are correctly and realistically integrated into the ego, the individual is able to use realistic methods of adaptation—that is to say, adaptation improves proportionately to our ability to have more realistic and clear representations of ourselves and the objects toward whom we have to adapt.

An "object" is a person—real, "out there", repeatedly experienced. When the significant objects—originally the mother of course—are not too painful or frustrating, object representations are fused into a realistic representation that one may adaptively relate to and deal with. By the age of eight months, the first capacity for self-object differentiation permits this process to begin. It is a process which develops into what we call object constancy and eventually, object love. A continuing interaction with significant objects, especially the mother and later the father, siblings and peers, is required for object constancy and object love to develop.

Notice the difference between object relations and object love. It is possible to have many object relations; a good politician knows the names and a little about many, many people. This is not the same as object love, in which there is a genuine affection and empathic feeling for other people as human beings with needs of their own. Notice also that we speak of the *epigenesis* of the ego (Erikson 1959) as an unravelling of inborn potential contingent on environmental interaction. Thus the individual comes into life with certain *anlage,* or primitive ego apparatuses, which unfold in their potential as a result of successful interaction with those around him, and furthermore, each stage of ego development depends on a successful experience and development in the prior stage.

In addition to debate about the concept of ego, there is debate about the concept of superego even within the ranks of classical psychoanalysts. With the exception of the Kleinians, most authors agree that the major phase of superego formation occurs during the resolution of the Oedipus complex, around five or six years of age. Of course, there are forerunners of the superego before that time. (The Kleinians conceive of the main structure of the superego as forming much earlier.)

There is a harsh critical aspect of the superego. The forerunners of the harsh critical superego are memory traces of punishment. The harsh critical superego is supercharged with internal aggression; there is a psychic connection between the id and the harsh critical superego that allows the draining of the aggressive energies from the id via the harsh critical superego. Thus we see people who are flooded with profound aggression turning this aggression upon themselves through the harsh critical superego.

A benign aspect of the superego also exists, based on memory traces of love and approval from the parents. The final precipitation of the harsh and benign aspects of the superego occurs under the influence of the Oedipus complex, and at this time there occurs the major internalization of parental values.

The ego-ideal aspect of the superego is less clearly understood. It seems to bridge the ego and the superego and to form out of micro-internalizations, which I have discussed already. Freud often uses the term *ego ideal* and *superego* interchangeably, and *he* means, by either, the internal values of the parents—goals and identifications that are formed in the interaction with the parents. Later authors have used the term *ego ideal* to represent a separate aspect of the superego. The traditional view was to see the ego ideal primarily as an aspect of the superego and as representing something that the individual would like to be. Thus, for example, shame is thought of as a tension between the ego and the ego-ideal aspect of the superego in which the individual has not lived up to his ideals; guilt is experienced as a tension between the ego and the harsh critical superego in which one has transgressed the rules internalized from the parents.

Later thinking such as of Kohut (1971) sees the ego ideal as coming from the search for an idealized parent imago. When the superego is formed the idealized parent imago is then placed in the superego. However, both the superego and the ego become infused with love and admiration for the idealized powerful parent. The idealized parent becomes an aspect toward which one aspires and in that sense becomes part of the ego ideal. We speak of the ego ideal as pulling the ego forward. Thus, for Kohut the ego ideal is not a separate functioning entity in the superego, but a kind of infusion of the superego with power and admiration and consequently with a wish to be like and to obey the beloved, internalized, idealized parent or superego.

The term *transitional object* was first introduced by Winnicott and later referred to by Modell (1963). For our purposes, we use Modell's definition of a "transitional object phase" of the development of object love, during which there is a clinging, dependent relationship to the object. This stands between the primary narcissism, where there is no recognition of the object as separate, and true object love, where there is the capacity to relate to the object as separate, human and having needs of its own.

The concept of *self-object* was introduced by Kohut (1971) to help distinguish between object relations and object love. The small child has object relations but not object love. It relates to others as self-objects in which the object is experienced as part of the self and having no life of its own. These are very important concepts, because they appear in the transferences of many patients and they help the therapist to understand certain aspects of behavior in psychotherapy that ordinarily would cause irritation and rejection on his part. If one understands a clinging, dependent transference in terms of the phase of object love that the patient is in at the time, or if one understands that the rage of a patient when he has to leave at the end of a session or when the therapist goes on vacation represents the total inability of the patient to think of the needs of the therapist or to tolerate any lack of control over the therapist, then a more appropriate response and interpretation can be presented to the patient.

The term *disavowal* was introduced by Freud late in his life to describe the splitting of the ego in the service of defense. The most recent description of this phenomenon in the literature is the so-called "vertical split" of Kohut (1971), involving grandiosity. In disavowal, both aspects of the ego are more or less conscious, but one part is really "unaware" of or glosses over the other. The important point is that repression is *not* involved. Disavowal is an important mechanism of defense that occurs before the establishment of the repression barrier and it stands along with such defenses as denial or hallucinatory omnipotence. There is disagreement whether disavowal ought to be called a splitting of the ego or a splitting of the self in the service of defense. The important point is that two contradictory perceptual or behavior systems are operating at the same time and are both conscious; an individual shifts back and forth between them. Freud's well known example was the denial of castration that the little boy experiences when he first sees the female genital; the perception that there are some humans who have no penises is kept in the conscious right along with the insistence that all human beings have penises. Both perceptions are reacted to and contained in the conscious mind at the same time.

Kohut's "vertical split" is somewhat different and has to do with the conscious presence of a grandiose self in the mentation and behavior of an individual who is also aware at the very same time that he is not grand. For example, the patient at times consciously behaves as if he were powerful and omnipotent and important in a manner far out of proportion to his real state; at other times he behaves appropriately but in a manner contaminated by low self-esteem, shame propensity and hypochondria.

The repression barrier is established firmly at the time of resolution of the Oedipus complex. Transference represents a crossing of the repression barrier in which an object representation or a self-representation is projected onto the therapist and he is then related to accordingly. This is the restricted definition of transference; there are others. Therapeutic alliance, on the other hand, is an attitude of expectation and cooperation based primarily on memory traces of previous experience with authority figures or doctors. It has nothing to do with the repression barrier, no crossing of which is involved. It is based primarily on memory traces of successful experiences with people toward whom the individual had turned for help in the past.

Clearly the style of defenses as well as the primary autonomous functions of the ego involved have a genetic or hereditary basis. To put it technically, Nagera (1967) speaks in terms of ego structures rather than ego apparatuses or ego functions, a view which postulates the existence from the very beginning of life of a number of ready-made primitive structures or organizations and which is completely in line with Hartmann's assumptions of inborn ego apparatuses belonging to the conflict-free sphere. "These structures exist at birth, while most other structures have to be created during the development; that is, further structuralization is taking place all the time as development proceeds."

Three factors are crucial as determinants of the rate and extent of acquired structuralization. First we have innate limitations, which differ from individual to individual—differences in inborn qualities. Second, human needs and human nature are involved; the various degrees and intensities of our needs serve as a triggering force to propel us along the path of structuralization and ego development. The third factor is the environment in which we happen to be born. Adaptation to a high degree of civilization also demands a great extent of ego structuralization. As civilization becomes more complex, it makes further demands on the ego's capabilities to deal with the ever-increasing complexity of propositions of the new order of things.

Thus, as Nagera points out, education is basically a system "devised to teach children in a condensed and simplified manner the means by which they can build complex psychological ego apparatuses capable of dealing with the complexities created in our world. All education does is to exercise a number of mental capabilities in special directions and combinations until the ego learns to perform a number of complicated functions in interaction."

I suspect that the capacity of the borderline to snap back and to move up and down the ego axis is related to these inherited styles of defense and primary autonomous functions as well as to the existence of at least some adaptive identifications with some significant parental or grandparental figure in the past. Sometimes these identifications don't occur until adolescence, during which the borderline patient is lucky enough to meet a relatively healthy individual that he can use for microidentifications.

Rapaport (1951) explains that the ego is born out of conflict and is a party to it. Certain apparatuses of the ego have primary autonomy and certain functions are outside of conflict in the conflict-free sphere of the ego. Now there is a certain constancy and reliability in the autonomy of the ego as an emergent organization which has laws of its own distinct from the elements which control it. Rapaport warns us that this autonomy, especially the secondary autonomy, is always relative. He indicates that the onslaught of drive motivations, especially when unchecked by therapeutic help or when aided by overzealous therapeutic moves, may reverse the autonomy and bring about a regressed psychotic state in which the patient is to a far-reaching extent at the mercy of the drive impulses. The higher-level autonomous motivations are dissolved and the allies that the therapist usually counts on—spontaneity and synthesis—are absent. He points out, "Thus we can see that the issue of ego autonomy is not merely a theoretical problem, but also a practical one of therapy, particularly in borderline and psychotic cases."

He doesn't say it, but the converse is obviously also true. Good psychotherapy enhances the core of autonomous ego function, leads to greater cohesiveness of the self—better overall ego function—and reduces the clamor and disturbances of the impulses which is always such a big problem in treatment of borderline patients.

Gitelson (1963) points out that it is very difficult to separate what is constitutionally given and what is acquired through introjection. The climate of the first relationship with the mother establishes the fundamental and typical mood of the person. The intimacy of the symbiosis of mother and child is what makes it so extremely difficult to be certain what is constitutionally given and what is acquired. Of course, everything is further complicated by subsequent identification with father and siblings and other significant persons later on. As a matter of fact, the latter, "including the parents as they are and appear in later years, impose various modifications for better or for worse, on the original identifications."

However, Gitelson's point is *that these original identifications are essentially indestructible and retain their effectiveness.* The earliest identifications enter into the formation of what we call ego nuclei, and a great deal in the therapy depends on the extent to which these are dissolvable and can be dealt with by therapeutic modification. It is not difficult to see, then, how complex the careful dissection of an individual's ego functions can be and how difficult it is to understand the basic nuclei of the ego in the borderline patient. Now we can also see that these ego nuclei, the earliest identifications, vitally affect what we call ego strength.

The understanding of so-called ego strength also depends on understanding of the superego. The internalization of the parents via identifications, which reaches its peak at the Oedipal stage, internalizes both critical and loving aspects of the parents. Thus there is both a harsh or critical superego and a benign superego. Obviously inner strength is based on the presence of the benign superego, which infuses the ego with approval. Day-to-day parental approval generates a whole system that causes the build-up of ego skills in the latency period. If the parent withdraws at that time, the harsh or critical superego takes over this function, and the unfortunate individual is quite vulnerable. I have noted that in adolescence the more malevolent of peers are often allowed to take over this function also.

The ego ideal is also in the superego and is related by some authors to the equivalent of the primary narcissism of the baby. Thus, one tries to live up to the idealized image of what one could be, and this is a part of the self-regulation system. For example, let us take ambition. From the point of view of libidinal drives, ambition can be understood as the wish on the oral level to incorporate the world, on the anal level to produce the largest bowel movement—to be productive—and on the phallic level to have the biggest capacity, to be outstanding and efficient. *Simultaneously,* ambition can be understood on the level of the ego ideal or narcissism as the wish to be magical, powerful in sublimated socially acceptable ways, and so to get love and approval from the self and others.

Therefore, if one has a good ego-ideal system, then one can mobilize one's ego potential. Otherwise one must search outside oneself for an idealized parent imago to be with and must use one's conception of what the leader (the idealized parental image) is in order to regulate oneself. This is a more technical description of Odier's "neurosis of abandonment" described in borderline cases in Chapter 2.

The secret behind ego strength, then, from the point of view of the superego lies in the presence of a benign, approving, self-regulating system made up of the expectations one has of oneself which come from the ego ideal and the approval of oneself coming from the benign superego.

Gitelson (1963) further explains that the primary influence of the parent is internalized and made permanent in the formation of the superego. He writes, "Aggressive and libidinal energy which is withdrawn from its original focus on the parents becomes available to the superego itself, providing it with powers which are exerted against the forces of the id and the derivatives in the ego. The superego originates in part from the conditionings which occur in the preverbal and pregenital relationship to the mother; it is transiently stabilized in the context of the Oedipus complex, in middle childhood; it appears in its ultimate form after puberty, and in this form it is crucial to the definitive molding of character. However, its strength is relative not only to the quality of identifications which have entered into its formation, but also to the strength of the id."

We see, therefore, that the metapsychological description of the borderline patient is extremely complicated; in our explanation of the symptomatology of the patient we have to take into account both the ego and the superego. More precisely we must study the four functioning subsystems of the ego—the primary autonomous functions, the secondary autonomous functions, the defensive functions and the adaptative identifications—AND the subsystems of the superego—the harsh critical superego, the benign superego and the ego ideal. The interaction of these subsystems produces the self-regulating system which the patient presents clinically and upon which he must rely in dealing with the vicissitudes of life.

Since there are a number of subsystems that can go wrong, we are dealing with a tremendous variety of possible permutations and combinations that produce a variety of metapsychological characterizations for the borderline patient. Thus, there is no reason to believe that any one metapsychological characterization can be applied to all borderline patients; it is more scientific to begin with a given borderline patient at the descriptive level of ego and superego functioning and then try to understand the nature of the various subsystems described above and the intrasystemic defects and conflicts that have led to symptomatology manifested by the specific patient.

Kernberg (1970b) proposes a classification of character pathology on the basis of careful examination of instinctual development, of superego development, of defensive operations of the ego, and of the nature of the pathological character traits as well as of the vicissitudes of internalized object relationships, and he outlines the structural characteristics of *higher, intermediate,* and *lower* levels of organization or character pathology. I won't take the space to review this paper in detail, but it gives the reader an idea of the number of permutations and combinations that take place, many of which fall under the general rubric of borderline patient. Clearly these combinations can fall at various levels on what one might call a continuum ranging from the well integrated to the almost disintegrated. In a way it is the existence of this continuum that has caused so much trouble, because there are no discrete diagnostic entitities here, but only more or less of this or that, and it is difficult at times to be certain that two authors who are talking about "borderline patients" are really talking about the same classification of patients on the continuum.

I think this accounts for a great deal of the profound disagreement in the literature. For example, Masterson (1972) has devoted a whole book to the basic theory that separation from the mother does not evolve as a normal developmental experience for the borderline patient. On the contrary, it entails such intense feelings of abandonment that it is experienced as a rendezvous with death. To defend against these feelings, the borderline patient clings to the maternal figure, thus failing to progress through the normal developmental stages of separation and individuation to autonomy (Masterson and Rinsley 1975). This is of course based on the concept of separation-individuation, which has evolved from Mahler (Mahler and Gosslinger 1955; Mahler and LaPerrier 1965; Mahler et al. 1975; Mahler 1963, 1971, 1974, 1975), who studied by direct observation the separation-individuation processes of normal children. It is based, therefore, on certain fundamental assumptions about the phases that normal children go through (the autistic phase, the symbiotic phase and the separation-individuation phases).

Great theoretical differences appear at once if one looks at the work of Kohut (1971). Mahler's work is based on a theoretical system defined by the position of an observer equally distant from the interacting parties of mother and child, occupying an imaginary point *outside* the experiencing individual. Kohut insists that the core area of psychoanalytic metapsychology is defined by the position of an observer who occupies an imaginary point *inside* the psychic organization of the individual, with whose introspection he empathically identifies. This is of course accomplished through the transference revival of childhood experience rather than through direct observation of children and through reconstructions of the inner life of the child on the basis of transference reactivations. This difference of viewpoint between Mahler and Kohut points to why there is such a profound theoretical difference between those who work from the classical psychoanalytic point of view and those who approach the borderline patient from a variety of other types of viewpoints such as interpersonal theory or social interaction or behavior theory and so forth.

The crucial differentiation among (1) narcissistically experienced archaic self-objects; (2) internalized psychological structures that perform drive-regulating, integrating and adaptive functions previously performed by external objects; and (3) "true objects" cathected with object-instinctual investments forms the foundation for recognizing the *profound distinction* between psychoanalytic metapsychology and *all other* points of view (Kohut, 1971).

CHAPTER 6

Metapsychology of Narcissism

The greatest current debate, of course, is on the subject of narcissism. We can distinguish two basic views about primary narcissism. Balint (1968) flatly states that there is no such thing as primary narcissism. In his view, the individual is born with primary object love—the kind of seeking is for an object that will gratify the person without his even having to first communicate the need to the object. It is in the wish for the intuitive, empathic all-loving maternal object. There is no room in the theory of Balint for primary narcissism, and he sees development as progressing strictly along the line of object relations, from primary object relations to mature object love.

Freud, on the other hand, beginning with his famous paper "On Narcissism" (1914), defined narcissism as the cathexis of the self or the ego with libido. Notice that Freud sometimes uses the terms *ego* and *self* interchangeably. There is only a dim notion in his theoretical formulations that a distinction is necessary between self and ego. This is usually called the "syphon theory" of narcissism, because it is thought of as a U-tube in which there is a fixed quantity of libido available. When more is cathected to the ego or the self, less is available to be cathected to objects, and vice versa. According to Freud's theory, the infant passes from a phase of autoerotism, in which there are simply body states before any ego nuclei have even developed, to a phase of primary narcissism, which begins with the formation of ego nuclei and represents an overwhelming cathexis of these ego nuclei with the libido. Then occurs a gradual transition from the stage of primary narcissism to the state of object love, as libido is divested from the ego and cathected to objects (object-representations).

Secondary narcissism is also defined differently by different authors. Freud defined secondary narcissism as a defensive withdrawal of libido from objects back into a cathexis of the ego or self, and that was the usually accepted definition of secondary narcissism until recently. Balint insists that all narcissism when it appears is secondary narcissism, since there is no such thing as primary narcissism. Disregarding the concept of secondary narcissism, Kohut, at the other extreme, would argue that narcissism follows an independent line of development and reaches levels of narcissism from primitive to mature.

In his theoretical orientation Kohut, in direct contrast to Balint (1968), stays closer to the classical psychoanalytic viewpoint, postulating a preliminary phase of autoerotism followed by primary or primitive narcissism. Kohut (1971) explains that in normal development, "The equilibrium of primary narcissism is disturbed by unavoidable shortcomings of maternal care, but the child replaces the previous perfection (a) by establishing a grandiose and exhibitionistic image of the self, the *grandiose self*; and (b) by giving over the previous perfection to an admired, omnipotent (transitional) self object: *the idealized parent imago.*" With much greater care and attention than any author has previously paid to this subject, Kohut elaborates and distinguishes the vicissitudes that occur as the equilibrium of primary narcissism is inevitably disturbed.

Ferenczi (1950) as early as 1913 points out that an analysis that reaches to the depths reveals that feelings of inferiority are reactions to the exaggerated feelings of omnipotence to which certain patients have become fixed in their early childhood and which have made it impossible for them to adjust themselves to any subsequent renunciation. The manifest seeking for greatness that these people have, Ferenczi explains, is the return of the repressed, a hopeless attempt to reach once more, by means of changing the outer world, the omnipotence that originally was enjoyed without effort. Those objects which are not as yet available to the immature psyche will be experienced in an intrapsychic world as if they were parts of the self. Freud would say these need-fulfilling objects are invested with narcissistic libido. Kohut feels that the line of development of object love proper can only begin *after* the secure differentiation of the self from objects. Before that time objects are not loved for their attributes, which are at best dimly recognized, they are loved as part of the self.

Modell's (1968) theory, which I have referred to previously, states this in terms of the child continuing to need to create illusory substitutes that he can control in place of the actual mother, who has an independent center of volition or will power. Modell, following Winnicott, calls this a transitional object relation, and he explains how by utilizing fantasies of omnipotence the infant is enabled to preserve in one aspect of his mind his illusion of symbiosis.

Now whether these archaic self-objects are referred to as transitional objects or part objects or self-objects seems to be mainly a matter of which author you read. The point is that these various object imagos are gradually sorted out realistically and, concurrent with the achievement of stable reality testing, they are consolidated into whole objects with stable characteristics. This opens the way to true object love.

Notice that this discussion of object relations is focused on the intrapsychic world and avoids a confusion of the early phases of development with later stages. The failure to make this distinction has been responsible for controversy and has been the source of one of the primary difficulties between the classical psychoanalytic approach and the attempts of Melanie Klein and Fairbairn and others. Modell is criticized by Kohut and his co-workers (Gedo and Goldberg 1973) for failing to attain the necessary metapsychological clarity in his view that cognitive differentiation of self from object marks the emergence of the self as a cohesive entity. By differentiating self-objects from those invested with true object libido, Kohut presents an evolving sequence of the child's objects and also the complementary issue of the development of the child's self. *Thus the central clinical discovery here is the overriding importance of the attainment of a cohesive sense of self.* Clearly, failure to achieve this cohesion is characteristic of various forms of severe psychopathology, and even in those cases that Kohut feels are analyzable there is a vulnerability to fragmentation of the self under stress.

Kohut believes that there is a separate normal developmental line for narcissism, whereas the other authors believe narcissism should essentially disappear and change into object love in normal development. For Kohut, then, after primary narcissism has been established, the next developmental stage is an attempt to retain primary narcissistic equilibrium in the face of realistic disappointing experiences. This stimulates two psychic formations, the grandiose self and the idealized parent imago. The child forms a fantasy of being himself as all-powerful and omnipotent, a sense of himself as grandiose. He also forms an imago of an all-powerful omnipotent idealized parent. Both of these formations occur around the same time and represent the attempt to retain primary narcissism either by imagined grandiosity or by connection with the omnipotent parent who will therefore meet all his needs.

The grandiose self and idealized parent imago are normally eventually integrated into the personality. The idealized parent imago, as already mentioned, becomes part of the ego ideal in the superego toward which the individual strives. The grandiose self becomes a part of the ego apparatuses and functions as ambition and drive regulation. Kohut explains that the grandiose self, when it is integrated into the ego, pushes the individual forward through ambition and drive regulation. The ego ideal, formed of the idealized parent imago, pulls the individual from above, so to speak, and becomes a goal toward which the individual strives.

A cohesive sense of the self as separate from others must occur in normal development, and it is based on the reality fact that one *is* separate as a mental and physical self. The cathexis of various self-representations determines how we think about and even behave towards our real mental and physical self.

The term *identity* is probably the most confusing of all and has been made even more confused by Erikson's use of the term "ego-identity." Identity is best thought of as a sociological term, referring to the individual as a coherent entity with direction and continuity at any given stage of human development. Identity is a vector term; thus it has both a magnitude and a direction in contrast to all these other terms, which are essentially scalar (only magnitude). There must also exist identity representations. The subjective feeling of having an identity that Erikson emphasizes would depend primarily on the cathexis of identity representations. The concept of identity is most complex because it depends on all the other concepts already defined as well as on the vicissitudes of the milieu and the culture in which one lives. For example, when we speak of "sexual identity," we are really including a host of other functioning aspects of the personality as well as interpersonal interactions and the influence of the social milieu, all of which form representations in the person's ego of his sexual identity.

Kohut explains how under ordinary circumstances, the grandiose self and the idealized parent imago—important for ambition, enjoyment and self-esteem—become integrated into the adult personality. With each of the mother's inevitable minor empathic failures, misunderstandings and delays, the infant withdraws narcissistic libido from the archaic imago of unconditional perfection (primary narcissism) and acquires in its stead a particle of inner psychological structure that takes over the mother's functions in the service of the maintenance of narcissistic equilibrium. Thus, tolerable disappointments in the primary narcissistic equilibrium lead to the establishment of internal structures that provide the ability for self-soothing and the acquisition of basic tension tolerance. However, if severe narcissistic traumas are suffered by the child, then the grandiose self and the idealized parent imago are retained in unaltered form, *not* transformed into the adult personality, and exert a pressure of their own.

Another way to understand the lack of inner sustainment (Saul 1970) in the borderline patient is to focus microscopically on the ego ideal. The core of narcissistic omnipotence in the ego ideal is the remnant of the positive, gratifying, mother-child relationship when there has in fact been good mothering. When this component is present it has a need-satisfying wish-fulfilling quality of its own, which continually bathes the ego with its own sense of narcissistic omnipotence, no matter what other conflicts there may be. This component of the ego ideal is either there or it is not there—and it has a profound influence on the further growth and development of other psychic structures.

Weiner (1973) explains, "If the mothering is poor or inconsistent and the substructures fail to develop, the resultant inability of the infant to deal with a feeling of abandonment and helplessness will distort ego growth and later object relations." Basic trust cannot grow and fear of abandonment and betrayal beclouds all later object relations. Internally, the ego cannot fall back on its own psychic friends in times of trouble, for on this level, there are none. At this time a feeling of hopelessness occurs, and this psychic state sets the stage "for the disposition to fall ill of melancholia" (Freud, 1917).

Weiner (1973) also calls attention to various "rescue operations for narcissism" described by Hartmann and Lowenstein (1962). These rescue operations are very important. They involve the idealization of positive aspects of the parents and other important people. In addition the ego may develop character traits which fulfill precepts of the ego ideal. The person may go through life having developed character traits that satisfy the ego ideal, but the loss of an important object or a breakup of these traits due to retirement, financial reverses and so on may occur, taking away the external narcissistic input, and then the person suffers a depression. At this point the patient feels mentally bankrupt and external reassurance becomes useless because "the poverty about which the patient complains is psychologically true. . . . Endless protestations from the family, friends, and well-meaning professionals are usually addressed to the conscious ego, which is weakened, while the unconscious ego is preoccupied in a fruitless search for inner nurturance." Many borderline patients come for psychotherapy at this point.

Kohut describes the difficulties between the child and the parent that lead to disruption of the normal trend of events in the vicissitudes of narcissism. Under optimal circumstances the child experiences gradual disappointments in the parent or idealized object; to put it another way, the child's evaluation of the idealized object becomes increasingly realistic, which leads to a "withdrawal of the narcissistic cathexes from the imago of the idealized self-object and to their gradual internalization."

If the child suffers traumatic loss of the idealized object or phase-inappropriate disappointment in it, then optimal internalization does not take place, and the psyche remains fixated on an archaic self-object:

> The personality throughout life will be dependent on certain objects in what seems to be an intense form of object hunger. The intensity of the search for and of the dependency on these objects is due to the fact that they are striven for as a substitute for the missing segments of the psychic structure. They are not objects . . . since they are not loved or admired for their attributes, and

the actual features of their personalities, and their actions are only dimly recognized. They are needed to replace the functions of a segment of the mental apparatus which has not been established in childhood.

The trauma suffered most repeatedly in these cases is severe disappointment in the mother, who because of her defective empathy with the child's needs did not appropriately fulfill her functions as a stimulus barrier, an optimal provider of needed stimuli, a supplier of tension-relieving gratification and so on, depriving the child of the gradual internalization of early experiences of being optimally soothed or aided in going to sleep. The mature psychic apparatus should later be able to perform these functions predominantly on its own.

This has been carried to a fascinating degree of further metapsychological refinement by Kohut. He writes, as noted above, *of phase-inappropriate disappointment in the idealized parent imago:* depending on the phase in which this inappropriate disappointment occurs we will see different clinical pathology. Thus in the very early stages of life with the predominant need for maximal soothing and relaxations towards going to sleep from the parent, a phase-inappropriate disappointment will lead to the search for this kind of soothing from the outside, since the proper "transmuting internalizations" have not built it in from the mother. The patient is left with a malfunctioning stimulus barrier, and we observe the search for drugs or other procedures (including psychotherapy) for the primary purpose of obtaining this soothing from an external source.

Disappointment in the late preoedipal period leads to a sexualization of pregenital drives and derivatives as development proceeds, with a resulting predominance in the psychic life of "perversions" of all sorts in fantasy or even acting out. Disappointment in the Oedipal or early latency period makes the internalization of the idealized parent imago into the ego ideal impossible (or, in early latency, undoes this internalization, which at this point is new and shaky) and results in a fixation on the search for an idealized parent outside of the patient. The result is an intense striving for a dependency on an idealized person, as if this person were a missing part of the self; approval from this person is required to maintain narcissistic equilibrium, and personal accomplishment brings no lasting satisfaction. Odier's "neuroses of abandonment" fall in this area.

As an example of the latter, Kohut presents a patient in which "the central defect of his personality was the insufficient idealization of his superego (an insufficient cathexis with idealizing libido of the values, standards, and function of his superego) and, concomitantly, the strong cathexis of an externally experienced idealized parent imago in the late pre-Oedipal and Oedipal stages." This led to a diffuse narcissistic vulnerability, the hypercathexis of his grandiose self occurring mainly in response to disappointments in the idealized parent imago, and the tendency toward the sexualization of the narcissistically cathected constellations. In such patients a hypersensitivity to disturbances in the narcissistic equilibrium takes place with a tendency to react to sources of narcissistic disturbance by a mixture of wholesale withdrawal and unforgiving rage, forming a very typical and frequent clinical picture.

According to Kohut, an unconscious attachment to, and failure in integration of, the archaic grandiose self or the idealized parent imago and their corresponding self-object representatives, result from impaired development of narcissism. Disturbance in integration of the grandiose self means that the primitive narcissistic impulses remain walled off from the reality ego, but they continue to influence the self, as manifested by wide oscillations in self-esteem and other phenomena.

A rather strongly opposing view is presented by Kernberg (1970a, 1974a, 1974b, 1975a, 1975b), who refuses to differentiate between narcissistic personalities and borderline personalities in the way that Kohut does. Their fundamental similarity, he insists, is in the predominance of mechanisms of splitting or primitive disassociation, as already briefly described in Chapter 3. Thus, from a dynamic viewpoint "pathological condensation of genital and pregenital needs under the overriding influence of pregenital (especially oral) aggression is characteristic of narcissistic personalities as well as borderline personality organization."

The difference between a narcissistic personality structure and the borderline personality disorder, says Kernberg, centers on the specific presence in the former of (1) an integrated grandiose self which reflects a pathological condensation of some aspects of the real self—for example, the specialness of the child that may have been reinforced by the parents; and (2) the ideal self—with fantasies and images of power, wealth, and beauty that compensated the small child for the experience of severe frustration, rage and envy—and the ideal object—the fantasy of an ever-loving and ever-giving mother in contrast to reality.

Kernberg argues that the integration of this pathological grandiose self "compensates" for the lack of integration of the normal self-concept and explains the paradox of relatively good ego functioning and surface adaptation in the presence of a predominance of splitting mechanisms and lack of integration of object representations.

The disagreement is about the origin of this grandiose self and whether it reflects the fixation of an archaic normal primitive self with a separate line of development (Kohut) or is *always* a pathological structure clearly different from the normal infantile narcissism. Kernberg emphasizes the pathology, and especially the repetitive chronic activation of intensive rage reactions that comes up in the psychotherapy of the borderline patient.

CHAPTER 7

Disputes and Disagreements

Theories of Melanie Klein. Jacobson (1964) made what might be called the first heroic attempt from the point of view of classical ego psychology and metapsychology to make sense out of Melanie Klein's confused concepts of ego, self and identity. She evaluated Klein's contributions and pointed out that there was a failure in her work to distinguish the endopsychic representation of external objects from introjects and from the infantile superego. In other words this differentiation, which I have mentioned previously, between archaic internalized objects, objects out there and representations of objects, is not carefully made. Jacobson points out that Klein fails to distinguish the constitution of self, and object representations, object relations, and ego identifications from superego formation. Jacobson makes a very careful attempt to describe the vicissitudes of self- and object representations as they enter both ego and superego formation.

An attempt to sharpen up the theoretical approach of Klein has been made by Fairbairn, Guntrip and others; these authors make an effort to bridge the distance between the Kleinian approach and the classical metapsychological approach. Fairbairn's theoretical contributions suffer from a confusion of concepts similar to Klein's. In addition, we have the criticism of Klein from the point of view of Winnicott and Balint, who theoretically are closer to Guntrip and Fairbairn but clinically point out that Klein's tendency to push farther and farther back the age at which mental mechanisms appear tends to neglect the influence of the environment.

Thus the vagueness and ambiguity of Kleinian terminology are major stumbling blocks preventing the clarification of Kleinian theory even by such brilliant minds as Guntrip and Fairbairn. There are internal inconsistencies within Kleinian theory, and because of them I am not going to spend much time discussing the Kleinian school and their approach to the borderline patient. In addition, there are shifts in the way the terms *ego* and *self* are used throughout Kleinian literature that make it very difficult to grasp the exact meaning of such important concepts as projective identification. Every time I give a course on the borderline patient this concept comes up, and it is very difficult to pin down just what Klein meant by it. She originally described it as the projection of split-off parts of the self into another person. One aim of the process, then, is the forceful entry into the object and control of the object by parts of the self. At this point she uses the concepts of ego and self interchangeably, whereas elsewhere she describes them separately. Her followers have broadened the concept of projective identification in a variety of ways that I won't go into at this point. We will discuss projective identification later in more detail (see Chapter 9).

Theories of Primitive Object Relations. The theory of primitive object relationships (see review by L. Friedman 1975) is the basic point of disagreement, and yet it is vital to any understanding of the borderline patient. A reasonable and relatively simple theory of primitive object relations and the application of this theory to the understanding of the borderline patient is presented by Modell (1963). Modell insists that the "borderline patient" is a homogeneous group, different than the schizophrenic patient on the one hand—where there is a significant disorder in sense of reality testing—and from the neurotic on the other hand. This is manifested by the primitive but consistent form of object relationship that the borderline patient forms in the transference.

To my knowledge this is the first serious attempt to differentiate the borderline patient on the basis of a consistent type of transference that he forms. Modell reminds us that he is using the term borderline as I have—not as ambulatory schizophrenia but as a separate group. The object relationship that the borderline patient forms in the transference, according to Modell, is midway between the transference of the neurotic and that of the psychotic. In the neurotic transference, the object is perceived as outside the self and invested with qualities that are distorted fantasies arising from the subject. But the object still exists as a separate individual. On the other hand, schizophrenics are unable to perceive that there is something outside of the self at all. Therefore, Modell sees the borderline transference as related to a transitional stage, and he compares the relationship of the borderline patient to his physician as analogous to that of a child to a transitional object, the blanket or a teddy bear. He states, "We can observe that there is a uniform, almost monotonous, regularity to the transference phantasies, especially in the opening phases of treatment. The therapist is percieved invariably as one endowed with magical omnipotent qualities, who will, merely by his contact with the patient, effect a cure without the necessity of the patient himself to be active and responsible."

The type of transference formed by the borderline, according to Modell, is also transitional because it stands midway between a state of affairs where there is an absence of the sense of self, as in the psychotic, and one where there is a distinct sense of self, as in the neurotic. There is a fusion or confusion of the sense of self with the object.

It is implied from this that there are three phases of object love that take place in early development. In the earliest phase the young infant responds to the mother but cannot make a psychological distinction between the self and the object. The middle phase is the phase of transitional object relations. Then mature object love, according to Modell, is the stage where there is a distinct separation between self and object. Thus the difference between the borderline and the neurotic patient resides in the fact that for the most part the psychic development of the neurotic patient has passed through the stage of the transitional object, whereas the psychic development of the borderline patient became arrested at the stage of the transitional object.

The cause of this arrest essentially has to do not with physical loss of the mother but with the kind of failure of mothering that I have already discussed in Chapter 2. Modell similarly describes from his clinical experience, not mothers who are lost, but mothers who are unable to make emotional contact with their children as they themselves are severely depressed or even psychotic. There is a significant comment that in some of these cases the usual amount of holding and cuddling was absent. In other patients, although the physical care was adequate, there was a profound distortion in the mother's attitude toward the child. For example, the mother could not perceive the child as a separate person, which induced a relative incapacity on the child's part to differentiate self from object. My clinical experience has been very much of the same nature from reconstruction in the intensive psychotherapy of the borderline patient.

Why is it that the borderline group does not slip into schizophrenia? Why do they hold on to the capacity of reality testing? According to Modell's theory, the schizophrenic patient is fixated at an even earlier stage of development, but in addition to that Modell postulates possible biological factors. There is no point in going into this, because it is an X factor that one could speculate on endlessly.

Self and Identity. Kohut's contribution, differentiating self objects from those invested with true object libido, makes it possible for the first time to meticulously clarify the overriding importance of the attainment of the sense of the cohesion of self. It is this consolidation of self that others, like Jacobson, have referred to as the stable sense of identity. Failure to achieve cohesion of self character-izes various forms of severe psychopathology. Regressive fragmenta-tion of the sense of the wholeness of the personality corresponds to what Freud (1927, 1938, 1940) called splitting of the ego in 1927. In some places he used the word ego differently from the way the word ego is used in the structural theory, since at the time "disovowal" (Freud, 1927) takes place, the ego is not firmly established. Here is a confusion again; Gedo and Goldberg (1973) point out that the correct terminology should be "splitting of the self." (We reject Jacobson's term *identity* because her usage of *identity* instead of *self* is some kind of an attempt to straddle the gap between two disciplines—social and individual psychology—and doesn't really belong to either.)

Erikson (1959) compounded this terminological muddle, and it is quite a muddle, by introducing the term *ego identity* to designate the ultimate maturation of the sense of self in adolescence. Therefore, it is best for us to drop the term *identity,* a social sciences term, and stay with the construct of self. Even *self* is very semantically difficult, and there are great problems in trying to impose it on the tripartite model of the mind (ego, id, and superego), but the cohesive sense of self *is* a very important aspect to clinically consider in working with borderline patients!

Adult Narcissism. The question remains unanswered whether pathological narcissism in the adult is a consequence of some sort of pathological narcissistic infantile organization or whether it is merely a result of interference with the normal evolution of infantile narcissism, leading to developmental arrest (see reviews of the debate by Ornstein 1973, 1974a, 1974b). Kernberg (1974b) insists that "pathological narcissism is strikingly different from normal narcissism." In his view, the grandiose self and the idealized parent imago represent pathological developments, *not* developmental arrests, and there are no "substantive agreements" with Kohut in this area (Ornstein 1974a).

Zetzel (1971, 1973) maintains that narcissism is a predominant element in the character structure of borderline patients; she believes, "This behavior often serves to cover a deep distrust and helps to defend against underlying paranoid traits which are based on the projection of a rather primitive oral rage." Thus Zetzel is in essential agreement with Kernberg, seeing the personality organization of borderline patients as "impulsive and infantile." She attributes this to "an underlying weakness of the structure and organization of the ego." The ego's overall capacity for neutralization of instinctual drive derivatives is poor.

I would suggest that we try to stay as close as possible to the practical situation through the scrutinizing of clinical material—begin with the clinical material and try to see which of these various theoretical formulations fit the given clinical phenomena. This means that the intelligent reader will have to juggle in his head these conflicting theories and be prepared to try to fit the theories to the clinical phenomena the way one fits scattered pieces together in a jigsaw-puzzle opening. You scan and try out several pieces, one at a time, to see which piece fits.

Projection and Introjection. Kohut's theory attempts to get rid of the concepts of projection and introjection in infancy altogether, as these are terms that have been utilized with very insufficient precision in the literature (Rapaport 1944). Thus the so-called projections of psychotics are caused by failure to maintain the boundary of the self.

The attribution of a thought or feeling of one's own to another is simply due to the lack of differentiation between the self and object.

A repression barrier is necessary before genuine projections can take place. Gedo and Goldberg (1973) attempt to differentiate what one might call less mature types of projections from more mature projections as seen in the neuroses. The latter occur after a reasonably firm repression barrier has been established. The repression barrier is not solidly established until the Oedipal phase of life has been worked through. These authors imply that since the irreversible establishment of the ego is not expected to take place until after the resolution of the Oedipus complex, the concepts of projection and introjection before that time are at least metapsychologically quite different, if not altogether incorrect. Thus it is much easier, relatively speaking, to characterize the borderline patient in a descriptive fashion than it is to understand the metapsychology involved.

According to Zetzel (1973), the defensive processes of internal splitting of the ego into good and bad parts is supported and engineered through the interplay of introjection and projection. Meissner (1974) describes the correlated aspects of introjective and projective mechanisms and how the interplay of introjective and projective mechanisms weaves a pattern of relatedness to the world of objects and provides a fabric out of which each individual fashions his own self-image. Out of this interplay comes the gradual emergence of differentiation between the self and object, according to authors Zetzel, Modell and Meissner, without postulating a second line of development for narcissistic libido.

However, Zetzel (1973) continues, the excessive operation of these primitive mechanisms in borderline patients prevents the ego from achieving any meaningful integration of both self- and object images "which have been built up out of libidinal derivatives, with the self and object images which have been built up out of aggressive derivatives." She sees a progression of cycles of the projection of aggression and "the subsequent reintrojection of hostile and destructive object and self images" as central to the development of both the psychotic and borderline personality organization. "In psychotic development, this process produces a regressive refusal of self and object images with the loss of ego boundaries and self-object differentiation. In the borderline however, the process does not reach that level of regression, but rather brings about an intensification and fixation of splitting processes."

In a complex metapsychological sentence Zetzel claims, "Thus splitting achieves an active separation of introjects of opposite quality—good as opposed to bad. The integration of such object derivatives is one of the major ways in which aggression is neutralized and detoxified." This is explained in terms of the fusion of libidinal and aggressive instincts in normal development, which permits a neutralization of aggression. The splitting mechanism on the other hand, results in an inadequate neutralization of instinctual energies; according to Zetzel, "Splitting is consequently a basic dimension of the borderline patient's ego weakness." Thus Zetzel and Kernberg seem to be in agreement regarding the dominance of splitting mechanisms and the importance of the rage or unneutralized aggression in the borderline patient.

Similarly, the idealization of the therapist and the shift back and forth between the idealization and the devaluation of the therapist and between overvaluation and devaluation of the self are explained on the basis of the splitting mechanisms and of the mechanisms of projection and projective identification—"at once expelling evil aspects out of the self and putting them on objects, leaving the self good and strong, or again taking them in again thus making the self weak, helpless, and evil." This is in sharp contrast to Kohut's approach as described above.

Zetzel's approach to the borderline patient is therefore based on an attempt to help the patient deal with the impaired ego. Due to this impaired ego, "In the therapeutic relationship, magical expectations, impairment of the distinction between fantasy and reality, episodes of anger, suspicion, and excessive fears of rejection are to be anticipated over a relatively extended period." This is a result of what Zetzel calls a developmental failure. The cure for this failure is to gradually establish "areas of relatively autonomous functioning which are more or less free of the toxic effects of evil and destructive introjects."

There is a certain atmosphere in this quotation about the effects of evil and destructive introjects that is reminiscent of medieval theology. There is a certain personification involved which is semantically, metapsychologically, and scientifically undesirable. This is the reason why attempts are being made to reconstruct and clarify these theories of early development in order to remove the moralistic and emotional overlay brought about by discussion of such things as evil, destructive and malevolent introjects—almost as if they were an infestation by the devil.

CHAPTER 8

Developmental Failure in
the Borderline Patient

The developmental failure in borderline patients, to summarize Zetzel (1971, 1973), includes a failure in each of the following developmental tasks: (1) the achievement of definitive self-object differentiation; (2) the capacity to tolerate frustration, delay, separation, and narcissistic injury; and (3) "the internalization of a positive ego identification which serves as a basis for a basic self-esteem and a relatively substantial sense of autonomy."

With respect to the first task, we see the difficulty in the borderline patient of distinguishing between fantasy and reality—especially under stress. According to Zetzel this also becomes a problem in placing the patient on the analytic couch, but there is an early report of a panel on the borderline patient (Rangell 1955) in which Zetzel herself points out that in England the couch is employed somewhat more freely and universally with borderline patients than it is in the United States; no undue effects have been reported. Zetzel explains, "It is possible that the difficulties here of the use of the couch stem to some degree from the analyst's fears of the consequences rather than from the patient, for the latter, if free association is becoming too threatening, will usually set up his own controls." This has been my experience in many instances also, and I have reported elsewhere on this in detail (Chessick 1971b).

I hasten to add that the use of the couch in the psychotherapy of borderline patients is *not* a procedure for a beginner. It should only be undertaken by the skilled, experienced and well-trained psychothera-pist who is aware of the difficulties involved. In some cases it is then definitely very helpful; in others, it has no effect one way or another. One of the clinical phenomena most impressive in differentiating the borderline patient from the schizophrenic patient is that schizophrenic patients usually do very poorly in unstructured and couch situations; they really fall apart or become unintelligible. Borderline patients simply usually do not.

With respect to the second developmental task, the intolerance of aggressive impulses is most typically shown, and both the aggressive impulses of the patient *and of others* are not tolerated. Zetzel sees the lack of capacity to deal with frustration, delay, and loss as due to the problem of splitting, which makes the patient particularly susceptible to "the toxic effects of destructive and hateful impulses and impairs their capacity to master ambivalance."

The third developmental path is seen as most impaired and Zetzel speaks of "an impairment of the capacity for identification," that is to say, the patient is seen as unable to effectively internalize whatever strength is to be had from the therapist. Zetzel sees this limitation and basic impairment in the capacity of the ego as setting a limit on the effectiveness of therapeutic effort regardless of how stable, realistic and consistent the doctor-patient relationship has become. Because of these problems, Zetzel concludes that borderline patients should be seen infrequently in order to avoid mobilizing the intensive ambivalence and unneutralized aggressive aspects which always threaten to disrupt the treatment. This is in contrast to Kernberg's view of treatment, although both authors base their conclusions on what seem to be essentially similar metapsychological descriptions of the borderline patient.

It is not really a metapsychological statement to say that the borderline patient has "a limited and vulnerable capacity to internalize a sufficiently stable ego identification and thus gain some level of stable and genuinely autonomous functioning." This statement does not explain *why* this phenomenon occurs—it is more of a clinical impression.

However, Zetzel's quotation is consistent with Giovacchini's (1967a, 1975) view: "Disruptive introjects do not lead to ego differentiation. They interfere with the development of specific areas of adaptation.

Such lack of development or maldevelopment may prevent the patient from obtaining gratification from persons who may be willing to help him. The patient is not able to utilize or assimilate experiences which another person that does not have the same type of constricting introjects finds indispensable for his emotional development."

There is little understanding and agreement on the exact method by which the introject is formed or on precisely how it functions in specific states of ego development to either enhance or impair the adaptative functioning of the ego and the synthetic functioning of the ego to produce the subsequent impaired development of a healthy sense of self.

The task of psychotherapy with the borderline and psychotic patient becomes infinitely complicated by the fact that the patient neither has a firm grasp of his own sense of self nor is able, because of the introjects, to respond to supportive, kindly or benevolent measures as we logically would expect a starved and lonely person to do. It is now theoretically clear why attempts at directly gratifying the borderline patient have been repeatedly shown to fail. Directly trying to mother the borderline patient causes serious chaos and often produces a paradoxical response, leading to frustration on the part of those who originally approached the patient with benevolence and good will.

Kohut divides the class I have described as borderline patients into those who form stable narcissistic transferences and are thus treatable by the method of formal psychoanalysis on the one hand, and all the rest on the other. The metapsychological differentiation here rests on the issue of the cohesive self. This is characterized in detail by Gedo and Goldberg (1973). It must be made clear that the fundamental and irreconcilable difference between Zetzel and Kernberg on the one hand and Kohut on the other is in the area of the importance and vicissitudes of narcissism. Zetzel and Kernberg see this narcissism as a pathological formation which is used by the patient to hide and deal with intense unneutralized aggressive drives and to compensate the patient for profound disappointments in childhood. When it is removed by suitable interpretation the primitive aggressive drives appear or are projected and are analyzed by interpretation.

Kohut, on the other hand, emphasizes narcissism as a form of normal development which has been arrested in certain types of patients. If they are to be treatable by formal psychoanalysis, these patients must have the capacity to form a stable narcissistic transference in the situation. If they do not have this capacity, then in the psychoanalytic situation they regress to a fragmentation of the self and the only form of treatment that makes sense is for the therapist to provide unification of the self by being a consistent reliable object for structure formation to the patient.

In these situations interpretative approaches have little to do with what happens, since if the patient is lacking a cohesive self-system and cannot conceive of others in terms of whole objects, then transference and interpretation make no sense. Gedo and Goldberg write: "It is sounder to conceptualize these events as consequences of the therapist's entry into a patient's narcissistic world as a transitional object; this intervention serves to bind and integrate the fragmented personality through gradual mastery of narcissistic injuries. This experience is usually not the reliving of any past relationship, however, but a real experience in the present which may have had no precedent." If the unification of the self is accomplished in this way, then there may be additional improvement by way of further maturation of various functions towards secondary autonomy.

Gedo and Goldberg argue that such therapy, in which unification and pacification are essential, is "nonpsychoanalytic." The treatment in such patients is utilized as a transitional object, and this is the key to the therapeutic success. The reason these therapies are called nonpsychoanalytic is that transference and interpretation do not really have an effect, although the therapist may think so; what is really helping the patient is the utilization of the therapeutic atmosphere as a transitional object around which the unintegrated nuclei of the self may cohere in order to allow the patient to find a solid sense of self and therefore a better capacity to distinguish between self and objects.

Even after this has occurred, the patient is still saddled with infantile narcissistic positions involving the split-off grandiose self and the search for the idealized parent imago described above. The treatment is that of formal psychoanalysis, but if the patient cannot form a stable narcissistic transference, then the therapist must be satisfied with the use of pacification and unification techniques.

There is no doubt that pacification and unification techniques have a very important role in the treatment of the borderline patient. Winnicott calls this "good-enough holding" the therapist provides, and we will go into this when we talk more specifically about treatment. Here we have an important clinical differentiation based on different theories of approach to the borderline patient. We will take up later in detail the question, "Should the therapist allow the patient idealization of the therapist without interpretation for a long period, or should such idealizations be interpreted somewhat vigorously as attempts to hide tremendous rage and aggression?"

It should be added here that even though formal psychoanalysis is advised for patients who can form stable narcissistic transferences, "Kohut has found it necessary to introduce a technical modification into this analytic technique. He advocates the acceptance of the patient's idealization of the analyst without interpretation for a long period. In this sense, the analyst offers himself as a new and real object for the purpose of permitting the mastery of a developmental defect."

The fundamental hypothesis of Gedo and Goldberg is that effective therapies of the borderline patient are based on the ability of the therapist to serve as a focus "around whom the clusters of unintegrated nuclei may coalesce into an integrated, cohesive self." With Kohut, Gedo and Goldberg apparently believe that there is no basic metapsychological difference between the schizophrenic patient in remission and the borderline patient. Both patients need the unification of a fragmented psyche through the continued availability of the reliable object—the presence of a real person or even of a reliable setting: "It is sufficient to establish an uninterrupted relationship." From this point of view it makes little difference what the therapist interprets to the patient, for what is most important is not the verbal content of the therapeutic transaction but the consistency, stability and reasonableness of the relationship to the patient.

Again we see a profound and irreconcilable difference between Kernberg's and Zetzel's approach on the one hand and Kohut's, Gedo's and Goldberg's on the other, both in terms of technical therapeutic principles and metapsychological description. Kohut places the focus on the narcissistic sector of the personality and introduces the technical modification of accepting the idealization of the patient without interpretation for a long time. Kernberg does not accept the idea of separate developmental lines of narcissism, and he aims to reach the level of an Oedipal transference neurosis in the treatment. The narcissistic structures revived in the analysis are interpreted by

Kernberg as defensive elaborations against primitive rage *and* against more mature object relationships. He attempts to resolve the pathological narcissistic structures through insight into the primitive mechanism of the splitting of the object into "good and bad." "He implements this aim by a direct confrontation of the patient with his splitting mechanism and by a consistent interpretation of all mani- festations of his narcissism as defensive" (Ornstein 1974a).

According to Kernberg, the patient needs to become aware of his need to devalue and depreciate the analyst as an independent object to protect himself from the reactivation of underlying oral-sadistic rage and envy and the related fear of retaliation from the analyst. Even in the use of the term *envy*, the difference between Kernberg and Kohut appears, because *envy* already implies the capacity to sense another person as a separate object. If a person is only a self-object, you don't envy that person; it would be like envying your right arm! So here again the theoretical differentiation is apparent: self and object differentiation is thought of as occurring significantly earlier in development in Kernberg's theory.

Kohut, on the other hand, focuses on what he conceives to be the patient's *inability* to perceive the analyst as a separate object, and therefore empathic appreciation of this inability is required rather than interpreting this phenomenon as a defense.

It seems to me that the closest approach to the resolution of this problem so far has been suggested by Wangh (1974). He feels that the discrepancy between these two views is largely apparent. The intrusions of aggressive drive manifestations described by Kernberg are the inevitable residues of the failure to develop of the ideal sequence described by Kohut. According to Kernberg, pathological narcissistic grandiosity carries with it the rage that accompanied the frustration of normal narcissistic grandiosity. Wangh writes, "In other words it seems to me that in clinical practice we inevitably meet, confront, and uncover both those phenomena described by Kernberg and those set forth by Goldberg. The degree and quality of the rage, often covered by stand-offish grandiosity, will determine the degree of pathology in the individual patient." Therefore, the seeming discrepency may occur not only from a particular approach taken by a particular therapist as a function of the personality of the therapist, "but also from the range of patients—that is, their degree of sickness—which each encounters in his practice."

To put it another way, the psychotherapist of the borderline personality disorders has to keep in mind three foci in understanding the patient. The first of these is the traditional problem of the formation of classical transference, in which those areas of ego function most advanced in the patient will participate. In addition to this, narcissistic transferences may form as described by Kohut; at any rate, varying degrees of narcissism will always be an important focus in the psychotherapy of the borderline patient, whether this narcissism is a defense against both primitive formations and object love or not. Finally, the focus on unneutralized aggression, splitting, introjects and projective identifications is vital; the therapist will be dealing with intense depreciation and hostility from these patients, which always threatens the therapeutic alliance. The therapist will have to develop the flexibility to deal with each of these foci in an appropriate manner as they arise and in addition be able to provide pacification and unification when fragmentation becomes a serious threat.

The relative preponderance of narcissistic structures in the presenting personality of the patient or of splitting mechanisms with a ready tendency to contempt, hostility and depreciation, as well as projective identifications and so on, determine the kind of patient that is being described from a clinical descriptive point of view. Whether or not the idealized parent imago and the grandiose self represent way stations in the normal and separate developmental line of narcissism or whether fixations in such formations are always pathological and defensive cannot be settled at this time.

In view of the therapist's having to deal with so much unneutralized aggression, it does seem that it is wiser, at least in the intensive psychotherapy of such patients, to accept the idealization and to watch for and interpret the shifts from the idealized parent imago to the grandiose self when there is disappointment in the idealization, rather than to sharply confront and break up the idealization by interpretation. The latter procedure, it seems to me, makes it harder for the patient to internalize the idealized therapist, which will be necessary to modify his attitude toward himself, and it will increase the rage with which the patient's already overburdened ego has to contend.

For a long time those patients who present primarily with
unneutralized aggression and depreciation and envy of the therapist
need to be helped to deal with these phenomena through an
identification with the nonaxious, tolerant and consistent approach of
the therapist. Those patients who present predominantly with
narcissistic pathology (often including a tendency to fragmentation
and the formation of at least a hint of cold paranoid grandiosity and a
sense of persecution) need to be helped toward an insight into their
narcissistic pathology and toward an understanding of what the
narcissistic pathology defends them against and/or toward an insight
into how phase-inappropriate disappointments in childhood generated a developmental fixation into the narcissistic pathology. There is no
reason why both of these phenomena cannot occur in a patient—thus a
pathological grandiose self could be based on a developmental fixation
in the area of the grandiose self but could also have a defensive
meaning which would hypercathect and distort even the normal
grandiose self. I conclude this chapter by warning the reader that these
authors are using "grandiose self" in metapsychologically quite
different ways.

Part III
DEVELOPMENTAL PATHOLOGY

CHAPTER 9

Early Ego Development
and Projective Identification

It would not be in the least surprising or perturbing to discover that by this time the reader is somewhat confused with the plethora of theories, all of which seem to be inconsistent and sometimes downright conflictual, that have been introduced in an attempt to understand early ego development—without which, of course, there can be no understanding of the borderline patient. So at this point I am going to pause and try to make some kind of a summary and side-by-side comparison of the principal theories that have been put forward in a capsule form, so that the reader can compare and contrast the various points of view.

Let us begin with the most objective observational kind of theory. Mahler has of course done meticulous observational work on the young infant and child. Using Mahler's timetable, from age zero to two months occurs the "normal autistic phase" during which the neonate is observed to be incapable of perceiving anything beyond his own body. He cannot distinguish himself from his mother and seems to live on a purely instinctive basis in a world composed solely of inner stimuli.

During this phase the mother serves as an external executive ego, replacing the child's initial incapacity to bind instinctual energies and to delay discharge (Mahler 1952). She must prevent the neonate from being overwhelmed and traumatized by internal stimuli and help him achieve gradual transition from an exclusive cathexis of processes within the body to an ever-increasing cathexis of sense organs on the surface of the body and thereby to an increased sensory awareness of the outer world. The great problem of this phase, then, might be labeled the threat of overwhelming traumatization from being flooded by unneutralized stimuli.

Observationally speaking, the second phase of life is labeled by Mahler the symbiotic phase and lasts from around two or three months of age to around six or eight months of age. During this phase, which is marked by the infant's beginning capacity to perceive at least fleetingly that satisfaction is dependent on a source outside his body, the mother is not yet perceived by the child as a specific whole person. She can still be replaced by a substitute. The specific smiling response at the peak of the symbiotic phase indicates that the infant is responding to the symbiotic partner in a manner different from that in which he responds to other human beings. He clings to a specific symbiotic relationship with the mother. This specific symbiotic relationship reaches its peak at about six months, and between six and ten months of age occurs the beginning of what Mahler defines as the separation-individuation phase.

The process of separation-individuation refers to a psychological growing away from the undifferentiated symbiotic relationship with the mother and a growing toward differentiation of the self from the mother. Thus at the very time when the infant's specific attachment to his mother is growing stronger and stronger, paradoxically his developing psyche and soma require him to begin to detach himself from her in a series of separating and individuating steps. This separation-individuation is completed, according to Mahler, by about three years of age.

The separation-individuation phase is divided into subphases by Mahler and her co-workers (Mahler and LaPerrier 1965, Mahler et al. 1975). Although the chronology varies somewhat in her work, it is important to be aware of these subphases:

1. *Differentiation* is characterized by increase in partial locomotion and much scanning; "he begins to express active pleasure in the use of his entire body, shows interest in objects and in pursuit of goals, and turns actively to the outside world for pleasure and stimulation."

The differentiation subphase of the separation-individuation phase lasts from about six to ten months of age, and during this period there is maturational growth of locomotive function, active pleasure in the use of the body and a turning actively to the outside world for pleasure and stimulation, but these emerging functions are still expressed by the child in close proximity to the mother, and we begin to have the appearance of the well-known stranger anxiety, or "eight-month anxiety" (Spitz, 1965), which appears around this time. In this phenomenon, the percept of the stranger's face is compared with memory traces of the mother's face. It is found to be different and rejected with disappointment: "What he reacts to when confronted with a stranger is that this is not his mother; his mother 'has left him.' "

The continuous investigation of the mother's features in a prolonged and sober visual and tactile exploration, and the comparing and checking this with the features of others, seems to testify the beginning of self and object differentiation.

2. *The Practicing Period* from about ten to eighteen months is characterized by great strides in locomotion. At the peak of this subphase, when the infant is one-and a half years old, the sense of inflated omnipotence, the idealized state of the self, is at its height and, in Piaget's terms, sensorimotor intelligence just begins to be replaced by representational intelligence. The first eighteen months of life lead, in a sense, to upright locomotion and to this grandiosity or self-inflation; the second eighteen months represent a corresponding deflation.

Arieti (1974) points out that Piaget's cognitive descriptions are always treated by other theorists as if they were autonomous ego functions, but in order to understand schizophrenic phenomena, cognitive descriptions *cannot* be treated as if they were autonomous ego functions. Their vicissitudes must be brought into our affective theories of early development.

There is an additional benefit to mentioning Piaget at this point, because if one follows his work (Piaget and Inhelder 1966; Pulaski 1971) it is clear that the *utmost caution* must be used to impute to the infant younger than two years old *any* capacity for symbolic representation of "good" or "bad" object representations or *any* kind of evocative images or representations for that matter! Before the infant is one-and-a-half to two years old, according to Piaget, cognitive development is characterized by coordination of action in the *absence* of representation. During this so-called sensorimotor period of Piaget, there is no symbolic activity and no evocative memory, and adaptation is based on recognition in action of familiar sensorimotor "schema" being experienced at the moment. The burden of proof, therefore, falls heavily indeed upon those who would postulate anything more than Piaget's studies have indicated.

3. *Rapprochement* begins as the child learns to walk and lasts from about sixteen to twenty-four months, the end of the second year of life. The very pleasure of mastery is followed by separation anxiety in the toddler as he becomes aware in the middle of his second year of his true physical separateness. "With this awareness, he begins to lose his previous resistance to frustration and his relative obliviousness of his mother's presence," and so he clings possessively to her.

4. The *Fourth Subphase,* essentially the third year of life, is "characterized by unfolding of complex cognitive functions; verbal communication, fantasy, and reality testing."

When we move into the metapsychology of these observational phases, it is important to understand that we have made a sharp shift in position (Kohut 1971). As explained previously, Mahler's position is defined as that of the observer who is equidistant from the interacting parties and who occupies an imaginary point outside of the experiencing individual. In metapsychology, our position is that of the observer who occupies an imaginary point *inside* the psychic organization of the individual with whose introspection he empathically identifies.

Freud's famous phases of libidinal development roughly correspond to Mahler's observations. Thus the stage of autoerotism corresponds to Mahler's phase of normal autism from about birth to two months. The phase of primary narcissism lasts during Mahler's symbiotic phase from about two to six months, and the beginning of rudimentary object love in Freud's sense appears at the beginning of Mahler's separation-individuation phase.

Kohut makes serious modification of this. He essentially goes along with the phases of autoerotism and primary narcissism of Freud. He explains that around the beginning of the separation-individuation phase, from about six to ten months, there is also a transformation of primary narcissism along its own line of development, first appearing at this point as the grandiose self and the idealized parent imago already described.

By the time the separation-individuation phase of Mahler is completed, that is at about the age of three, the formation of the cohesive self, according to Kohut, is ready. Rudimentary object love is possible, the transformations of narcissism have begun in such a way that the grandiose self and idealized parent imago have started to be substantially internalized, and a cohesive sense of self has been formed. The individual becomes capable of beginning mature object love, and the rudimentary primary narcissism becomes eventually transformed into as such things as humor, wisdom, serenity and so on.

Modell's theory is somewhat more simple. His phase of "no self-object differentiation" roughly corresponds with Mahler's autistic phase—about zero to two months. A transitional object phase follows. The objects during this phase are not perceived in accordance with their true or realistic qualities, and he compares this with Winnicott's (1951) discussion of the transitional object. Winnicott dates the phase of the transitional object at four, six, eight or twelve months, that is to say, the phase of the transitional object occurs around the beginning of the separation-individuation phase and lasts through that first differentiation subphase. Object love becomes more mature, according to Modell, when separation and individuation are completed, again in Mahler's terminology at about three years of age.

Kernberg (1966, 1972a, 1973) distinguishes four stages of early ego development, briefly outlined here and discussed in detail later. His first stage precedes the establishment of the primary undifferentiated self-object constellation and corresponds roughly with Mahler's phase of autism from zero to two months. In his second stage, which corresponds roughly to Mhaler's symbiotic phase from about two to six months, there is an undifferentiated self-object image (or representation) present. The third stage, which corresponds to Mahler's differentiation subphase of separation-individuation, from about six months to ten months, is when good and bad self-object images are differentiated. At this point a stranger is greeted with anxiety, and Kernberg interprets this as the first efforts on the part of the infant to externalize the bad self-object image (compare the explanation of Spitz given in Chapter 8). The fourth stage, according to Kernberg, occurs between one and two years of age, around the time that cognitive object permanence occurs. Affective object permanency perhaps occurs a bit earlier. According to Kernberg, affective object permanency occurs through the coalesecence of good and bad self-object images into images that begin to correspond to the real object out there.

Finally, we have the English school, for example, Balint, who claims that rudimentary object love with primary cathexes to primary objects is present shortly after birth and gradually extends into mature object love. More theoretically, Fairbairn claims that libido is simply a function of the ego and the ego is fundamentally object-seeking. This is presented as a total and complete supplanting of Freud, so one must choose between Freud and Fairbairn. Klein postulates sophisticated object relations established shortly after birth.

Modell and Kernberg essentially agree that the late symbiotic stage or the early separation-individuation stage (Mahler's differentiation subphase, from about six months to one year) is where the damage is done in the borderline patient. Kohut places the onset of narcissistic disorders at around the age of one year, lasting perhaps to three years, at a time when the grandiose self and the idealized parent imago are supposed to begin to be substantially internalized and integrated into the ego and the superego. If this process does not take place correctly, the developmental arrest leads to the formation of the narcissistic personality disorder.

The appearance of classical eight-months anxiety, or stranger anxiety, in the development of the infant marks the achievement of cognitive self-object differentiation, a physiological as well as a psychic achievement. At this point there begins an appropriate coalescence and separation, according to Kernberg, of self- and object representations and the development of rudimentary object love. Kohut (1971), on the other hand, speaks of this as the era of separation anxiety. *The fact that cognitive self and object differentiation becomes possible at around eight months of age, according to Kohut, does not mean that a coherent sense of self has occurred.* Only nuclei of self-representations begin at this time. Certain intermediate phases still have to be passed through.

Thus between around eight months of age and three years of age, Kohut postulates an *intermediate phase* of powerful cathexis of the grandiose self and the idealized parent imago. These psychic formations are gradually internalized and integrated within the psychic structure, and by the age of three the grandiosity becomes confined to phallic narcissism; at the same time a cohesive sense of self forms. With the resolution of the Oedipus complex at around six to eight years of age, there is superego formation; moral anxiety replaces castration anxiety. At this time the repression barrier is established and consolidated, and after eight years of age anxiety becomes confined to function as signal anxiety (Gedo and Goldberg 1973). From the age of eight years, further *transformations* of narcissism occur, as well as a separate development of object love.

From the development of cognitive differentiation between the self and object at eight months and until the attainment of a cohesive sense of self at age three, the object is utilized as part of the child's narcissistic world. Only after the establishment of a cohesive sense of self can object love begin to develop.

Until the cohesive sense of self develops, disavowal or splitting of the ego, as Freud calls it, is a major and important defense—in Kohut's terms, the splitting of the self. What happens in regression to periods before the cohesive sense of self has developed is a fragmentation of the self. Kohut's concept of fragmentation of the self is crucial to understanding psychotherapeutic technique.

It follows from this that borderline patients are not treatable by classical psychoanalytic methods. There is no cohesive sense of self, there is no self-object differentiation, the self is fragmented, and only pacification and unification (so that the ego nuclei can coalesce) are possible.

On the other hand, when one postulates intrapsychic images and representations and introjects as occurring during the phase when the damage has been done that produces the borderline patient, then the psychoanalytic method makes sense. For then the projection, projective identification and reintrojection involving these intrapsychic images can be interpreted to the patient and so worked through and understood by him. Again, it is clear that there is an absolutely irreconcilable difference involved here, between theoretical preconceptions and corresponding treatment recommendations.

I am ruling out the English school. Klein's use of various vague concepts has already been discussed, and her discussion of the paranoid and depressive position (postulating the death instinct as the motivation for the anxiety behind these phenomena) seems to me to be a considerable stretching of philosophical concepts and to engage us in a semantic confusion. Her idea is that the infantile ego is in danger of disintegration unless it can extrude destructive parts of itself onto the maternal object, who is then seen as a persecutor; this is known as the paranoid position. Later, to preserve the maternal object itself, the object is split into good and bad portions, and then we get the depressive position. It is difficult to accept the idea that these complex intrapsychic processes occur shortly after birth! Similarly, Fairbairn's concepts require a total abandonment of all the basic premises of psychoanalysis developed by Freud and a complete new theoretical orientation; this makes them impossible to accept. Modell (1975a) presents a heroic attempt to bridge this gap between Fairbairn and Freud—his effort is the best in the literature so far.

We do have to look with greater care, however, at Klein's concept of projective identification. This is used in many places in the literature, and no two authors use it alike! Originally it was meant to mean a forceful penetration in which the object was actually in phantasy either injured or turned into an enemy. It was used also to explain the emotional states that some patients may produce in the therapist. This affect is claimed to exceed even countertransference and has to do with the manifestation of the most primitive means by which a baby can communicate emotions to its mother. If they are disagreeable emotions, the baby can be experiencing relief by so manifesting them. The motive is to evacuate or extrude the stress, and the angry infant (patient) forcefully projects the hatefulness into the mother (therapist).

Kernberg (1967, 1968, 1971, 1975a) repeatedly picks up the concept of projective identification. The main purpose of projection in the borderline patient, he points out, is to externalize the all-bad aggressive self- and object images, and the main consequence of this need is the development of dangerous retaliatory objects against which the patient has to defend himself. This projection of aggression is rather unsuccessful. As Kernberg explains, "While these patients do have sufficient development of ego boundaries to be able to differentiate self and objects in most areas of their lives, the very intensity of the projective needs, plus the general ego weakness characterizing these patients, weakens ego boundaries in the particular area of the projection of aggression." This leads these patients to feel they can identify with the object onto whom aggression has been projected and therefore increases the fear of their own projected aggression. They have to control the object in order to prevent it from attacking them, and they have to attack and control the object before, as they fear, they themselves are attacked and destroyed. At the bottom of this projective identification is the lack of differentiation between the self and object, so that one continues to experience the impulse as well as the fear of that impulse while the projection is active and feels the urgent need to control the external object.

It is a projection in which the projection has not thoroughly worked, leaving the patients with a feeling that they must fear the projected aggressor and at the same time that they have not really been able to get rid of their own rage and aggression so they must attack the projected aggressor also. They identify with this aggressor that they project, and they must attack the aggressor just as they fear to be attacked. They project out this aggression and they identify with the aggression when it is projected out. This is a difficult concept but is already modified from Klein, because at this point the projection out of the aggression is not seen as a forceful penetration a la Klein, it is seen as an attempt to deal with the enormous rage and aggression of the borderline patient. Kernberg thinks this is the essential difficulty and basic problem in treating such patients.

According to Kernberg, then, the projective identification is understood as a consequence of the failure of the projection of so much aggression in a person with a weak self-object differentiation. On the one hand, he projects the aggression; on the other hand, he identifies with the so-called aggressor that he himself has set up. This leads to fear of attack and a need to attack and, of course, has obvious crucial clinical consequences in terms of what happens between the patient and the therapist in psychotherapy, both in transference and countertransference. For example, "In dealing with borderline personality organization, dedicated therapists of all levels of experience may live through phases of almost masochistic submission to some of the patient's aggression, disproportionate doubts in their own capacity, and exaggerated fears of criticisms by third parties." (Kernberg 1975a).

In borderline patients, according to Kernberg, the higher-level ego structures are missing and early conflict-laden object relations are activated prematurely in the transference. He tries to modify Klein's theories because of her lack of precision and even notes the confusion in her use of the term *splitting* (Kernberg 1972b). He does accept a concept of introjection and projection somewhat related to Klein, but he rejects the concept of introjection as having to do with oral incorporation (it is never made entirely clear what Klein meant by this anyway).

The ego states in the borderline patient represent an affect linked to certain types of object representation images and certain types of self-representation images. Kernberg's concept of introjection really has to do with a fixation of an interaction with the environment forming an organized cluster of memory traces, leaving an image of an object, an image of the self in interaction with that object and the affective coloring of both the object image and the self-image.

Furthermore, it is postulated that these images occur quite early. For instance, the well-known reciprocal smiling response at about three months of age may mark the first beginning of an organization of the psyche. It is important to realize, Kernberg explains, that such formations and images can take place quite early. He asserts that splitting as an active mechanism comes into operation around the third month of life and reaches its maximum several months later, only gradually disappearing in the latter part of the first year of life. The later developments of the ego presuppose an important overcoming of the splitting processes. Kernberg disagrees with Klein and Fairbairn in their assumption that an ego exists from birth, however.

In the borderline patient the splitting has never been resolved and the weak ego falls back easily on the splitting, creating a vicious circle in which ego weakness and splitting reinforce each other. This leads to the observed clinical phenomena in the psychotherapy of the borderline patient. Kernberg here and there also suggests a constitutional factor of perhaps extreme aggression or a constitutionally determined lack of anxiety tolerance which may interfere with the synthesis of important introjects of opposite balances, as I will explain later. This is never made quite specific in his theory and remains vague as the postulation of a constitutional "X factor".

Wolberg (1973) stresses Klein's concept of projective identification in the psychodynamics of borderline patients even more than Kernberg. In general she considers the concept of ego defect in the borderline patient as giving way to a new concept of "defense," in which the individual is shielded from perceiving the true nature of the reality situation in the parental home. A sadomasochistic role is assigned to a child by his parents. The child becomes enmeshed "as a transferential object in service of the parent's defenses. The ensuing neurotic and psychotic processes are defenses against a harsh reality with which the individual tries to cope, and the crucial mechanism is identification with the parents." In projective identification there is passive and masochistic behavior with sadism as its goal; the insistence on a sadomasochistic position is a defense against intense oral aggression. The patients deny their autonomy and, out of rage, force others to do for them what they should do for themselves.

According to Wolberg, identification in this situation is not a form of development or ego growth but a substitute for object relations, and in psychotherapy this projective identification has to be unravelled and broken up. "For example, the therapist may be regarded as a sadistic mother-image, while the patient experiences himself as the frightened, attacked child; then, even moments later the roles may be reversed." The goal of the therapy is to show the patient that in his projections he sees in others what is also in himself. This serves to externalize the introject and makes it possible to discuss the unconscious motivations, the fantasies and the defenses of the other. These goals are accomplished essentially by confrontation at appropriate times. Thus, for example, a woman patient quoted by Wolberg, "denies the sadistic side of the controlling mothering mechanisms and says that she is really 'good'. She would never have acted that way with her mother if her father had not made her do so. She denies that she acts this way today with her husband, although in previous sessions she has alluded to this."

What Wolberg calls projective interpretation is the first step in outlining an interlocking defensive pattern between two people; as in Kernberg's conception of narcissism, the purpose of the projective identification is to defend the patient against both his own powerful unneutralized aggression and his fear of destructive retaliation from others as a response to this aggression and as a projection of this aggression onto others.

All seem to agree that treatment involves modifying cold, unloving and archaic ego and superego introjects with new warm, loving and reasonable introjects. The patient learns an adequate way of life through identification with the analyst, i.e. through "analytic introjects"; this identification must be fostered if the patient is to gain an understanding of reality. One must be very careful in emphasizing this technique to avoid the use of confrontation as a disguised form of countersadism on the part of the exasperated therapist, for everyone agrees that narcissistic and borderline patients produce tremendous countertransference reactions in the therapist, which vary all the way from sarcastic putting down of the patient to actually acting out in a massive retaliatory and destructive way toward the patient.

Kernberg (1975a) states that in addition there is "quantitative predominance of negative introjections stemming from both a constitutionally determined intensity of aggressive drive derivatives and from severe early frustrations." As a consequence, the child never does give up the splitting and in turn creates a serious problem in the development of the autonomous ego functions. Thus we have an emphasis on bringing forth and interpreting the negative transference in terms of the projection and on the breaking loose of severe oral aggression, which is kept under control by a careful structuring of the therapeutic situation through the use of so-called parameters.

A frank dealing with the manifest and latent negative transference is absolutely necessary, and trying to avoid this under the guise of building a "therapeutic alliance" leads only to a vicious circle: "Projection and reintrojection of sadistic self and object-images in the transference." This is Kernberg's objection to Kohut's allowing the idealization of the therapist to develop without interpretation. He argues that this avoids the mobilization of the latent aggression, which can only be worked through by its becoming manifest in projections and direct hostility toward the therapist. Unless this basic aggression is allowed to surface and is worked through in the psychotherapy, no fundamental structural change can take place in the ego of the patient, since all the energies are bound up in dealing with this archaic, magical and frightening aggression.

CHAPTER 10

Internalized Object Relations

For Kernberg, projection, introjection, projective identification and pathological narcissistic formations are all defense used by the patient to deal with aggression. The narcissistic personality structure then becomes a form of borderline personality organization in which the primary operation for maintaining the splitting is the formation of a highly pathological grandiose self. "The integration of this pathological grandiose self ... explains the paradox of relative good ego functioning and surface adaptation in the presence of a predominance of splitting mechanisms, a related constellation of primitive defenses, and the lack of integration of object representations." (Kernberg 1974a).

Again, the disagreement is about the origin of this grandiose self—whether it reflects the fixation of an archaic primitive self in the course of normal development or a pathological structure clearly different from normal infantile narcissism. Those patients who function on an overt borderline level characteristically show repetitive chronic activation of intensive rage reactions replete with demanding and depreciatory attacks on the therapist; the pathological grandiose self enables the patient to avoid this, but when it is broken up through interpretation the rage appears again.

The decision for Kernberg as to whether the borderline patient is amenable to uncovering intensive psychotherapy rests, therefore, not on whether or not stable narcissistic transferences form, but on whether the nonspecific manifestations of ego weakness are so great that they rupture the treatment. Thus, in the presence of a severe lack of anxiety tolerance, generalized lack of impulse control, absence of sublimatory channelling and strongly predominant primary-process thinking, as well as a tendency toward delusion formation, we have the danger of transference psychoses and destructive acting out which can only be treated by a supportive and authoritative psychotherapeutic approach, at least until structure has been provided for the patient that holds these reactions within workable and socially acceptable limits. After this has been accomplished, it may then be possible to go forward in an intensive uncovering psychotherapy. The outbreak of dangerous, aggressive paranoid rage as well as intense depression and guilt—even with the possibility of suicide—represents the important prerequisite of the working-through process but can only be allowed if the therapist is confident that the patient is able to keep these manifestations within the safe boundaries of the psychotherapy.

Notice again the main thesis that the structures determined by the *internalized* object relations constitute a crucial determinant of ego integration, and an abnormal development of internalized object relations determines varying types of psychopathology. Kernberg (1972a) outlines four stages of development of internalized object relations which, *if* one can accept the early existence of such intrapsychic structures, is the least objectionable and confusing of all the theories. These stages are, as already mentioned briefly in Chapter 9, as follows:

Stage One, in which the primary undifferentiated self-object constellation is built up under the influence of pleasurable gratifying experiences of the infant in interactions with his mother, occurs somewhere in the second to third month of life.

Stage Two consists of the establishment and consolidation of an undifferentiated self-object image or representation of a rewarding type under the organizing influence of the gratifying experiences of the child-mother unit. Thus, "A primary intrapsychic structure is built up, with early traces fixating the primitive coenesthetic constellation and its gratifying 'all good' affective quality; this constitutes the primary, undifferentiated, self-object representation." Simultaneously, a separate intrapsychic structure representing an undifferentiated "all bad" self-object representation is built up under the influence of painful and frustrating psychophysiological states. At this stage there is no separation between self and nonself.

Stage Three is reached when self and object have been differentiated under the influence of perceptual and cognitive growth. Ego boundaries stabilize and self-images become separate from object images, but there is not yet an *integrated* concept of the self, for good and bad images are separate. Thus, object constancy is not yet possible.

Stage Four, the final stage of integration of good and bad self-images occurs in the second year of life with a coalescence into an integrated self-concept. Affects become integrated, toned down and differentiated. At the same time a coalescence of good and bad object images takes place, fostering better discrimination among object images stemming from interpersonal relationships and a more realistic representation of significant others. Thus, "An integrated self-concept 'surrounded' as it were, by an integrated conception of others, with ongoing modifications of self concept and concept of others in the process of interpersonal relationships, constitutes 'ego identity' in the broadest sense."

The transition from Stage Three to Stage Four is where the disaster has occurred in the borderline patient. Differentiation of self-images from object images has occurred to a degree sufficient to permit the establishment of integrated ego boundaries and concomitant differentiation between self and others. However, the coalescence in integration of good and bad self-images and object images fails because of the pathological predominance of primitive aggression. The intensity of aggressively determined self- and object images and of defensively idealized "all good" self- and object images makes integration impossible, for bringing together extremely loving and extremely hateful images of the self and significant others produces an unbearable anxiety and guilt. The result is active defensive separation of such contradictory images, and splitting becomes a major defensive operation.

The integration of loving and hateful feelings in the context of internalized relationships with others is a major precondition for neutralization of instinctual energy, according to this theory. Lack of such neutralization deprives the ego of an important source of sublimatory potential and of the conflict-free emotional sphere. It brings about a persistence of primitivization of emotions with secondary lack of impulse control. Thus premature sexualization and oedipalization of relationships with parental figures leads only to aggressive contamination of the sexual life of the patient.

Similarly, correct superego development cannot occur, leading to an overdependency on external sources of reassurance, praise and punishment. The channeling of aggression into the psychic apparatus from which the ego and the self develop serves the biologically protective function of avoiding external discharge onto the mothering figure upon whom the infant is so dependent. This inward direction of aggression is normally elaborated into stable internalized object relations that successfully neutralize the aggression, but this mechanism fails in patients with borderline personality organization. It is not clear whether it fails because of a constitutional weakness or defect or because of the profound phase-inappropriate disappointment that takes place at the time, generating larger quantities of rage and aggression than the psychic apparatus is able to handle.

The remobilization and discharge of this aggression in the therapeutic situation lightens the burden on the psychic apparatus and permits the eventual fusion of good and bad self- and object images, providing the remobilization does not lead to psychotic or destructive behavior that ruptures the treatment entirely.

Kernberg, as stated, feels that the grandiose self described by Kohut is always pathological and that even the idealizing transference of Kohut is simply the projection of the grandiose self onto the therapist. This pathological configuration, according to Kernberg, defends the patient against profound oral rage and envy, paranoid fears (due to the projection of sadistic trends onto the therapist, who becomes the hated and sadistically perceived mother image), loneliness and hunger for love and guilt over aggression. Thus one of the *big clinical questions* is whether the grandiose self as it appears in the patient and develops in the mirror transferences should be allowed to remain until it is gradually broken up and, through transmuting internalizations, be brought into integration in the personality or should be directly interpreted as a defense.

In pressing his point of view about the grandiose self, Kernberg (1974b) differentiates infantile narcissism from adult pathological narcissism in at least five ways: (1) the child's narcissistic demands are more realistic; (2) in the child these demands coexist with object love when they are not frustrated; (3) the child's demands relate to real needs; (4) there is a certain warm quality about the child's self-centeredness; and (5) the exclusivity and totality of wishes for admiration, wealth, power and so on are far greater in adult pathological narcissism. The child wants more in the way of loving and sharing.

The combination of high inborn intensity of aggressive drives and a mother who is cold, narcissistic, overprotective and includes the child in her narcissistic world gives him a sense of specialness around which the grandiose self crystallizes and which leads to a pathological grandiose self-formation in adult patients.

Thus the intrapsychic world of the borderline patient with these kind of problems (Kernberg 1974b) consists solely of a pathological grandiose self, devaluated shadow images of the self and others, potential persecutors which are nonintegrated, sadistic superego forerunners and primitive distorted object images onto whom the intense oral sadism has been projected. Laboring with this nightmare in the intrapsychic world, a pathological grandiose self provides better social adaptation than in the usual borderline patient and compensates the patient for inner suffering, but the price is a grandiose isolation and a loss of true human contact. In addition to that, adult superego formation is prevented, so a sadistic superego represents a constant danger to the ego, even to the point of self-destruction.

Thus, Kernberg sees a lack of interpreting of the mirror transference and idealizing transference as "supportive tolerance of the narcissistic constellation," while Kohut implies that to insist that the idealizing transference hides profound hostility and exists solely for that purpose represents a countertransference in the therapist!

Finally, the presence of "all good" and "all bad" object energies which cannot be integrated interferes seriously with *superego* integration as follows (Kernberg 1967): "Primitive forerunners of the superego of a sadistic kind, representing internalized bad object images related to pregenital conflicts, are too overriding to be tolerated, and are reprojected in the form of external bad objects." We see the same problem underneath the pathological narcissistic configurations, for at the bottom of these pathological structures is a "hungry, enraged, empty self, full of impotent anger at being frustrated, and fearful of a world which seems as hateful and revengeful as the patient himself" (Kernberg 1975a).

CHAPTER 11

Unresolved Metapsychological
Problems: My Views

We turn now to a resolution of the differences between two eminent groups of psychoanalysts on very important issues, from the point of view of the psychotherapist who practices predominantly intensive psychotherapy. We need answers to the following questions:

1. Is idealization of the therapist a defense against rage and a projection of the pathological grandiose self, or is it a search for the idealized parent imago due to a developmental arrest?
2. Does narcissism undergo a separate developmental pathway and do narcissistic disorders thus represent an arrest of development, or does the presence of the grandiose self simply represent a pathological structure developed to defend the patient against profound rage and envy and so on?
3. Are the differences between borderline patients and narcissistic personality disorders fundamental or not? That is to say, is the narcissistic personality disorder separate from the borderline patient and treatable by formal psychoanalysis, or is the borderline patient simply a psychotic who is not manifesting overt symptomatology and who is not treatable by formal psychoanalysis or modified psychoanalytic psychotherapy?
4. Should the mirror and idealizing transferences (Kohut) be interpreted as defenses against negative transference or should they be accepted as manifestations of developmental arrest which

will be spontaneously broken up through the process of the psychotherapy and reintegrated through transmuting internalizations?

5. Are Kernberg's outline of the phases of early ego integration and object relations and his postulation of the basic pathology in the borderline as that of splitting and the presence of nonintegrated good and bad self- and object images correct?

6. Is the grandiose self shown by the adult patient in psychotherapy a developmental arrest of the normal child's grandiose self or is it fundamentally different than the grandiosity of the small child?

7. Is there a fundamental difference between the borderline patient and the psychotic patient with important ramifications for the psychotherapy of each?

8. As Ornstein (1974) asks, are these experts talking about the same level of observation or are they not even talking about the same patient population?

It seems to me that this last question may contain the secret of the discrepancy. Perhaps it is clarified when we look at the way that the two authors deal with the problem of aggression. Ornstein writes, "For Kernberg, the raw id-derivative of aggression in the form of oral rage and envy is inevitably intertwined with the earliest projectively and introjectively internalized object relations. ... For Kohut, the id-derivative of aggression becomes activated or psychologically elaborated as it arises experientially from the matrix of archaic narcissism."

From the review of my own clinical material I have come to certain conclusions, and I will state these conclusions in advance for clarity. They are:

1. I think that two different patient populations are being discussed by Kohut and Kernberg and that this is causing a lot of the confusion. On the whole, the kind of patient that comes into a psychoanalytic institute asking for formal psychoanalysis or at least gets through the institute's sophisticated intake procedures and is referred to a certified psychoanalyst is different from the run-of-the-mill borderline patient who comes in seeking psychotherapy from therapists who are struggling to make a living out in the field.

2. There is no reason to believe that the kinds of transference formed have to be restricted either to the purely narcissistic stable transferences described by Kohut or to regressive fragmentation. It is possible that other kinds of workable transference can form, for example, the transitional-object type of transference, as described by Modell, and this can be more characteristic of the run-of-the-mill borderline patient and yet stable enough to lend itself to psychoanalytically informed intensive psychotherapy, if not to formal psychoanalysis.

3. In general the theoretical conceptions of Kohut seem to be the more acceptable and believable. They don't postulate as much sophisticated, intellectual and cognitive functioning for the small baby, and they allow the formation of the narcissistic disorders to take place a little later. Although Kernberg has modified some of the Kleinian concepts, his theoretical formulations still assume a considerable sophisticated capacity on the part of the six- or seven-month-old infant to form and retain self- and object representations.

4. There is no doubt that the splitting Kernberg describes seems to be present in the adult clinical material. The question is whether what is described as due to splitting—that is to say, the projecting out of malevolent introjects—is not really a *telescoping* that the patient undertakes for the purpose of communicating primitive affect. In this way, later feelings and later self and object representations, which form after the stage of the cohesive self, are invested with primitive and early affects, especially aggressions, for the purpose of communicating and externalizing the unbearably intense current affects of rage nad so on.

5. On the other hand, Kohut's theory has certain unsatisfactory aspects to it, because it is only half a theory, as he himself admits. In Kohut's monograph (1971) he deliberately discusses the libidinal aspects of narcissism. Only in a paper (1972) does he discuss narcissistic rage. The enormous rage in these patients is not sufficiently explained by the theory of narcissistic injury. There is something not quite worked out in Kohut's formulations, and we look forward to his later and more complete formulations of aggressive aspects of narcissism.

The answer to all of these questions can only be found by reference to clinical material. For some patients the descriptions of Kernberg seem very appropriate, whereas for others Kohut's approach seems much more to the point. The dividing line seems to have fundamental significance for psychotherapy in terms of the clinical appearance of raw aggression in the form of oral rage and envy with an apparent splitting into good and bad self- and object representations.

It is usually possible to identify patients who are using narcissistic defenses against primitive disintegration as a consequence of oral aggression, because these forms of aggression intrude themselves in a variety of subtle and sometimes not-so-subtle demands in spite of the narcissistic formation. Usually this type of patient is more accurately labeled the borderline personality organization and appears more fundamentally to fit the psychodynamic descriptions of Kernberg.

You will notice that in describing my cases I am using Kernberg's psychodynamics wherever it is appropriate, but please remember that I think a *telescoping* goes on, so that when these patients seem to show projection of good and bad self- and object images, it is *not* necessary to conclude that that comes from what went on in the infant's psyche at age six months. Rather, what the therapist is experiencing is the communication of extremely primitive affect, which is presented with ideation that is borrowed from a later phase of development at a time when there *is* adequate cognitive capacity, including the capacity to form, retain and re-present self- and object images.

The primary problem in borderline patients is really founded upon the development of enormous undifferentiated primitive rage that goes way back to the patient's earliest days. Such overwhelming negative affect disrupts the development and smooth functioning of the psychic apparatus. Its origin can be traced to a devastating enemalike intrusiveness and massive inconsistency primarily based on lack of empathy on the part of the mother. It is then later attached to and appears clinically in phantasies and projections of destructive archaic bad unintegrated self and object images, among others.

There *also* seems to be a type of patient described by Kohut who functions at a better and more integrated level and is not struggling so pathetically and constantly with these intensive early unintegrated affects. As Kohut has pointed out, attempts to interfere with the development of mirror or idealizing transferences in such patients, for example by insisting to the patient that such transferences hide hostility, do produce hostility, but a hostility *not* attached to structures that were hidden by the narcissistic pathology; it represents rather a withdrawal into narcissistic rage as a consequence of lack of empathy from the therapist. This kind of interpretation breaks up the treatment primarily because it is not correct!

It is very important to make as clear as possible a distinction between the two kinds of patients, because in one kind, the rage produced when the grandiosity is interpreted is appropriate in the therapy and facilitates a release of material previously repressed, whereas in the other kind, the rage produced signals a failure of empathy on the part of the therapist; the consequent narcissistic rage is a repetition of what happened between the patient and his mother. I believe the difference in patient populations is the solution to the disagreement between the authors under discussion, and it is a very important clinical distinction. I also fully realize that this solution leaves many metapsychological questions unresolved, and I cannot attempt to resolve these problems here. The reader is referred to the increasingly sophisticated metapsychological discussions in the literature that attempt to distinguish the borderline patient from the narcissistic personality disorder (Modell 1975a, 1975b), and I will offer only some clinically pertinent comments.

An increasing focus on the precise failures in mothering that produce these two kinds of patients is taking place in the literature. The concept of the *intrusiveness* of the mother was discussed by Heimann (1966) a number of years ago. She suggested that "the bad internal objects do not arise as a result of *active introjection* by the infant, but as the result of *passively endured intrusions* of an unloving mother, beginning during the undifferentiated stage when the infant is maximally helpless." Mahler et al. (1975), in summarizing her findings on the subject of "middle-range" pathology, emphasize how, in the rapprochement phase of separation-individuation especially, the more intrusive and unpredictable the mother is, the less the modulating and negotiating functions of the ego gain ascendency. Thus, *predictable emotional involvement, consistency and minimal intrusiveness* are the primary ingredients of mothering necessary to avoid fixation in a rapprochement crisis, using Mahler's terminology. When such fixation takes place, coercive behavior, such as temper tantrums to force mother to function as an omnipotent extension, and desperate clinging, with a splitting of mother representations in order to protect mother against aggressive drives, must take place, leading to the eventual clinical picture of borderline pathology.

The patient is highly vulnerable to separation anxiety because of the "precocious hatching" necessitated by the uncomfortable symbiotic stage. Aggression tends to be aimed at the self in order to preserve the mother, and a poor internalized mother representation is available for inner sustenance under stress. Mahler emphasizes the total body experiences (Spitz's concept of coenesthetic global experiences) necessary for a successful symbiosis and the importance of the "internal mother," defined as "the inner image or intrapsychic representation of the mother," who in the course of the third year becomes available as a soothing mechanism in the mother's physical absence. In borderline pathology, in place of the internal mother there exists a set of "bad experiences" intruded into the helpless infantile ego—a destructive substructure perhaps formed by "cumulative trauma" (Kahn, 1974).

Masterson and Rinsley (1975) point out how Kernberg's and Mahler's timing of the occurrence of the fixation underlying borderline personality development differ significantly, "the former citing the period of 4 to 12 months and the latter the period of the 'rapprochement subphase', coinciding with 16 to 25 months postnatally." They agree with me that, "the preponderance of evidence would appear to be more favorable to Mahler's timing," but they emphasize more the mother's withdrawal of her libidinal availability as the child makes efforts towards separation-individuation during the rapprochement subphase. The "borderline mother," according to these authors, has the defensive need to cling to her infant, and therefore the child's separation-individuation represents a major threat. I fear the tendency to oversimplify in this viewpoint, leading to another devilish personification like the "schizophrenogenic mother."

Modell (1975a, 1975b) builds on the concepts of intrusion and inconsistency in the most careful effort to date to distinguish, in this middle-range pathology, between the borderline patient and the narcissistic personality disorder. He sees all these disorders as representing "the psychopathology of object relations," related primarily to an actual failure of the human environment. Thus, bringing the above authors together, he writes, "The environmental failure may be massive and obvious, such as a failure of a constant and reliable maternal object in the first and second years of life, or the failure may take more subtle forms such as a failure of the mother to accept the growing autonomy and individuality of the young child, thus interfering with its sense of identity and separateness."

In Modell's view, the more massive failures in the preoedipal period leave the patient with an intense persistent object hunger and lead to the clinical picture of the borderline patient. The subtle failures allow the patient to internalize something, but due to a premature disillusionment with the mother, a precocious and fragile sense of self develops. This leads to the narcissistic character with the "false self," as described by Winnicott. He is led theoretically to a revision of psychoanalytic theory and to a postulation of the instinctual nature of object relations, which brings us once more to the highly controversial metapsychological disputes reviewed recently, for example, by Friedman (1975).

For the clinician, what is important to keep in mind are the issues revolving around the terms *defect* and *developmental arrest!* I believe those cases marked by massive failure in the maternal environment show borderline pathology and are grounded on an intrapsychic defect, primarily the lack of strong positive identifications to neutralize and modulate aggression. Narcissism and introject formation in such patients are related to the patient's effort to set up his own substitute structures in order to deal with aggression and other drives and achieve some kind of adaptation to life. The narcissistic personality disorder, on the other hand, has achieved some internalized psychic structures, although these are primitive, and is responding to a more subtle form of failure of the maternal environment. Disillusion with the mother in a precocious or phase-inappropriate manner is the central factor leading to substantial developmental arrest in the area of narcissism.

This is a clinically vital distinction, because clearly the therapeutic strategy for patients suffering from an intrapsychic defect will be substantially different than for patients with a developmental arrest; furthermore, these are theoretical poles and our patients actually present with a combination showing the preponderance of one or the other. The secret of successful treatment depends on meticulous evaluation of the patient so as not to confuse defensive or substitute structures with pristine or archaic psychic structures as they manifest themselves in the patient's personality and behavior.

CHAPTER 12

Clinical Material

Let me turn directly to a series of brief vignettes from my practice to illustrate what I am talking about. Needless to say, this discussion is of *fundamental importance* in approaching the intensive psychotherapy of the borderline patient.

Patient #1: Very soon after being placed on the couch he reported the fantasy that I was going to cut his throat and kill him. At first I became very alarmed by this fantasy, arising as early as it did in the therapy, and sat him up for a year or so of treatment. As I got to know this man I realized that he was actually quite intact and able to function; there was no history of psychotic breakdown or behavior in his past life, nor in any way could there have been attributed to him a narcissistic personality disorder. He showed none of the characteristic features of such patients, but presented rather with a depression secondary to homosexual preoccupation with a friend who had moved away. This was worked through in long-term intensive psychotherapy, and gradually the rage deep in this patient began to show itself again in the father transference and later in the mother transference.

His early childhood was an absolute nightmare and the psychodynamics of his homosexual interests and his depression were clear. At the point where the early enormous oral aggression and envy threatened to emerge in a more primitive form (as they had instantly appeared in a delusion early in the therapy), the patient developed a series of narcissistic defensive configurations related to his work capacities and his sense of entitlement from the world. At this point the clinical material appeared to be that of a narcissistic personality disorder. In this patient the interpretation of the narcissistic configurations as a defense against the frightening rage was appropriate and helpful, and the patient was able to go forward through a series of projections onto myself and his wife (during psychotherapy his homosexuality had profoundly diminished and was replaced by heterosexuality and marriage) so that his rage and fear of his sadistic intrusive aggressive mother could be worked through.

Patient #2: A woman entered psychotherapy after her husband turned from her to a perversion, leading to a subsequent divorce. The presenting situation was one of a profound narcissistic injury and deep overwhelming narcissistic rage as a response to her husband's choice of a perversion over her. Here the picture described by Kohut seemed extremely accurate. Even the patient's acting out by sexual promiscuity fit Kohut's (1971) formulation that the acting out in the narcissistic personality disorder represents a process similar to symptom formation in the neuroses. He writes, "The acting out of narcissistic personalities is a symptom which is formed in consequence of a partial breakthrough of repressed aspects of the grandiose self. Thus, although usually maladaptive and often disruptive, it may nevertheless be regarded as an achievement of the ego which amalgamates the grandiose fantasies and exhibionistic urges to suitable preconscious contents and rationalizes them, analogous to the process of symptom formation in the transference neuroses." This patient acted out sexually by conquering a whole variety of men and at work by taking on an enormous burden of responsibilities, behaving as if she were the president of the company.

The psychotherapy was marked by the characteristic countertransference problems (described by Kohut) in dealing with a mirror transference, which problems developed fairly rapidly: boredom, difficulty in emotional involvement with the patient and precarious maintenance of attention, leading to overt anger at the patient, a tendency to exhortations, forced interpretations, and tension and impatience on the part of the therapist. The patient's verbal and nonverbal behavior were not object-directed and contained the demand for total enslavement of the therapist as a prestructural object in order to help maintain her narcissistic equilibrium.

Following Kohut, and with his insights, it was possible through allowing the mirror transference to develop—in this case an archaic merger transference—for the patient to restore her narcissistic equilibrium, relinquish the acting out, resume her social life and remarry and return to her previous level of functioning. This satisfied the patient, and no attempt at an extensive psychotherapy of her narcissistic disorder was made, since the patient was pleased with her former level of functioning.

Patient #3: She presented as a typical borderline patient with no evidence of a narcissistic personality disorder or symptoms centering on the problems of narcissism. Kernberg's psychodynamics seemed very appropriate, and the patient needed a lot of help in dealing with split good and bad self- and object images, which were constantly projected and reintrojected so that the patient's life became an alternating cycle of periods of relative peace and periods of rage and paranoid fears. At no time were narcissistic defenses predominant in this case, and the psychotherapy centered around providing an accessory structure to the patient to help her deal with those periods when the pressures from the unintegrated bad self- and object images disrupted her functioning level. It was not possible for many reasons for this patient to be treated at more than a supportive level, but this form of treatment enabled her to function successfully and stop her alcoholism. The essence of the technique was to bolster the ego's defenses and to support the less pathological defenses so that the patient could deal with her aggressive and destructive impulses and continue to function.

Patient #4: This man presented as a schizoid personality who gradually revealed a variety of narcissistic and exhibitionistic fantasies. He came into psychotherapy because his marriage was failing and he was beginning to realize that he could not ever achieve anything remotely close to his primitive fantasies of total grandeur, admiration and exhibitionism as a world-famous musical performer and a chess genius. Nothing more was possible with this patient than to allow a therapeutic alliance to develop and to become the patient's only friend and confidant, seeing him infrequently and sharing his concerns as well as pointing out reality and providing some structure to his life. This enabled him to function at his schizoid level but removed his serious depression, which had dangerous suicidal components to it.

To assume that under his profound narcissistic fantasies were enormous fragmented bad and good self- and object images would be simply a speculation; he never gave any evidence that this was a problem. What he constantly presented was a deep longing for love; when someone paid attention to him he was happy, and when he was ignored by everybody he became depressed. Here I felt it was best not to be a "bull in a china shop," as Kohut describes it, and simply to promote the patient's functioning at his schizoid level.

Patient #5: Over a period of many years she had had two or three acute psychotic episodes with delusion formation of a paranoid nature and innumerable hypochondriacal preoccupations. The tendency toward fragmentation was continually present under stress. In spite of therapeutic efforts the patient slowly drifted to a lower and lower level of personality functioning. The great problem was the tendency to fragmentation of the self under stress which displayed itself by the appearance of the hypochondriasis, by delusional reconstitution of the grandiose self in a cold, paranoid grandiosity, and by profound narcissistic rage. There was a persistent theme of delusional reconstitution of the omnipotent object in terms of a powerful persecuting system against her. Even antipsychotic medication seemed to have no effect on these fragmentations, nor did anything else; it was as if the basic glue holding her personality and her self together was defective. In this case the regression was to a stage prior to that of the cohesive self. The narcissistic configurations appeared to be a desperate attempt to protect herself against fragmentation, an attempt analogous to her innumerable visits to innumerable doctors for her hypochondriacal complaints. The psychotherapy consisted primarily of providing a consistent structure to the patient around which she could reintegrate each time she fragmented.

Patient #6: She demonstrated the classical mirror transference of Kohut and suffered from a profound defect in internal soothing mechanisms, which resulted in her being addicted to holding as described previously in the literature. The patient varied from time to time in the form of the mirror transference from an archaic merger to considering us as twins to an expectation of echo and approval. At times this was replaced by an idealizing transference, and sometimes I had the feeling that both were present in oscillation in the same session, as described by Kohut. This patient, with totally unempathic parents, suffered from a severe narcissistic personality disorder. She was able to talk about rage and envy, but it was clear in examining her relationship with her father that any effort to break up the narcissistic transferences would have resulted in her experiencing a severe lack of empathy exactly parallel to what she had experienced from her parents. There was a serious danger of suicide.

In this case, perhaps the most clearly of all the cases, the narcissistic problem appeared to be a developmental defect and the narcissism as it displayed itself in her personality was remarkably similar to the narcissistic demands of the small child. In this case there was no essential descriptive difference in the grandiosity of the patient and the grandiosity of the small child. It is possible that this is a signal to the therapist, namely, *the more his empathic perception of the patient is that the patient's grandiosity resembles the narcissism of a small child, the more likely it is that the therapist is dealing with a narcissistic personality disorder.* When narcissistic configurations approach the bizarre and the delusional, one becomes suspicious that these are restitutive attempts to deal with unintegrated, sadistic and aggressive self- and object images that threaten to overwhelm the patient's personality and fragment the self.

Patient #7: He is an example of the latter. He was apparently not psychotic but presented a long history of tremendous hostility and even aggressive acting out, although he never committed any serious crime. At a point where he was suddenly and unexpectedly disappointed in a warm mothering relationship with a woman (which he had unrealistically expected from her), he developed a vivid delusion that he was the second Christ. This lasted a few weeks and disappeared and never appeared again, but it shook him up and caused him to seek therapy. Even with the vivid delusion there was some insight that it was a delusion.

In this case the narcissistic fantasies were extremely grandiose as they emerged in the long process of intensive psychotherapy. Furthermore, they were clearly related to bitter disappointments in the mothering function and represented the kind of dynamics described by Kernberg in which the patient split people into good faces and bad faces; when a person who was "a good face" failed to come through, he became instantly transformed into "a bad face" and became the object of powerful aggressive fantasies as well as powerful feelings of fear of retaliation for the aggression. The use of "faces" as images in this manner is, in my experience, very common in the intensive psychotherapy of borderline patients.

In this case the distant, cold and aloof grandiosity was quite different from that of a child; the patient after a while was able to discuss his deep, idealizing transference with me as clearly a projection of his own grandiosity, in which I was to be used as a stepping stone to his achieving divinity. First he and I would be above everyone in the world, and then as he used up all my strength, he would leave even me far behind. There was constant enormous chronic anxiety over the tremendous aggression attached to these unintegrated bad self- and object images and a corresponding superego defect as described by Kernberg, quoted earlier (Chapter 10).

Patient #8: She presented a cold, aloof grandiose self, bristling with antagonism, hostility, suspicion and paranoid fears. The pathology here was that of a starved, lonely, hungry little girl, and the whole therapy centered around dealing with rage and mistrust of a very primitive nature. There was clearly a search for a soothing parent, but no ability to accept any adult for that purpose because of the paranoid fears. At times I thought a merger transference was appearing, but whenever the patient got wind that in any way she might need me, there were immediate denial and paranoid accusations. The problem was complicated by the fact that her husband supported her paranoid feelings and her denial and seemed to need her as dependent, sick and alcoholic. In this case, simply through the therapist's becoming a vehicle for the discharge of her rage and hatred during the therapy sessions, the patient was enabled to "mellow" (her term) in her relationships to other people. At the center of the therapy was a tremendous fear of rejection and abandonment as well as of destruction from her projected sadistic preoccupations.

The patient was suffering from a threatened inner disintegration because of the presence of unbearable highly charged aggressive affects. Notice that the expression of communication of these highly charged aggressive affects doesn't *have* to take place as a projection of bad or good self- or object images onto the therapist and their subsequent reintrojection or by projective identification. It can take place in a number of ways, and it is incumbent on the therapist to pick up empathically the presence of this volcanic aggressive affect in the patient and to help the patient to deal with it.

This patient also illustrates another important principle in the treatment of borderline and narcissistic disorders that has not sufficiently been emphasized. Simply accepting the patient over long periods of time, not rejecting him, not getting rid of him, listening to all the raging, interpreting the projection, and still continuing to accept and work with the patient often seems to have a very important therapeutic effect! These patients feel that no one could possibly accept them or be with them because they know they are so unpleasant. The great rage makes them feel terribly unlovable, very anxious and interested in attacking before they are rejected. My clinical experience has been that the rage these patients present mellows and calms down just because the therapist does not disappear, remains consistent and does not retaliate and reject the patient for it. This is much harder than it sounds, for obvious reasons; I will discuss countertransference problems in detail later.

Patient #9: She illustrated similar dynamics to those described by Kernberg, but in this case the narcissistic aspects were minor and what was at the center of the defensive structure was a severe obsessive compulsive set of defenses that appeared after some quasi-schizophrenic disorganization had been resolved in the psychotherapy through the provision of consistent structure. The patient continued to function, but at a severe obsessive compulsive level, for many years. At the center of her problem was a clear and profound fear of the hostile sadistic intruding mother, which partly represented the projection of the patient's own aggressions but partly was also true of the mother.

In this case we see how a different series of defenses can protect the patient against the same problem as the use of a pathological grandiosity. In these cases as with many other cases, the problem is to help the patient deal with overwhelming aggression and fear of retaliation, as described by Kernberg. This is done in psychotherapy through the interpretation of transference projections as well as by providing structure and reality testing for the patient when the aggressions threaten to fragment the personality. The more serious the danger of fragmentation, the more the therapist has to provide himself as a structured introject to help the patient control the situation. In these cases the patient borrows the strength of the therapist in the alliance to help buttress the ego's defenses against the disruptive rage.

Patient #10: A classical type of highly successful narcissist, she came into treatment when a number of friends who were her late-middle-age acquaintances died. As a result of this she became aware that ultimate narcissistic injury—sickness and death—could not be avoided even for her. The psychotherapy was clearly that of a narcissistic personality disorder in which a deep archaic merger transference appeared and sustained the patient for years, resulting in a gross improvement in her functioning outside the treatment hours. Gradually there was a transmuting internalization and the patient became increasingly integrated and healthy, showing clinically the classical transformation of narcissism described by Kohut. Rage, when it appeared, was clearly narcissistic rage involving some narcissistic injury. Profound splitting, described by Kernberg, was not present.

Patient #11: She presented herself with "identity confusion" (her term) and a terrible problem in choice of career after having tried a whole variety of occupations. In due time, it became clear that there was a profound grandiose self demanding to know, to understand and to be everything that made it impossible for her to be satisfied with any career choice. In this case an archaic merger transference formed, and the patient was gradually able to resume her development. At no time did the profound splitting of object and self- representations occur or show itself, but rather there clearly appeared to be a developmental arrest. The case was complicated by an extremely pathological identification with a schizophrenic father that made the patient appear much more bizarre and weird than she actually was and much sicker than she actually was.

Patient #12: She was almost a converse of the previous patient in that she presented herself as what appeared to be a classical narcissistic disorder. Interpretations involving her fear of merger with the idealized parent imago had no effect, even though the patient seemed to suffer when such a merger threatened what Kohut has described as "traumatic states." Only when a discussion and working through of her profound rage took place was the patient able to resolve the pathology or the phenomenology of the traumatic state and resume functioning.

Here the patient's narcissistic pathology seemed clearly aimed at protecting her from the frightening emergence of magically charged archaic aggressive affect. The situation was complicated by the fact that one of her parents had cancer and was close to death; the patient felt that the emergence of her archaic rage would literally cause the death of her parent. This forced a massive repression of sadistic impulses, which could then only be released in the therapy process, often by projection. In addition to narcissistic configurations, the patient had such a problem in dealing with sadistic impulses that she had to have recourse to a variety of chemicals, including alcohol, marihuana and others, in order to literally provide a physiological soothing of the threatening disruptive aggression. It was a good prognostic sign that the patient was able to give up these chemicals early in the therapy and focus the problem in the transference.

Her other common defensive technique was withdrawal and retreat, which sometimes literally meant hiding in her room for days; at other times it could be experienced within the therapy hour as a sudden withdrawal of object cathexis from the therapist and a return to a cold, aloof and grandiose narcissistic state. After a while, I learned that interpretation of her rage at this point would reverse this process and allowed the therapy to continue. The serious danger of suicide was always present in this patient, as one might expect with so much unneutralized affect.

Patient #13: She entered therapy with the presenting problem of frigidity, but it soon became clear that her main aim in life was to render all males impotent and frustrated and to injure their narcissism in every possible way. This was clearly a problem of narcissistic rage in which the attempt was to reverse the real narcissistic injuries she had suffered at the hands of her father. For example, every time she reached out as a child to her father for affection she would be teased and pinched. In this case we were dealing with a borderline patient with many hysterical features, but the basic psychodynamic configuration was the tremendous aggression. The narcissistic problem represented an announcement and an acting out of the severe aggression, which also manifested itself in many other ways, such as bowel movements before and after the sessions, overt raging, constant attacks on and devaluations of the therapist and so on. The therapeutic problem was clearly to help the patient develop ego structures to deal with, if not to neutralize, the profound aggressions.

Patient #14: He was in therapy allegedly because of a depressive masochistic character disorder. The pathology appeared to be due to a narcissistic personality disorder as described by Kohut, and the presence of deep disintegration was not demonstrable. My contention is that it is possible in many cases—although from time to time one is fooled—to differentiate between the presence of the narcissistic rage which is part of any narcissistic personality disorder and the presence of rage and aggression communicated as infusing archaic unstructured and unintegrated self- and object images. This differentiation represents *two different types of patients;* one suffering from a developmental arrest in one area of the personality and another suffering from a defect that formed before the stage of the cohesive self. *The psychotherapist's empathic perception of the quality of the rage and the quality of the narcissism forms an important source of information to distinguish between the two types of patients.*

Patient #15: He clearly fell into the borderline type, although he showed no surface rage at all. He presented with extreme grandiose fantasies accompanied by fears of world destruction, which were attached to a series of religious fanatical radio broadcasts. These represented a carefully guarded secret, and he could not be diagnosed as schizophrenic on clinical examination! His only relationships were to inanimate objects, especially cars, radios, television sets, etc. His secret grandiose fantasies were extremely bizarre and vague, and it was not difficult to understand that they protected him against the total fragmentation which would have resulted without them. He was suffering from an incipient inner disintegration due to total inability to tolerate extreme rage. This patient's example shows that the patient does not have to present the rage directly in the psychotherapy for the therapist to catch onto the type of patient he is dealing with.

Patient #16 presents an interesting variation: She broke down when an ambivalently loved husband was killed in the Vietnam War. This sudden event confronted her with her own murderous wishes toward the archaic mother, which she had defended herself against by complete denial—she "loved" her mother and she was "sure" to the point of delusion that her husband could never be hurt by anybody. For a long period she could not even bring herself to admit that he was killed, and there emerged a long-standing grandiose fantasy that she was a princess of royal birth, which was in some ways fed by (a) the mother's insistence that her family was superior to ordinary people and perhaps had some noble blood and (b) her father's worship of her as a small child, which suddenly stopped when she came into the Oedipal period and showed some manifestations of sexual interest toward him.

Here we have a *combination* of profound childhood narcissistic injury with developmental arrest *and* a problem of apparent archaic unintegrated self- and object good and bad images in which the grandiose exhibitionistic fantasies represent *both* a defense against the totally destructive rage *and* a developmental arrest. It was as if one narcissistic configuration was layered upon another! In these cases the treatment has to be directed to deal with the profound pathological splitting so that the patient can function without fragmentation, and the developmental arrest aspect must be relegated to a later phase of the therapy.

Patient #17: There was a similar development of pathological archaic rage, but narcissistic defenses were not used. The patient used instead withdrawal from life into a convent and reaction formation by doing good works. Here again we see how the narcissistic defenses are only one set of defenses among others that are used by patients against similar basic problems of dealing with rage and aggression. Breuer's famous patient Anna O. is a similar case (Breuer and Freud 1895).

Finally, it is of the greatest interest to contrast *Patients #18 and #19:* Both patients presented with the *same* chief complaints of a deep sense of being meekly inferior among human beings, depression and paranoid suspicions. There the similarity ended, for Patients #18 was functionally paralyzed at the beginning of treatment, whereas Patient #19 was a successful person, well-thought-of, efficient and married. Both patients presented in due time important narcissistic and exhibitionistic fantasies, and both patients had been profoundly narcissistically injured by their parents for different reasons.

Patient #18 constantly struggled with the problems of fragmentation. His rage was extreme and his narcissistic preoccupations were bizarre and total; for example, he wanted to be the dictator of the world and kill millions of people. He was infused with hatred and constantly suffered from the projection of this hatred onto others, including the therapist. Even the most successful interpretations, when followed by functioning improvement, were often followed by dreams in which the therapist was murdering him.

Throughout the therapy he stayed faithfully with his treatment, made new gains, was able to work successfully, get married and take care of a wife and children, and yet, there was no change in his basic narcissistic preoccupations or in his inner feelings of rage. When the rage became overwhelming, he even had to resort to exhibitionism, which clearly analyzed itself into a hostile attack on the archaic intrusive mother. The therapy consisted essentially of the ventilation of his tremendous oral aggression in a nonretaliatory situation; his destructive fantasies were filled with parallel fears of retaliation. For example, he could not drive a car, because he was afraid that if he was stopped for a ticket by the police an altercation would occur and it would end up with his being destroyed by the police. Thus the therapy enabled him to function through a ventilation of the overwhelming rage, but no basic change in the pathology was possible.

Patient #19, on the other hand, formed a merger transference and was gradually able to reveal important narcissistic exhibitionistic fantasies from childhood, which were worked through. She showed the classical oscillation between an idealizing transference and a merger transference as well as a retreat into cold and aloof grandiosity when there was a disappointment in the empathic perception of the therapist. A gradual resolution in her narcissistic pathology took place, and she showed the classical transformations of narcissism described by Kohut.

Patient #20 represents an insufficiently recognized narcissistic personality disorder that presents clinically with a psychosomatic disaster consequent to the internalized undifferentiated rage (Chessick 1977c). The case has been described in detail in *Agonie: Diary of a Twentieth Century Man* (Chessick 1977b).

Part IV
PSYCHOTHERAPY—GENERAL APPROACH

CHAPTER 13

Overview of the Psychotherapy
of the Borderline Patient

What are the answers to the unresolved metapsychological questions raised at the beginning of Chapter 11?

1. Idealization of the therapist can be either a defense and a projection or a search for the idealized parental imago or both, depending on the pathology of the patient.

2. The narcissistic configurations may represent a separate developmental pathway in which there has been an arrest or, in other patients, may represent desperate attempts to protect against a fragmenting splitting of the personality.

3. There is a fundamental difference between borderline patients and narcissistic personality disorders. In the former, for the most part, we are dealing with affect *clinically expressed* as associated with more primitive and unintegrated self- and object images, whereas the narcissistic personality disorder appears clinically to have progressed farther toward a stage of the cohesive self.

4. The transferences should be interpreted as defenses only in those cases where an effort is being made in the therapy to help a patient in his struggle with fragmenting rage but should be allowed to develop without interruption in other cases and in the intensive psychotherapy of a narcissistic personality disorder.

5. Kernberg's formulations of the borderline personality organization are very useful, but they do not apply to the classical narcissistic personality disorder. Furthermore, the appearance of good and bad

self- and object representations in the therapy does not indicate these
are present in the infant under two years of age! At this stage of life
there are at most preverbal, preconceptual, affect-laden memory
traces. When these appear in psychotherapy, they are attached to
representations as they are communicated by the ego working on a
much more advanced level of cognition and operation. There is no
good reason to postulate the existence of such complex images in the
two-year-old, and most developmental psychology militates against
such postulates. One should keep in mind the powerful *synthetic*
function of the ego in telescoping analogous psychological experiences, especially for the purpose of communication and being understood.

6. The grandiose self in the borderline patient is crudely different
than that of the child, whereas in the narcissistic personality disorders
it is much more similar and reflects a developmental arrest.

7. The difference between a borderline personality disorder and a
psychotic seems to have to do primarily with the tendency toward
fragmentation and the cohesiveness of the ego in terms of coming back
together. The borderline personality fragments to an alarming degree,
but it snaps back rather quickly and without heroic measures. The
psychotic patient fragments into innumerable pieces; there is a total
loss of the observing ego, and reintegration, when it occurs, is rigid and
brittle. Thus the fragmentation in the schizophrenic patient is a much
more serious and ominous matter and carries a far worse prognosis.

The psychotherapy of the profoundly schizophrenic patient has to
deal with far greater danger of fragmentation, and only after the
therapist has been built into an important ego structure can the
intensive psychotherapy of the schizophrenic take place. In fact this
may never be possible, because the danger of total fragmentation is so
ominous. It is as if we are dealing with a certain basic glue which is not
present in the schizophrenic, is partially present in a kind of elastic
amount in the borderline personality disorder, but is relatively strong
and cohesive in the narcissistic personality disorder. The limitation of
intensive psychotherapy in these three kinds of disorders is based on
the strength of this glue. Fragmentation always has to be attended to
before anything else, because when it occurs there is a loss of the
observing ego and the fragmented parts of the personality are not
available to the patient for therapeutic work. Because of this they

threaten to disrupt and destroy the treatment in a malevolent fashion.

The threat of such fragmentation is always ominous and accompanied by great anxiety in the patient, often along with psychosomatic symptoms. The alert psychotherapist attends to this before anything else, and he must constantly assess the danger. In the schizophrenic patient the danger is always present, and it forms a profound limitation to the treatment. In the borderline patient the danger is variable, and careful history taking and experience with the patient can help the therapist to assess (a) the seriousness of the risk of fragmentation and (b) the cohesiveness, in terms of how long it will take for the patient to recover from impending fragmentation.

At the same time one must be careful not to read one's own anxieties into the fear that the patient will fragment. It is typical in the psychotherapy of the borderline patient for lots of anxiety to be stirred up in the therapist, and this sometimes appears as a projected fear that the patient is on the verge of fragmentation and collapse. This causes a misjudgment of the psychotherapeutic situation with a result of backing away from the patient, an avoidance of uncovering, aborted attempts at support, writing of prescriptions and a therapeutic stalemate.

In the narcissistic personality disorder the danger of fragmentation is minimal in a well-conducted psychotherapy and the closest we get to it are Kohut's "traumatic states." These are due to a flooding of unneutralized narcissistic libido, and if this understanding is appropriately presented in nontechnical language to the patient, the excitement usually subsides. As Kohut points out, "The analyst should tell the patient that it is sometimes very hard to become aware of the intensity of old wishes and needs, that the possibility of their fulfillment may be more than the patient was able to handle all at once, and that the present state was an understandable attempt to rid himself of his excitement . . . it can be made clear not only that under such circumstances the child is in need of a tension-dispelling adult, but also that the patient is temporarily reexperiencing this old state since the personality of his mother had not permitted such optimal experiences in childhood." Eventually the patient with the narcissistic personality disorder who is experiencing the reemergence of these powerful feelings in the transference learns to handle these increasingly familiar tension states more smoothly, without the direct aid of a therapist.

It is vitally important that the therapist be aware of what is happening when these states take place during the psychotherapy! If these states do not respond to such interpretative work, the therapist should be suspicious that he is dealing instead with the danger of fragmentation and the disruptive reemergence of archaic oral aggressions projected onto the therapist as a mother figure. This in turn serves as an important tip-off to the therapist of the nature of the basic pathology with which he has to help the patient struggle.

Clearly the basic problem of intensive psychotherapy with borderline character disorders is how to deal with the fact that the patient has not received what Winnicott calls good enough holding in infancy. There are almost as many varieties of recommendations for the treatment of the borderline patient as there are authors on the subject. General agreement is only found on a few basic issues. First, ordinary encouragement or supportive therapy as practiced in the general physician's office produces either no effect at all or a dramatic remission soon followed by relapse with the same or new symptoms accompanied by the angry demand for more magic. Second, the typical administration of various pharmacological agents to these patients often complicates the situation in many ways. They abuse the dosage instructions, and the side effects produced by improper dosage complicate the symptom picture. They collect medications from various physicians and take these in various amounts and combinations. Suicide attempts with these medications pose a definite risk.

Rapid shifts and changing, with all the excitement, storm, and panic they cause the patient and those around him, often accompanied by either missing appointments and failures to pay the bill or spending session after session in talking about various symptoms and the constant introduction of extraneous problems and extraneous matters, soon make both physician and patient feel that no progress is being made. There is typically an exasperation on the part of the therapist as well as a developing barrage of complaints about the treatment from the patient, which may lead to an impasse, and a referral for hospitalization or a variety of other ways are employed to get rid of these patients.

However, if one is willing to put up patiently with a great deal of frustration and disappointment, it is possible to successfully treat borderline patients. Four basic approaches to the psychotherapy of the borderline patient are found. The first type emphasizes a very authoritative and direct approach with much psychological pushing and shoving of the patient in order to get him moving. Emphasis is placed on controls, socialization and reality testing, and therapy deals mainly with the symptoms and attempts to produce a personality who modifies himself to please the therapist in order to function socially. Unless interminable contact is maintained with the patient, relapses are soon to be expected, especially when life stresses arise. If this approach can be made to work, it is certainly quicker and cheaper than long-term intensive therapy. An excellent write-up of this approach may be found in the first edition of the *American Handbook of Psychiatry* in an article on the borderline patient by Melita Schmideberg (1955). It may interest the reader to compare this article with my article in the second edition of this handbook (Chessick 1975) to see the advances and the changes in thinking over a period of fifteen years about our approach to the borderline patient.

The second type of approach is a formal psychoanalysis, seen by some as a desperate heroic measure and by others as the treatment of choice. Most psychotherapists reject this approach out of clinical experience in which many borderline patients show a complete intolerance to the ordinary psychoanalytic situation, reacting with suicide attempts, transitory psychoses, dramatic chaotic symptoms or acting out that finally interrupt the treatment. To say the least, a formal psychoanalysis of the borderline patient should not be attempted by anyone except the most experienced and well-trained psychoanalyst who is willing to assume great risks.

The third type of psychotherapy attempts to combine an uncovering psychotherapy with providing a directly gratifying experience of some kind for the patient. This direct experience can vary from taking the patient's hand to examining the patient in the nude or letting the patient bite and suck on the therapist's hand or breast or what have you, in a direct attempt to provide "better mothering experiences" within the particular psychodynamics of the patient. Needless to say, the danger of massive countertransference acting out is quite rampant in these situations, and the most hair-raising and destructive behavior by the therapist can be excused as attempting to provide a corrective experience. From a theoretical point of view, this approach has additional dangers in that the use of such heroic measures, which are essentially a primary-process kind of interchange, works directly against the stated aim of diverting the patient's ego functioning away from primary-process and toward secondary-process-based thinking and behavior. Even more than in authoritative and directive psychotherapy, the patient can easily become hung up on the primary gratifications involved, leading to a demand for more and more and at best a subsequent stalemate. I have seen this repeatedly occur when attempted by inexperienced or poorly analyzed psychotherapists.

I have collected a series of cases from supervision, from the reported experiences of other therapists and from patients' reports that I considered reliable, which detail psychotherapists' attempts to treat borderline patients by giving direct gratification of all varieties, from handholding all the way to hugging and kissing the patient. I have not seen *one single case* where this has had any lasting benefit in the psychotherapy. It sometimes gives the patient a temporary sense of soothing but invariably leads to a fixation on this kind of gratification, and always—which is most interesting—at some level the patient develops a profound hatred of the therapist, because the patient *intuitively recognizes* (a) that there is an exploitative aspect to this— the therapist is getting some kind of acting-out gratification—and (b) there can be no possible future for this kind of relationship with the therapist—it is bound to end in loss and rejection for the patient.

This leads to an intense ambivalence in the patient in which he becomes tremendously hung up on getting the primary-process gratification from the therapist and at the same time develops a greater and greater hatred of the therapist. This is usually resolved by massive acting out outside of the therapy of all sorts and kinds, sometimes without the therapist even being aware of it. It is very hard for such patients to leave therapy, because they are so hung up on the gratification, and when the time comes that the therapist is sick and tired of hugging the patient or whatever, explosive reactions occur.

I emphasize this because it happens all too often that the tremendous anxiety stirred up by borderline patients in therapists is resolved by massive acting out on the part of the therapist toward the patient. Again I emphasize that I have never seen a borderline case where any kind of direct gratification of a patient had a lasting or useful therapeutic effect. In every instance it has caused more harm than good. Invariably the reasons given by the therapist for what he is doing represent rationalizations of acting out.

The treatment offering the greatest potential with the least serious risk for borderline patients goes under the various names of psychoanalytically oriented psychotherapy or psychoanalysis with parameters or, best, psychoanalytically informed psychotherapy. I will now review this in more detail.

CHAPTER 14

Psychoanalytically Informed
Psychotherapy

The initial problem of psychoanalytically informed psychotherapy of the borderline patient is getting the patient to form a therapeutic alliance in spite of all the storm which his symptoms lend to the relationship. In fact, the patient must at first be very tightly locked (Chessick 1966) into the therapy to enable him to maintain the relationship in spite of the terrific anxieties of abandonment, penetration and annihilation that invariably arise and must be worked through along with the primitive rage. A very long period of "being there" from a psychotherapist with high empathic capacity and great frustration tolerance is at times necessary before the patient begins to build a sense of confidence and becomes locked into a symbiotic relationship with the therapist. This is facilitated by concentrating at the beginning on reality problems instead of getting lost in fancy or highly intellectual dream interpretations or psychodynamic formulations, and also by a certain deep inner attitude toward his patients on the part of the therapist.

This deep inner attitude is described in a poetic little one-page paper by the French psychoanalyst Selma Nacht (1969): "It seems to me that what is most important to obtain such a result is not so much what the analyst says as *what he is*. It is precisely what he is in the depths of himself—his real availability, his receptivity, and his authentic acceptance of what the other is which gives value, pungency, and effectiveness to what he says."

Now, of course, this is very very difficult to teach for it is based partly on one's innate capacities and partly on the thoroughness with which one has had a psychotherapy of one's own. One must remember, as Nacht explains, that the activity of the therapist is aimed at helping man master the incessant whirlpool created by the clash of constructive and destructive tendencies within him. "If he can manage to escape the zone of conflict, man is able in this way to escape the ambivalence which constitutes the most pernicious poison to his psyche, the major obstacle to the blossoming of the forces of love within him." These forces of love are infinitely more powerful in man than he may guess, provided that they are no longer constantly opposed, used or destroyed by conflictual currents.

Thus, as in the treatment of the adolescent, a certain sense of optimism and confidence in the outcome and in the forces of love within the patient is necessary if one is to successfully treat borderline patients. Especially at the beginning of the therapy, this kind of optimism and confidence helps one withstand the tremendous vicissitudes which otherwise would make one either retreat into a passive withdrawal from the patient or surrender in a kind of masochism to the patient's berating activities or even act out by directly gratifying the patient or by getting rid of him.

If the initial locking in takes place, strong transference manifestations appear, affording the opportunity to correct or at least to ameliorate the preverbal disaster without the use of dangerous heroic measures. This correction takes place in the context of the transference through empathic understanding and interpretation by the therapist as well as through a deep emotional interaction between therapist and patient. Success or failure in treatment depends on this process.

Various kinds of transferences take place, as I have already discussed. One sometimes sees Modell's type of transitional-object transference or one sometimes sees Kohut's type of mirror transference or idealizing transference. As long as these transferences are workable we have hope for progress. Some of them are analyzable, resulting in structural change, and some of them are not analyzable, in which case we get amelioration of the defect and a certain amount of resignation. We also have to face the fact that there are limitations as to how much we can do. In general, the literature is overly optimistic, and tends to ignore the warnings of Anna Freud (1969) regarding the intensive psychotherapy of pregenital disorders.

When you get into the discussion of the psychotherapy of the borderline patient, the work of Strupp (1973) becomes especially interesting and timely and important. Strupp feels that it is arbitrary in psychotherapy to pin the preeminent therapeutic influence on the interpretation of the transference. I think there is general agreement about this as long as one is not talking about formal psychoanalysis. In the psychotherapy of the borderline patient, except in those cases that form a transference neurosis that is stable and analyzable, a variety of factors influence the therapy and they are very nicely reviewed by Strupp, essentially in terms of learning process. It is often less important what the therapist considers theoretically to be causing the change than what the therapist is actually engaging in with the patient; the latter is often what leads to the therapeutic change.

Thus the psychotherapy of the borderline patient provides an excellent area for the research and investigation of therapeutic "influence." Strupp reviews a variety of factors that lead to influencing the patient in psychotherapy, for example, the importance of a solid, reliable and trusting relationship with the therapist. They are what Strupp calls learning experiences in constructive living, that is to say, in creating a situation where the patient is willing to listen to the therapist. In overcoming mistrust and resistance to accepting the therapist's guidance, the patient experiences a corrective type of meaningful experience, and this is important in terms of influencing the patient to change. There is even what Strupp calls moral suasion, which is implicit in the therapist's apparently neutral clinical stance, and I will talk more about this in detail later.

Thus the therapist, according to Strupp (1975), establishes himself as a good parent or authority figure: "... he creates conditions that maximize the chance of his being listened to and he seeks to neutralize or undercut road blocks the patient places in the way of his teachings; he points out maladaptive patterns of behavior and their underlying infantile assumptions; he sets an example by remaining calm, unruffled, reasonable, and rational; he refuses to get entangled in the patient's neurotic machinations; he conveys the message that the patient must learn to accept *personal responsibility* for his own actions instead of blaming others and life circumstances for his predicament; he teaches the basic lessons on how people in Western civilized society interact productively and nonneurotically; he teaches the patient to be less demanding and grandiose, to scale down his expectations of others, and to accept a more *active* role in managing his life; he conveys a philosophy of reasonableness, rationality, moderation, mutuality and fairness as the guideposts of the 'good life'; and, in broad terms, he combines love with discipline in helping the patient become a more autonomous, self-directing, and responsible adult."

This becomes most controversial when one is talking about classical psychoanalysis, in which the analysis of the transference neurosis makes the major changes, but in psychoanalytically informed psychotherapy it is *not* necessary to do what Strupp calls smuggling in these lessons on constructive living through the back door! We know that these are important therapeutic influences in psychoanalytically informed psychotherapy, and if one is to be successful in bringing about the very difficult task of inducing anyone to change deeply ingrained habits and beliefs, one is going to have to present one's self (Havens 1974) by involving the patient in an emotionally charged relationship and utilize the dependency and the transference to influence the patient in desired directions.

One of the most theoretically important questions is *whether*—if one wishes to bring about basic structural change—*this is enough*. Does there not also have to be some semblance of a transference neurosis, which can be analyzed in order to resolve infantile conflict?

Assuming that we are sufficiently analyzed ourselves and are not directly influencing what is happening in terms of transference formation, we don't have much choice as to whether a transference or a transference neurosis will form or as to what kind of a transference will form when we are working with borderline patients. Certain types of transferences are not desirable and they threaten to destroy the therapy entirely. The transference manifestations in general can be extremely frightening and strong and the patient resorts to many unusual measures to deal with them.

Perhaps the most dangerous problem comes from acting out in the transference relationship. Greenacre (1963) describes a type of massive acting out in the transference that is frequent, repetitive and sometimes lasts over a considerable period of time. In her cases it mainly occurs in the analytic relationship and in the analytic hour, but she mentions that for some patients it may even extend into relationships outside of the immediate contact with the analyst. This acting out usually occurs in the form of *attacks,* but not invariably in the form of attacks, and consists primarily of provocative or seductive behavior, taking many forms.

For example, the patients may present themselves as suffering and mistreated, with a constant worrying about some current grievance which even has a core of a kernel of truth in it, but which becomes brooded over in an obsessional way with a quiet drama aimed at getting the therapist to make an emotional response or intercede on behalf of the patient. More frequently the other side of the coin is up and the therapist is represented as the misunderstander. Then there is persistent, insidious nagging accusation with taunting ridicule. Anything the therapist says is taken out of context and distorted; if the therapist says nothing this is interpreted provocatively as indicating the justification of the complaint. There is a trying out of the therapist by a wearing-down effect to see where the limit of his tolerance really is.

This whole performance has the form of a tantrum of a special kind in which there is a relentless demand for reciprocation and discharge through the therapist. Greenacre interprets this as being connected to projective identification and implies that there is a beating fantasy behind this provocativeness, but she doesn't discuss it at any length. The psychodynamics may be controversial and may vary, but the therapist doesn't forget this kind of experience very easily.

One must be constantly aware of the potential for such attacks. Sometimes they occur outside the therapy, so the therapist must keep a constant eye on what is going on in the patient's real life or he will be suddenly confronted with explosive developments in the therapy of the borderline patient.

Two such typical dangerous transference developments seen in the psychotherapy of the borderline patient are the erotized transference and the involvement of a third person in the transference, developments both of which must be quickly recognized and dealt with or the treatment will be ruined. The erotized transference, which was even recognized by Freud (1915) early in the development of psychoanalysis, manifests itself by the stormy demand for genital contact with the therapist and so on. When this is rejected, the patient experiences deep and *sincere* hurt and humiliation. It is not amenable to interpretations and persists as a demand for direct gratification. Empathy, consistency of approach, patience, understanding the patient's sense of rejection and not reacting with fear or hostility to his or her demands can eventually lead to a resolution of this problem. It is very important in such situations not to make the patient feel humiliated or put down. If the therapist does not recognize the genuineness of these feelings and makes light of them or ridicules them, it is experienced by the patient as a profound narcissistic blow and generates a situation from which the therapy itself can never recover.

Similarly, borderline patients often cannot stand the intensity of their longings for the therapist in the transference and they may quickly dump all of this onto a third person and engage in massive acting out. In addition to that, they tend to sexualize these longings, which of course are really much more primitive and pregenital, but they are more acceptable if they are sexualized and the chances of acting them out are better. If this is not recognized and interpreted and stopped, sometimes emphatically, situations such as impulsive marriage or pregnancy may result.

A word is in order here about how one goes about emphatically stopping such massive acting out. It is always presented to the patient in terms of, "This will be a danger to you or to your psychotherapy. It is not in your best interest." It is never presented as a moral command of any sort, for the major responsibility the therapist has in preventing acting out has to do with the preservation of the psychotherapy itself. This rule is only violated in situations where the patient is a physical threat to himself or others, in which case the therapist must feel that his duty as physician or citizen comes first, but most of the time the problem is to emphatically present to the patient the idea that he is ruining his own psychotherapy by acting-out behavior and that he must delay it or the psychotherapy will be destroyed.

If this acting out persists and the patient insists in going ahead with plans that are clearly involved with transference acting out, the therapist must confront the patient with the choice of either stopping his behavior or foregoing treatment until he is willing to control himself better. In no way should the therapist implicitly condone or accept behavior on the part of the patient which he knows is a massive acting out in the transference. Everything else in the therapy has to come to a halt while this problem is dealt with, as it is a very dangerous situation for the patient and his psychotherapy. Alertness to the potential problem and constant active concentration on the patient's life situation are necessary. The use of a third person is not always undesirable to help the patient withstand the tense transference longings—it depends on what extremes the patient has to go to with this third person. Too energetic interpretations of transference longings can throw a patient into a chaotic panic and also disrupt the treatment entirely.

If disruption does not occur, the transference is properly understood and interpreted, and anxieties are gradually worked through, the patient is often able to uncover grandiose core fantasies in a protective atmosphere. Borderline patients live around their early infantile narcissistic fantasies which permeate and contaminate all ego operations. They cling tenaciously to these narcissistic fantasies, which represent a consolation for the deprivation of affect from the mother and also the patients typically attempt to produce the longed-for affect through satisfying *all* confusing, conflicting and unrealistic parental expectations. The patient lives as if he had already secretly accomplished these fantasies, producing a set of poorly adaptive responses to life.

Sometimes these grandiose core fantasies are apparent even at the beginning of treatment, but direct assault upon them simply results in vigorous denial or even breakup of the treatment, since they represent substitutes for gratifying human relationships and they cannot be given up until the annihilation and abandonment fears are worked through in the transference. A sarcastic approach to such fantasies, which is a typical beginner's mistake, *always* represents countertransference difficulties.

It is clear that the basic factor in successful psychotherapy of borderline patients has to do with how the psychotherapist handles the crucial dilemma produced by the intense transference longings and also by the associated deep fears and rage. Frosch (1971) points out the thin line the therapist has to walk between the gratification of the patient's wishes and the imposition of limits. One must bear in mind that the borderline patient himself frequently is caught on the horns of a dilemma, namely his need and wish for the object—in this instance, the therapist—and his fear of engulfment if such wishes are gratified. The whole problem of giving and receiving permeates the patient's relationship with his parents and subsequently with his therapist.

In agreement with what I have written, Frosch essentially points out that this very state requires structuring and the imposition of limits to help the patient deal with the multitude of confusing factors that make it so difficult to structure for himself, and he explains that it is possible to do this more firmly after the distrust which frequently permeates the feelings of the borderline patient for the therapist has been diminished and a good psychotherapeutic relationship has begun to evolve. Thus the building up of a feeling of trust is the crucial aim of the earliest steps in the psychotherapy of the borderline patient.

In a paper (Chessick 1968) written before that of Frosch, I pointed out how the therapist has to walk a tightrope in this crucial dilemma. On the one hand, it is clear that direct ministering to the patient's needs by behavior such as caressing or feeding or giving gifts to the patient constitutes a form of "acting in," as I have described (Chessick 1974a). It is undesirable except in the most minor and socially acceptable forms, such as allowing a cigarette to be borrowed and so on, because it prevents ego expansion by fixing the patient on the omnipotence of the therapist. On the other hand, a therapy without parameters will not hold the patient in treatment. The crucial dilemma the therapist always faces has to do with the question of where to draw the line.

For example, watching neophyte therapists it is easy to show that hiding behind rigid adherence to technique or rules of treatment is a defense against feeling the anxiety engendered in them by the massive pregenital strivings of borderline patients. Analogous, perhaps, is society's tendency to treat such people with rigid rules, for example, "The army will make a man out of him." On the other hand, dangers to intuitively approaching such patients are obvious. The therapist must genuinely know himself and not engage in countertransference acting out. The patients are only too eager to act out or "act in" in the therapy, and they pose a threat to the neophyte from that point of view alone. Thus, the key factor behind improvement is the therapist's ability to be emotionally responsive without predominantly using the patient for his own needs. In a similar fashion the therapist must be able to draw away and permit separation and individuation at the proper time.

Obviously, this depends primarily on the self-understanding of the therapist. Careful study of case material shows that it is actually possible to keep a secondary-process check on what is going on so as to avoid a wild and disorganized therapy. The more thoroughly understood the patient is, the more accurately it is possible to know whether our emotional interaction with him is on the beam from session to session. Improvement in the patient appears to be directly related to this emotional interaction, and to the degree to which it is consistently genuine, on the beam, and originates from a healthy and positive deep inner attitude of the therapist.

CHAPTER 15

Therapeutic Regression

The task of psychotherapy with psychotic and borderline patients becomes infinitely complicated by the fact that the patient neither has a firm grasp of his own sense of identity nor is able, because of his primitive narcissism or his need to project malevolent introjects, to respond to supportive kindly or benevolent measures as we would logically expect a starved and lonely person to do. It is now theoretically clear why attempts to directly gratify the borderline patient repeatedly fail. What is necessary instead is for the therapist to empathically grasp the nonverbal, unconceptualized affect-laden memory traces as they are communicated in subliminal inflections and behavior, to call attention to these and to help the patient conceptualize and verbalize them and explore their origins and meaning. A long period of working at this primitive level of "education" is often necessary before any interpretations make *any* sense to the patient.

We must begin at the level of ego function and perception the patient is at and gradually enable him to move forward developmentally to a level of cognitive and intellectual function where thought and abstraction make sense at all. This is the secret of the frequent impulsiveness of the borderline patient; it is not malevolence—there is simply no thought barrier developed between the impulse and the act. First of all we must literally help the patient bit by bit, through focus on his behavior, to develop a stronger and stronger thought barrier and capacity to wait and delay action.

The key to any successful uncovering psychotherapy with the borderline patient is in the capacity of the therapist to permit and enable the patient to unfreeze disruptive and restrictive introjects warping the basis of his early ego function, a function of the therapeutic atmosphere the therapist creates for all his patients. The major source of resistance to psychotherapy, as pointed out by Guntrip (1968), is ". . . the extreme tenacity of our libidinal attachments to parents whatever they are like. This state of affairs is perpetuated by repression in the unconscious inner world, where they remain as subtly all-pervasive bad figures generating a restrictive, oppressive, persecutory, inhibiting family environment in which the child cannot find his real self, yet from which he has no means of escape."

The only reasonable approach to these patients in uncovering psychotherapy will have to be in ultimately unfreezing the early ego formation, an unfreezing which can occur only if a controlled regression is permitted to take place. It must be pointed out that regression cannot be *forced* by the therapist. It must occur as a natural consequence of the sense of security within the therapeutic alliance that is allowed to form between a relatively healthy therapist and whatever mature aspects are available in the observing ego of the patient. Winnicott (1958) enumerates some of the obvious factors that allow this regression to take place. It might be first mentioned that "the whole thing adds up to the fact that the analyst *behaves* himself or herself, and behaves without too much cost simply because of being a relatively mature person."

The factors encouraging a regression useful in psychotherapy are

1. A consistent and frequent being at the service of the patient, at a time arranged to suit mutual convenience
2. Being reliably there, on time, "alive, breathing"
3. For a limited period of time, keeping awake and becoming preoccupied with the patient
4. The expression of love by the positive interest taken and "hate in the strict start and finish and in the matter of fees"
5. The attempt to get into touch with the process of the patient, to understand the material presented and to communicate this understanding by interpretation
6. Use of a method stressing a nonanxious approach of object observation

7. Work done in a room that is quiet and not liable to sudden unpredictable sounds and yet not dead quiet; proper lighting of a room, not by a light staring in the face and not by a variable light (In some instances the patient lies on a couch (Chessick 1971b) that is comfortable in most instances, depending on the situation, a face-to-face situation with the patient is necessary)

8. Keeping moral judgment out of the relationship as well as any uncontrollable need on the part of the therapist to introduce details of his personal life and ideas

9. Staying, on the whole, punctual, free from temper tantrums, free from compulsive falling in love and so on, and in general neither hostile and retaliatory nor exploitative towards the patient

10. Maintaining a consistent, clear distinction between fact and fantasy, so that the therapist is not hurt or offended by an aggressive dream or fantasy; in general eliminating any "talion reaction" and insuring that both the therapist and the patient consistently survive their interaction (Winnicott feels that this setting reproduces the earliest mothering techniques and invites regression. If it is consistently offered, an unfreezing takes place as a natural consequence of the regression that occurs)

The crucial unfreezing of malevolent introjects through a controlled regression contains within it two major constructive and therapeutic events. The first of these is the loss of destructive introjects; the second is the substitute introjection of the psychic field offered by the therapist.

However, the regression also contains a major potentially *destructive* event, for such a regression stirs up omnipotent expectations on the part of the patient; a yearning for what the therapist can do, magically and in a primary-process manner, to restore to the patient all the missing experiences from his infancy and to make good for the patient all the negative experiences of his infancy. I shall proceed to discuss first this potentially destructive event and then the constructive events in detail.

Either the inevitable frustration of the omnipotent expectations of the patient stirred up by regression *or* narcissistic blows that occur to the patient in real life during the long process of psychotherapy can lead to a series of events that result in a failure of the treatment. The psychotherapist must be aware that the danger of regression induced by the therapeutic setting can lead to failure, and he must have an understanding of the typical kinds of consequences that are produced as a result of the frustration of the omnipotent expectations and from serious narcissistic blows.

Such consequences are typically:

1. Acting out, in which the patient quits the treatment or in which he quickly finds a third person to meet his unbearable infantile cravings for holding and body contact as described by Hollender (1970; Hollender et al. 1969, 1970)
2. The need for revenge, in which the patient through passive aggression stalemates the treatment, stalemates his life or allows his life situation to fail, making psychotherapy impossible
3. Projection of destructive introjects onto the therapist with fear and hatred of him, all coming as a consequence of the frustration of the patient's omnipotent expectations, which may lead to a breakup of the therapy
4. An autistic retreat on the part of the patient into sadistic sexual fantasies
5. At worst, hallucinations and delusions as a consequence of self fragmentation, which may even require hospitalization

Let us turn now to the therapeutic and constructive consequences of regression in the treatment setting. The loss of malevolent introjects as a consequence of regression can be noted if the therapist carefully studies changes in both ego function and superego function in the patient. Destructive introjects in the ego manifest themselves by poor adaptative techniques. Introjects of the parents include many elements of the relationship with them that involve methods of mastery. As there is a loss of destructive and restrictive introjects, there is a corresponding improvement in the patient's capacity to adapt to the external world, to function more efficiently and to observe himself more realistically. Similarly, as introjects are discharged from the superego by projection and then interpreted, there is a lessening of the hostile punitive aspects of the superego, and the patient becomes more reasonable with himself and others and begins to develop a sense of beloved self.

Our basic tool in intensive uncovering psychotherapy is introspection and empathy. Kohut (1959) explains that consistent introspection in the narcissistic disorders and the borderline states leads to the recognition of "an unstructured psyche struggling to maintain contact with an archaic object or to keep up the tenuous separation from it." In borderline states, "archaic interpersonal conflicts occupy a central position of strategic importance that corresponds to the place of structural conflicts in the psychoneuroses." Thus Kohut points out that the analyst is introspectively experienced "within the framework of an archaic interpersonal relationship. He *is* the old object with which the analysand tries to maintain contact, from which he tries to separate his own identity, or from which he attempts to derive a modicum of internal structure."

Giovacchini (1965) points out that the acquisition of adaptive techniques by the ego leads to a higher state of integration and involves the process of incorporation. The ego develops by acquiring introjects that lead to more efficient functioning. He continues, "Such introjects may have several modes of action. On the one hand, the introjects may act defensively, reducing the disruptive potential of intrapsychic conflict or ego defect and permitting the ego to achieve a more stable homeostasis; as a consequence areas of functional autonomy may develop. On the other hand, the ego may utilize an introjected positive experience not only in regard to its defensive potential; it may benefit from the experience directly by having 'assimilated' an adaptive technique. ... The ego's 'armamentarium' is expanded and its functional range is increased."

Now when the desired controlled regression takes place in psychotherapy, a dissolution takes place, giving the ego the capacity to incorporate new objects, a capacity it did not previously have because of hostile destructive introjects leading to constriction. By regressing to such a level of disorganization, the ego has also lost its capacity to maintain the structured introjects when it progresses into a slightly advanced position. "It has gained from the loss of such introjects insofar as it has the capacity to incorporate experiences which can expand its adaptive potential."

Insofar as the child experienced an assaultive and rejecting external world before there was self-object differentiation, adult levels of ego functioning will reflect disturbances in structure instead of the id-ego conflict of the psychoneurotic. On this point there generally seems to be considerable agreement. Any attempt on the part of the therapist to directly gratify the patient will be offering the incorporation of an interaction that is based on primary process and thus cannot become a basis for ego development. If we attempt to give primary-process gratification by responding to irrational demands, we are contributing to the maintenance of an infantile organization and an equilibrium which contained a preponderance of primary-process elements. As Giovacchini points out, "the therapeutically desired development and synthesis *always* heads in the direction of the secondary process."

To put it another way, we want to do anything we can to enhance the ego's drive towards autonomy. In a later paper Giovacchini (1967a) discusses the need for acting out and what he calls externalization. The patient cannot tolerate the helpfulness of the therapist. By providing a setting to facilitate regression, the analyst situation sometimes causes the patient to believe that gratification is possible and reinforces the expectation of primitive satisfaction. The patient hopes to be rescued from his assaultive and depriving introjects, a megalomanic expectation of rescue which leads to bitter disappointment. As a result the therapist is viewed as insincere and is converted into a replica of the frustrating environment the patient once knew. This transformation involves a projection of a bad self as well as externalization; I have discussed externalization in detail elsewhere (Chessick 1972b, and in Chapter 20).

Giovacchini (1973) conceptualizes the borderline state as one in which the patient lacks adaptational techniques because he lacks memories of early gratifying experiences that later should have developed into methods of dealing with the problems of the outside world. The functional introjects which later contribute to the ego's executive techniques of mastery were never formed or, relatively speaking, only imperfectly formed. Giovacchini points out how these patients often create a situation of tension and urgency by expressing a need to be helped which cannot be met, since neither the patient nor the therapist knows what kind of help the patient seeks. The needs are so primitive that they cannot be articulated, and the therapist, if he tries to respond directly to them, experiences the same frustration and helplessness as the patient.

Giovacchini feels that the diagnostic evaluation of borderline patients is best made on a combination of various qualities of ego structures, behavioral characteristics, and possible courses of the disorder, a combination which also takes into consideration therapeutic outcome. I am in agreement with this approach. Giovacchini concentrates on ego systems, because he is interested in the formation of ego systems through the process of introjection. He divides these ego systems into three general categories—perceptual, integrative and executive—but states the behavior and adjustment of the patient considered borderline indicate that the primary defects are in the integrative system of the ego. "The integrative system coordinates perceptual stimuli, either inner needs or demands from the outer world, with appropriate executive responses. These appropriate responses depend upon memories of past satisfying experiences. If such experiences are lacking one does not know how to respond."

The lack of functional introjects in the borderline patient further leads to constrictions in the executive system of the ego, although the perceptual and integrative systems are also involved. This leads to a conflict between the ego and the demands of the outer world and to a tendency, because of this, for the patient to withdraw and have tremendous feelings of vulnerability.

Speaking of the symbiotic stage, Giovacchini continues, "One need not conceptualize this stage in terms of subtle mental representations, since the infant has neither the emotional nor the neurological structure for complicated mentation. In terms of needs—that is, a reestablishment of homeostatic equilibrium—he need not distinguish between himself and the person who administers his needs." Emergence from the symbiotic phase results in the establishment of a "structured identity so that eventually boundaries between the inner and outer world are clearly established. Insofar as the borderline patient has suffered frustration and deprivation during the stage of symbiotic fusion, his self-image is imperfectly formed. Since he has received little gratification, he has very few adaptational techniques to cope with even pedestrian problems." Note here that it is during the symbiotic phase and the vicissitudes that take place during it that Giovacchini places the beginning development of the borderline state.

Thus the borderline patient's early transference represents an effort to experience a symbiotic relationship with a strong, powerful person who will supply him with the adaptive techniques denied him by an inadequate, weak mother. The patient hopes to experience a magical rebirth and be the master of the now-threatening outer world. How the borderline patient reacts to the disappointment of magical expectation is a very critical issue. Giovacchini (1973) feels it distinguishes the borderline from other patients suffering from characterological problems, and he sees the typical reaction as poignant sadness, with the patient believing that he simply cannot be helped by treatment.

The reaction to the patient's frustration is counterfrustration in the therapist. This often leads the therapist to become anxious, because he has identified with the patient's desperation, feeling that he must respond almost blindly, giving advice or management. At this point the therapist abandons his analytic role because of his sense of urgency and anxiety. Sometimes the patient accepts this abandonment of the analytic role, but more often he feels that such intervention is an intrusion, or at least he eventually feels frustrated by it, since it is not really an appropriate response. It is felt more as an assaultive foreign body, and in Giovacchini's experience and also my own, *it often stirs up a tremendous amount of rage which may not show itself until much later.*

Many treatment failures marked by the patient's sudden withdrawal from treatment are caused by the therapist's anxiety. Giovacchini points out that the therapist attempts to defend himself against anxiety, by being "professional," which may result in forced interpretations. The situation becomes unmanageable and filled with quarrels and defensiveness. Then both patient and therapist feel helpless and therapy becomes increasingly confused and chaotic. Since the patient feels even more helpless than usual, demands for rescue increase and the therapist feels even greater anxiety. A vicious circle is created with an atmosphere of frustration and counterfrustration.

It must be made clear that if the therapist, on the other hand, refuses to abandon the analytic attitude and observational viewpoint, he may cause unmanageable amounts of frustration and run the risk of losing the patient. If the patient terminates treatment under these circumstances, it is doubtful whether intensive psychotherapy can help him. Patients sometimes feel they need "something more" than psychotherapy, and when the therapist refuses to modify the treatment and begin gratifying them, they leave. In my experience this "leaving" is either poignant or filled with rage and recrimination; either way it constitutes a sincerely painful experience for both therapist and patient.

More is internalized from the therapist in a properly conducted treatment than the healthy experience of a correct interpretation. First of all, the therapist's nonanxious observing attitude, his compassionate, studious and sincere approach to the patient, becomes a part of a healthy introject in the patient's ego. Most tricky of all, it seems imperative that we recognize the countertransference structure (Tower 1956) as an important aspect of the therapist's attitude, forming a psychic field that is also introjected by the patient. If this countertransference structure is not, for the most part, malevolent and murderous, at least it does not represent a serious impediment to ego growth through introjection of the therapist's psychic field. We hope then, that through the introjection of the psychic field of the therapist—based on correct interpretations, a compassionate secondary-process approach, a nonanxious observing attitude and a relatively benign countertransference structure—there is ego growth, manifested by better functioning of the various subsystems of the ego.

This view is supported by research at the Menninger Foundation (Appelbaum 1975) in which internalization is viewed as made up in long-term psychotherapy of a number of "part processes" that are the result of a growing working relationship and that act in a reciprocally enhancing manner with the therapeutic relationship, contributing to its development. "These interrelated part processes are: (1) the enhancement of self-esteem; (2) the corrective emotional experience; (3) transference cure—i.e., changed behavior in order to impress the therapist; and (4) identification with the therapist's attitudes." The Menninger group believes that all of the mechanisms—which are conceived of in Kernberg's terminology—produce "structural" change, which becomes reinforced by the environment's favorable response and so becomes increasingly stable. The surprise in the research was "the extent of change that occurred in patients unable to utilize insight." This again emphasizes the crucial importance of the actual experience the patient has with the therapist in long-term intensive psychotherapy.

CHAPTER 16

The Psychic Field of
the Psychotherapist

It is ego growth through this process that allows the destructive dangers of the regression induced by the therapeutic setting to be overcome by the patient's gradually increasing ego strength. They *will* be overcome providing certain ominous situations do not occur:

1. If the omnipotent demands are not too overwhelming and immediate
2. If the patient does not immediately quit or unconsciously set out to destroy therapy before any work can be done
3. If the destructive introjects that have made up the early ego formation of the patient are not so constricting and malevolent that a total rigidity and incapacity to get free of them is present
4. If the psychic field of the therapist is mature enough

It is clear that a certain realistic limitation is placed on our therapeutic efforts by the first three of these factors, and some cases will inevitably fail because of them. It is in the area of the psychic field of the therapist that the most hope exists for an improvement of our results.

In *Why Psychotherapists Fail* (Chessick 1971c) I have already discussed in detail the production of the optimal psychic field of the therapist. In addition to this generally optimal psychic field, there is certain specific work that the therapist must do with every patient and in every psychotherapy. It is easy to see that a countertransference structure is stirred up in the therapist (a) by each regressive step in the patient, confronting the therapist with a new set of feelings, demands and reactions; (b) by intercurrent realistic or narcissistic blows in the life of the psychotherapist—after all, this is long-term psychotherapy, during which both therapist and patient are experiencing numerous events in their actual living; and (c) by the very length of time of therapy, representing a "time frustration" to the secret omnipotent hopes of the psychotherapist.

All these factors operate to provoke the tendency in the therapist to exploit or retaliate or both, even in such minor ways as the tone of his voice or letting the patient out a minute early. Thus a constant *self-analysis of the countertransference structure* must be going on within the therapist in order to keep the psychic field up to a maximum of maturity. This should take place at the same time as efforts are made to understand the patient and to interpret this understanding back to him. So, *in the language of scientific understanding,* "learning from one's patients" means expanding one's own ego capacities through the continual self-analysis of countertransference structures precipitated either by the various phases of the patient's regression or by intercurrent events in the real world of the patient and/or the therapist.

This is not enough. *In the language of the humanistic imagination,* the patient must continuously experience the "presence" of the therapist. Each therapy session must "count," as Saul (1958) puts it. Each session must represent an encounter between the psychic field of the therapist—which in its maturity, extends trust, confidence and hope—and the need-fear dilemma of the patient, who has fallen away from authentic living and being with another person. This deep inner attitude on the part of the therapist can be maintained only as a function of continual reduction of constricting countertransference structures, just as a healthy nervous system permits the maintenance of an alert and attentive mind. The purpose of this for the patient is described by Saul (1970):

> For the unsustained, the analyst must provide the experience which the patient lacked in childhood: that of having an interested, sympathetic, understanding person always available in his life. Without such an attitude, technically correct

interpretations may be interpreted by the patient as disapproval. Accurate interpretations also require an attitude of human understanding, of being on the patient's side, of having confidence in him. ... The analyst's confidence is partly internalized and can move even the "hollow" ones in the direction of a sense of sustainment, of identity, a good self-image and self-acceptance.

It follows from these theoretical considerations that the phenomena described in the language of the humanistic imagination such as "presence" or "being there" or "I-thou" and so on represent *epiphenomena* of the successful working through in the psychotherapist of the various phases of countertransference structure called forth by the phases of the patient's psychotherapy.

The reverse is *not* true; here is where an increasingly common amateur error takes place. One cannot force "presence" or an encounter down a patient's throat. Hugging and touching and going through all kinds of "immediacy" gestures with a patient will not fool the patient; they mask serious countertransference problems in the therapist. Only the natural and inevitable unfolding of a human encounter in the forward progress of psychotherapy, as both the patient and therapist work through their respective tasks, can produce a genuine growth experience for both. *There are no shortcuts.*

Balint (1968) insists that in some cases in which words—that is, associations followed by interpetations—do not seem to be able to induce or maintain the necessary changes, additional therapeutic agents should be considered: "In my opinion, the most important of these is to help the patient to develop a primitive relationship in the analytic situation corresponding to his compulsive pattern and maintain it in undisturbed peace until he can discover the possibility of new forms of object relationship, experience them, and experiment with them."

According to Balint, the task of the psychotherapist with patients who are not classical neurotics, but whose disorders have begun before the consolidation of the repression barrier, is essentially to supply a "new beginning" to the patient. He attempts to provide an atmosphere in the psychotherapy that in a sense is a corrective emotional experience to the early nonempathic mothering the patient had. Those who follow Balint emphasize the patient's absolute need for empathy from the therapist and stress the danger that inappropriate verbal interpretations may be produced, because it is the empathic interactions that are essential for the successful treatment of such patients rather than interpretations of a transference.

Balint gives a few examples of how the "unobtrusive analyst" can foster this process. For example, the more the analyst can reduce the inequality between his patient and himself, the better are the chances of a benign form of regression. The analyst also provides time and a milieu that has a holding or therapeutic function. The environment "should be quiet, peaceful, safe, and unobtrusive . . . it should be there and . . . it should be favorable to the subject, but . . . the subject should be in no way obliged to take notice, to acknowledge, or to be concerned about it."

Again, Balint warns us that by providing this special therapeutic relationship the analyst must avoid becoming an omniscient and omnipotent object, and he must be sure that the gratification will result not in a further increase or excitement in the patient, but in the establishment of a tranquil, quiet well-being and in "a better safer understanding between the patient and himself." He adds, "None of the details of the therapeutic attitude outlined here are essentially different from what the analyst adopts when dealing with patients at the Oedipal level, and even the topics worked with are usually the same; but there is a difference, which is more a difference of atmosphere, of mood."

Fundamentally, I do not think that there is any necessary connection between Balint's (1953, 1968) theoretical conceptions and what he is advising the clinical therapist to do. If one carefully follows his recommendations, one is not carrying out an active therapy in the sense of Ferenczi at all, but simply permitting and tolerating a controlled regression of importance during the psychotherapeutic process. The therapist is simply being a decent human being who understands when to push the patient with interpretations and when to allow the patient some time for peace, quiet and working through. I do not think that this differs in clinical practice from how any sensitive, humane and feeling physician would act with his patient. Thus, there is a substantial gap between Balint's highly controversial theoretical considerations and the general office practice of psychoanalytically oriented psychotherapy. The difference seems to be an emphasis on a theoretical explanation of what is and is not important in therapeutic process rather than any fundamentally different approach to the patient.

Kernberg (1972b) brings to our attention that Balint sharply criticized the Kleinian use of conventional language mixed with nouns (like breast, milk, inside of the body) the meaning of which became so extended and comprehensive from Klein's clinical work, and he suggested that the Kleinian analysts tend to develop what he called a "mad" language. As reported at scientific meetings and in the literature, these kinds of interpretations create the impression of a confident, knowledgeable and perhaps even overwhelming analyst. "He wondered if this might be the reason why there is so much aggressiveness, envy, and hatred in their patients' material and so much concern about introjection and idealization," since these are common defense mechanisms in a partnership between an oppressed, weak person and an overwhelming powerful one. This deserves some careful thought in terms of psychotherapeutic technique. When powerful rage reactions show themselves in the psychotherapy of our patients, we must be extremely careful that they may be related to the therapeutic technique, language or countertransference structure rather than simply to the projection of primitive bad self-object representations.

Kahn (1974) refers to Balint's contention that there are really *two styles* of relating to the patient:

1. Listening to the patient, to what he verbally communicates in the classical situation, and deciphering its meaning in terms of structural conflict (ego, id and superego) and through its transference expression in the analytic situation.
2. What Kahn calls "a psychic, affective and environmental *holding* of the person of the patient in the clinical situation." The alleged result of this style is to "facilitate certain experiences that I cannot anticipate or program, any more than the patient can. When these actualize, they are surprising, both for the patient and for me, and release quite unexpected new processes in the patient."

My big objection to this second style is that it is too mystical. Even Kahn agrees that it is very personal to the style of living of the patient and of working of the therapist; as such, it becomes very difficult to teach and can be used or abused as license to do just about anything to and with the patient that the therapist wishes to do.

Balint, of course, is extremely careful to avoid this sense of license. He distinguishes between two important types of regressions, which he calls malignant and benign regression. Regression for the sake of gratification, which has the qualities of despair and passion and aims at gratification by external action with a suspiciously high intensity of demands and needs, is Balint's conception of *malignant regression.*

He sharply distinguishes this from a regression in which what the patient needs is the "arglos" state. What is desired in this state is the analyst's *recognition* of the patient's needs and longings for satisfaction which are the essence of a "new beginning" and the patient's recovery from his basic fault. The arglos state, which Balint (1968) considers to be an absolutely necessary precondition for the new beginning, is explained by the craving of the patient for "primary love" (Balint, 1953). It is clear that the special atmosphere provided during this state has more to do with recognition than massive gratification. Only token satisfaction of need is provided, and in the evolution of Balint's views the tokens of direct gratification become less and less; the recognition of the patient's need and the unobtrusiveness of the therapist are the essential ingredients.

Balint's approach to the arglos state is given indirect metapsychological support by Zavitzianos (1974), in my opinion, although he does not mention Balint in his paper. Zavitzianos postulates that an inborn developmental drive of the ego exists, which propels further development under favorable conditions. When this ego developmental drive is dominant in the therapy, the ego is *not* inclined toward a demand for transference gratification, but rather toward experience of the understanding and human decency of the therapist. At such points the offer of direct transference gratification would be refused and would constitute a complete failure of empathy on the part of the therapist. For this reason seemingly unanalyzable patients, explains Zavitzianos, respond to psychoanalysis because the analyst by his personality and the atmosphere he provides meets the needs of this ego striving and thus allows further development to occur from within. This explains in Balint's terms why the recognition and understanding by the therapist of the patient's profound needs and problems produces a "new beginning" and why attempts to directly gratify in the transference are actually destructive and miss the point.

Balint has called attention to the fact that an important theoretical change in the classical conception of psychotherapeutic technique is at hand and that this is determined by the increasing importance given to the actual experience of after-education that the patient in a benign regression has with the therapist. Such an experience, of course, is far more important when one is dealing with borderline or narcissistic personality disorders than when one is dealing with classical neuroses. Balint recognizes this quite clearly in his division of types of treatment into those suitable for patients who are essentially at the Oedipal level and those suitable for patients who are at the level of the "basic fault."

Unfortunately, his theoretical formulation is based on adultomorphic errors and there is also a mystical aspect to it in terms of the kind of atmosphere that the therapist is supposed to provide. *All patients* should be presented with the physicianly vocation (Stone 1961; Chessick 1977a) and the authentic self of the therapist, and it is not clear what special techniques are really involved in somehow trying to provide the patient with totally empathic mothering. We try to provide all our patients with as much empathically based understanding as we can, but we are always bound to make some empathic errors.

It is perhaps more realistic and practical to turn to Modell's technique of allowing a transitional object transference to take place so that the development of the patient can resume. Winnicott (1965, 1968) introduced the notion of the true and the false self, and this is associated with Modell's ideas. The *false self* develops in response to early nonempathic mothering and has to do with learning to be compliant, a certain inherent rigidity and lack of autonomy or spontaneous feeling. This often has to be broken down via therapeutic regression (Chessick 1974a) so that the pathological false self-compliance can disappear and a real exchange of affect and feeling can emerge in the therapeutic situation. If the therapist himself is a true self this will become clear to the patient, however, without any special alterations in the analytic process.

Kohut's (1971) therapeutic preoccupation involving regression and transference formation is: "How is one to differentiate the psychopathology of the analyzable narcissistic personality disturbances from the psychoses and borderline states?" For Kohut the answer seems to rest almost entirely on the type of transference that is formed when the patient is taken into a formal analysis. Thus, a differential diagnosis on the basis of initial interviews or symptomatology is almost impossible, if I understand Kohut correctly. He writes, ". . . the spontaneous establishment of one of the stable narcissistic transferences is the best and most reliable diagnostic sign which differentiates these patients from psychotic or borderline cases on the one hand, and from ordinary transference neuroses, on the other. The evaluation of a trial analysis is, in other words, of greater diagnostic and prognostic value than are conclusions derived from scrutiny of behavioral manifestations and symptoms."

Thus, as previously explained, Kohut places the unanalyzable psychoses or borderline states on the one hand and the analyzable cases of narcissistic personality disturbances on the other. The former tend toward the chronic abandonment of narcissistic configurations and toward their replacement by delusions; the latter show only minor and temporary oscillations, usually toward partial fragmentation.

The schizoid patient, whom Kohut includes among the borderline cases, keeps his involvement with others at a minimum as the outgrowth of a correct assessment of his regression propensity and narcissistic vulnerability. Such patients correctly evaluate their assets and weaknesses. "The therapist should thus not be a bull in the china shop of the delicate psychic balance of a valuable, and perhaps creative individual, but should focus his attention on the imperfections in the defense structures." To put it another way, the appropriate therapy for schizoid or borderline patients is not formal psychoanalysis, because a transference regression will take place that will lead to a severe fragmentation of the self. Instead, a psychoanalytically sophisticated form of insight therapy is called for that does not require the therapeutic mobilization of the self-fragmenting regression.

In this manner Kohut distinguishes among three groups of patients:

1. The ordinary psychoanalytic treatment patient who forms a transference neurosis
2. The borderline or schizoid or schizophrenic patient who is an unsuitable candidate for psychoanalysis and for whom a regression will lead to self-fragmentation

3. The patient with a narcissistic personality disorder, who forms certain definite types of stable transference in a formal psychoanalysis and, thus, is analyzable

Kohut has described what I would call *one type* of borderline patient, the type who develops an analyzable narcissistic transference in a classical psychoanalysis. It does not follow from this that all other borderline patients are to be labelled borderline schizophrenic or schizoid patients. To put it another way, it is not reasonable to say that if a borderline patient is put into psychoanalysis *either* he will develop a narcissistic transference of the type described by Kohut *or* he will develop a fragmenting regression. Other kinds of transference can also develop. Whether these other kinds of transference are amenable to a classical psychoanalysis remains an open question, but I think it is simply not true that borderline patients who are put on the couch either develop a fragmenting regression or develop the kind of narcissistic transference described by Kohut. There are other alternatives.

This in no way contradicts the formulations of Kohut, with which I am substantially in agreement. It merely indicates that borderline patients have various predominating features in their psychic organization which sometimes show themselves in the formation of a classic narcissistic transference as described by Kohut, sometimes show themselves as a regressive fragmentation, and sometimes show themselves in terms of other kinds of transferences that may or may not be amenable to analytic interpretation.

Following Kohut's formulations to their conclusions with Gedo and Goldberg (1973), we can establish a hierarchy of treatment modalities. Phase One, from zero to six months of age, represents the time from birth to cognitive self-object differentiation. Primary narcissism reigns supreme. Primary repression is the crucial mechanism of defense, and the primary anxiety is that of annihilation through overstimulation. Patients who have to regress to Phase One experience traumatic states or panics. The treatment of these cases is *pacification,* which represents the control of excitation, controlled catharsis and, if necessary, the use of medications and hospitalization. The essence of pacification is tension reduction and mastery through partial discharge.

A second phase of life, between eight months and three years, is the phase during which self-object differentiation progresses to essentially irreversible cohesion of the self. During this phase the grandiose self and idealized parent imago are utilized, separation anxiety is the characteristic anxiety, magic is the kind of reality testing used, and massive projection and introjection are employed. Patients who regress to such a phase present clinically what we call psychotic disintegration, and the treatment is that of *unification.* Such patients require a cohesion of the self through the therapist's providing reliable and consistently available objects and settings. An uninterrupted relationship with the therapist is crucial. As the therapist becomes a transitional object and puts himself in the life of the patient, there occurs what Balint has called repair of a basic fault, and the therapy is a real experience for the patient in which he is having an uninterrupted relationship with a real object. The therapist sometimes must even force himself into the life of the patient as a real object.

The third phase of life, from around three to six years, is from the time of the cohesive self to the solid formation of the superego. Narcissism becomes more confined to the phallus and castration anxiety is typical. Disavowal or splitting of the self is the mechanism of defense, but the self and object are perceived as whole and different. Patients are characterized by narcissistic personality disorders when they have regressed to or are fixed in this phase of life. The treatment then is *optimal disillusion*—confrontation with reality—and perhaps Kohut's kind of psychoanalysis in which stable narcissistic transferences are allowed to form and are gradually interpreted. The patient is helped gradually to give up the narcissistic fantasies, and the grandiose self and the idealized parent imago are integrated into the personality.

The final phase of childhood, between six and eight years of age and puberty, is the phase of consolidation of the ego and the repression barrier after the superego has been formed. The reality principle becomes prominent; the person is guided by his ego ideal and pushed by his ambitions. Moral anxiety is typical, repression occurs, and we have the era of the infantile neuroses. The treatment of this kind of disorder is *the psychoanalytic method,* using interpretation in which there is strengthening of the ego and mitigation of the severity of the superego and in which small quantities of dammed up inner energies are discharged.

One might add a fifth phase of life from puberty to adulthood that we could call the era of the fully differentiated psychic apparatus.

Signal anxiety is typical at this time, and narcissism has been transformed to wisdom, empathy, humor and creativity. Difficulties during this time are hopefully resolved by careful introspection and even self-analysis (Gedo and Goldberg 1973).

This neat division of the kinds of therapy necessary into phases of regression or developmental fixation that are appropriate is not quite satisfactory, because most patients present a mixed clinical picture. Obviously, patients who present traumatic or panic states must be given pacification. However, for those patients in the second, third and fourth phases, the treatment should present interpretation, optimal disillusion and unification together in the psychotherapy, with shifting emphasis during the treatment depending on where the state of regression is in the patient.

The therapist must empathically be able to tune in to where the patient is and provide the kind of treatment modality that is optimal for the patient at any given time. The danger of hierarchical formulations lies in the tendency to fit the patient to the treatment rather than the treatment to the patient. That is to say, they do not take into account fluctuations of the ego along the ego axis on a day-to-day basis (Chessick 1973) in every ongoing intensive psychotherapy.

Attacks on psychoanalytic psychotherapy that minimize the importance of interpretation make the same mistake; they tend to ignore the fluctuations of the patient's ego state on a day-to-day basis. There are times or phases in the psychotherapy where unification and optimal disillusion, usually loosely referred to as "education," are predominantly necessary. Education is always going on in every psychotherapy, since there is always, if the therapist "behaves himself" (Winnicott 1958), an uninterrupted relationship. On the other hand, interpretation is also always going on at one level or another. If it is skillful, it has a more or less important effect depending on the particular regressive phase that the patient is in at a given time during the treatment.

This explains the kind of criticism that is constantly aimed at psychoanalytic psychotherapy by such workers as Strupp. In a recent paper Strupp (1975) utilizes a case of an at best borderline, probably ambulatory schizophrenic, patient reported by Balint, and he demonstrates that interpretation, although claimed by Balint to be the therapeutic agent, was not the crucial therapeutic agent in the case. For such patients, as Strupp points out, it is gratuitous to argue that interpretation is the crucial factor: "... every patient is being influenced by the therapist in a wide variety of ways, of which interpretations are only one subject, and ... it is arbitrary to elevate the latter to a position of preeminence. On the contrary, I believe that the weight of the therapeutic influence is brought to bear in numerous modalities and that interpretations of all kinds are a relatively minor factor in the total change that is wrought over the short as well as the long term." This kind of argument is used to attack the psychoanalytic method and interpretation in all cases, and it is based on a confusion between patients who do not have a cohesive sense of self and patients who do.

Anyone who works in the area of narcissistic personality disorders or borderline states must maintain a continual special awareness of the kind of atmosphere he provides for his patients, and this is consistent with discussion of optimal disillusion and unification along the lines of Kohut's theory. Whether this "education" kind of treatment is to be labelled psychoanalytic or not seems to me a semantic question and one which is fraught with overtones of prestige and status; certainly, no one could deny that it constitutes optimal psychoanalytically informed psychotherapy.

Part V
PSYCHOTHERAPY—SPECIAL PROBLEMS

CHAPTER 17

Transference in the
Borderline Patient

I. Symbiosis

Much debate about the treatment (and even identification) of the borderline patient revolves around consideration of the kinds of transference they develop. These cannot be described in a simple manner, and furthermore it is not possible to understand the kinds of transference that borderline patients develop without as thorough as possible an understanding of the symbiotic phase of development and the separation-individuation phase, as already described.

Some confusion exists about the exact times of the symbiotic and early separation-individuation phases. Revision of Mahler's thinking took place between the 1950s and 1960s; the beginning emergence from the symbiotic phase was finally believed to occur earlier. For our purposes we could say that the height of the symbiotic phase is reached at about six months of age, and from that point on there begins the separation-individuation; with Mahler we could say that it is the general task of about the second year of life to reach at least some solid separation-individuation, although the process is far from completed and it takes another year yet before there is sharp differentiation and a sense of self is accomplished. That is to say, only by the time the child is three years old can we say that separation-individuation has been passed through in solid fashion.

Now the core of ego development, the first orientation toward external reality (as Schilder had pointed out already in 1938), is the differentiation of the body image, which is the psychic representation of the body self. "Through the rhythmically recurring experience of painful accumulation of tension in the inside of his own body, followed by regularly repeated experiences of gratification, which the infant cannot provide for himself hallucinatorily beyond a certain point, the infant becomes eventually dimly aware of the fact that satisfaction is dependent on a source outside of his bodily self." So Mahler (1952) points out that the infant recognizes "an orbit beyond the boundaries of the self, that of external reality represented by the mother. Bodily contact with the mother, fondling and cuddling, is an integral prerequisite for the demarcaton of the body ego from the nonself within the stage of somatopsychic symbiosis of the mother-infant dual unity."

It is very important to try to think about what goes on as the infant begins to experiment with the feel of his mother's body, comparing it with the feel of his own, learning about his body contours as separate from his mother's, distinguishing between himself and his mother. During the symbiotic stage the mental representation of the mother remains fused with the mental representation of the self and it participates in the delusion of omnipotence of the child.

In the symbiotic child psychoses, as described by Mahler (1952), "unneutralized libidinal and aggressive forces have remained narcissistically vested in fused systems of mother-father-child unit, reminiscent of the primary unit (mother-infant)." The world is seen as hostile and threatening because it has to be met as a separate being. Thus separation anxiety becomes the crucial issue in the symbiotic psychoses as described by Mahler. The boundaries of the self and the nonself are blurred.

We get into difficulty when we try to understand what has gone on intrapsychically during the *transition* from the symbiotic stage to the early stages of separation-individuation. Mahler (1975) feels that during the second year of life the maturational growth of locomotion really precipitates the separation-individuation. But what goes on within and among the psychic representations as we shift from a totally fused self-object representation to separation-individuation? It is not possible to reasonably assume that there is no autistic phase and that the child comes at birth with a ready-made ego, as Fairbairn assumes, or with ready-made capacities for forming introjects and so on, as

Klein assumes, and it seems to me that it is also stretching things a great deal to depend heavily on the clinical material of adult patients to make assumptions about self- and object representations being split in a preverbal child, an infant around one year of age.

What happens has more to do with a splitting of affects; the self- and object representations that appear during the therapeutic process in the transference are already a later accretion to which these affects are attached. This is more consistent with the cognitive capacities of the one-year-old than the assumption that self- and object representations are sitting in his undifferentiated psyche that can be sharply projected out onto a therapist years later.

Giovacchini (and also Kohut implicitly) differentiates between adaptative techniques which have been introjected (or as Kohut would call it, "microinternalized"), have become part of the child's ego and do not form a discrete entity like a foreign body, on the one hand, and disruptive introjects on the other. That is to say, during the phase of separation-individuation, the ego begins to differentiate itself from maternal introjects. The child sees himself as separate and distinct. He learns the mother's adaptative techniques, and this enables him to achieve further separation and strengthens the ego boundaries. As this occurs, the maternal introject, if you want to call it that, becomes part of the child's ego, and insofar as it promotes psychic harmony rather than disruption it loses its boundaries and becomes assimilated. This is a functional object relationship; Kohut uses the complex term *transmuting microinternalizations* to distinguish these experiences from the abruptly precipitated and disruptive introjects which occur when the experiences with the mother are basically ungratifying.

What happens when these experiences with the mother are ungratifying during the stage of separation-individuation is first of all that this stage is not successfully traversed, leaving the individual with immense separation anxiety, annihilation anxiety and a tendency to invest massive amounts of anxiety in all kinds of situations—typical of the borderline patient. It also leads to an ego which is poorly adaptive and has to use a variety of clumsy techniques to deal with situations that more fortunate individuals are able to handle in a much smoother fashion.

However, the worst consequence of the ungratifying experiences has to do with *the incredible hatred that is set up, the relentless, boiling, chronic rage.* I see no reason to postulate a constitutional aggressive factor! Sometimes this rage has to do with the infant's perception of the mother's rejection and hatred of it, but there are also situations where the mother doesn't hate the infant but is emotionally absent for other reasons or shifts back and forth or cannot empathize with the infant because it is needy, dirty, noisy and so on. The rage and the hatred are absorbed into the personality structure along with feelings of worthlessness and inadequacy, a sense of feeling unlovable and vulnerable, a profound lack of self-esteem and a sensation of being in danger. This sense of danger, which really has to do with fear of the explosion of hatred into the conscious mind, is either sensed as danger from some foreign attacking power within or projected out onto the therapist or others and experienced as coming from without. Often the wish is to kill this power, to "wipe it out" by the use of chemicals or alcohol or to identify with it and destroy somebody else.

In this situation there are no successful transmuting microinternalizations, but rather there are what Giovacchini (1975a) calls hateful maternal introjects, which have a disruptive influence and which must be kept under control or denied in various ways. During the process of psychotherapy of the borderline patient, these hateful maternal introjects, which primarily produce a sense of combined profound hatred and terrible intense helplessness and anxiety, may in their various aspects be projected into the therapeutic situation.

For example, Giovacchini (1972) writes, "The patient or child must maintain a facade of control and autonomy within the framework of a helpless and vulnerable ego. In order to maintain this control the child has to be isolated from the threatening introject which he can achieve by defensive splitting. On the other hand, he must cling to an external object because of the intense helplessness he feels. He requires both nurture and rescue from inner assault by the frightening, disruptive introject. But insofar as his self-representation includes derivatives of the primitive symbiosis, an inner assault also seems to emanate from those hateful aspects of the self that are *precipitates* of the mother-child fusion. The child then turns to the outside world for anaclitic nurture and salvation from a raging, self-destructive self."

This is the foundation of the kinds of transference one sees in the borderline patient, a turning to the outside world for anaclitic nurture and salvation from a raging self-destructive aspect of the self. It is important to keep in mind what we mean by the term *introject,* a badly misused term. It is best to think of it basically in terms of feelings rather than of some kind of personified image or phantasm in the mind. In the psychotherapy of the borderline patient, what is most impressive is the unneutralized feelings of all kinds that emerge, which frighten the patient and which the patient finds very difficult to deal with. Many such patients don't have these feelings attached to specific fantasies or these fantasies may change and shift in fleeting ways in dreams and projections and so on. For example, one patient would "hear" or remember the voice of her mother calling her name in a disgusted tone.

Giovacchini explains that as the patient projects these terrific feelings onto the therapist, the fact that the therapist responds to the patient, not with terror or helplessness, but with analytic calm and interpretations brings the therapist's secondary organization to the patient's primary-process chaos. This helps the patient achieve organization both through self-understanding and by incorporating the therapist during the regression. Giovacchini (1972) writes, "The regression to the symbiotic phase during analysis can lead the patient to regain parts of the self that had been split off, and the catalytic effect of the analytic introject causes them to be synthesized into various adaptive ego systems—not to be dissociated as they were in childhood."

II. Transference

With these considerations of the symbiotic phase in mind, we can look a little more at the kinds of borderline transference specifically described in the literature. One aspect of the transference is the intensity and seriousness of it, as described by Little (1966), for instance. She begins by agreeing with my basic contention that *borderline state* is an imprecise and descriptive term for a wide range of patients. She emphasizes the sliding back and forth on the ego axis as I have described it. The separation anxiety in such patients has to do with fear of annihilation; it is also often accompanied by a literal psychosomatic chaos. The patient may develop a whole variety of severe psychosomatic difficulties at the point where he begins, in the depth of the transference, to experience this annihilation anxiety (Chessick 1972b)—that is to say, the differentiation between psyche and soma begins to break down and the primitivity of the kind of anxiety involved makes itself known.

Similarly, as Little points out, the more primitive the form of anxiety, the more primitive is the form of defense against it and of course the less effective too, so we see a lot of magical thinking, omnipotence and simple rigid denial. These are the primitive defenses against annihilation anxiety: magical thinking, hallucinatory omnipotence or narcissistic omnipotence and simple denial.

Little stresses the tremendous degree of sensitivity, stability and flexibility necessary in the therapist working with borderline patients, because of the tremendous anxieties that are involved: "Freedom of imagination, ability to allow a free flow of emotions in oneself, flexibility of ego boundaries, and willingness to consider the views and theories of colleagues whose approach may be different from one's own (which is perhaps the same thing) may all prove to be vitally important in the treatment of any patient." I have tried to illustrate in the case reports how sometimes the views of one colleague appear to be most appropriate to a borderline patient; at other times one applies the views of another. I don't think this is an accident. It has to do with the variety of patients that are loosely labelled borderline.

So one aspect of the transference in borderline patients is the intensity of the annihilation anxiety and the primitive defenses of magical thinking, denial and narcissistic omnipotence that are used against it. The other aspect of the transference, which is fairly consistent, as already discussed from Modell, is the transitional-object nature of the transferences. The therapist is experienced as an object, perceived somewhat outside of the self, whose qualities are distorted by fantasies arising from the subject, and this object, the therapist, has a *real role* in the life of the patient in what I would call primarily a soothing kind of function. Borderline patients will put the therapist in this role no matter what he says or does, and whether he likes it or not.

To give a clinical example, a patient comes in session after session and reels off a long list of irritations and complaints that she has accumulated during the week. We discuss these various complaints, sometimes we discuss how she will deal with them, and she feels better when she leaves. The next session the same thing happens again. This goes on in an apparently endless series. For a long time I felt a growing sense of confusion with this patient because I could not understand why this was happening. The patient simply didn't seem to be catching on to what psychotherapy was all about. In fact, she rarely seemed to be listening to anything I said, and yet she came regularly; she felt that the therapy was helping and her life was even improving. Finally, *after very careful listening,* it occurred to me that what we were dealing with was the equivalent state of a six-month- to one-year-old infant. A cycle is reenacted in which the infant awakes from sleep, gradually gets tired, gradually gets hungry, gradually gets wet, becomes irritable, picks up a variety of complaints along the way and finally starts crying. Then the mother appears and cleans it up, holds it, cuddles it and feeds it. Then all is well and the infant goes back to sleep, and then the cycle begins all over again. The patient was using me in this sense from week to week as a transitional object for soothing and tranquillization, touching base to feel that all was well and I hadn't disappeared or lost interest. Then she was able to go out and face the outside world, which was perceived as dangerous, attacking, threatening and separate from the dyad that the patient had formed of herself and me, experienced as a part of herself, like a blanket or teddy bear.

If the therapist doesn't understand and catch on to this aspect of the transference, the result can be a destructive countertransference, because it is very irritating to be used this way, as a self-object (Kohut 1971). In the first place, one has the feeling that one does not have a self of one's own. The patient is not responding with affectual contact to one's own self but is simply, deliberately, and selectively ignoring the human aspect of the therapist and using him as an object. This always stirs up hostility in another person. In the second place, it all seems to go against what we try to do in psychotherapy, where we look for the effect of our interpretations in improving the person's life, leading to better adaptation, enhanced ego strength and so on. When the kind of transference I am describing is in effect, however, it doesn't matter very much what we say! The patient is not interested in the *words* at all, any more than when the mother picks up the baby, the baby cares which lullaby the mother is singing. This is a narcissistic blow to the therapist, who likes to think of himself as doing something to help the patient grow and as having thoughts and ideas which are useful to the patient and helpful in the psychotherapy. This kind of patient is simply not ready to utilize interpretation.

The therapist has to be aware of the tendency to retaliate and drive such patients away. If he does not retaliate, transferences which are characterized by massive annihilation anxiety, by the projection of tremendous rage and affect onto the therapist, or by the use of the therapist as an object occur and are often quite stable transferences when they appear in psychotherapy. Are they workable and do they respond to interpretation? There is a great deal of debate and disagreement on this point. Clearly, a tremendous amount of patience is necessary to work with these kinds of patients. A calm, consistent approach, not getting sucked into the dramatics, and a consistent interpretive approach are mandatory. Always staying with the material, not getting too deep or too fancy or too caught up in Kleinian terminology over a very long period of time, not only provides pacification and unification, but also does eventually provide insight which the patient gradually begins to use in many cases.

It is not possible to predict which patients can get more out of the psychotherapy than simple pacification and unification, but surely every patient should be given a chance. Neither the impatience of the therapist nor the narcissistic blow of being utilized as an object nor the great slowness of the treatment is sufficient cause to give up on the patient or to come out with a prescription pad and tranquillize him.

In my experience from supervision of residents and even with presenting cases to colleagues, I find two great pitfalls in such transferences. First of all we must face the therapist's fear of these transferences. It looks as if the patient is exploding, and unless the therapist has a fairly thorough dynamic grasp of what is going on, he can become panicky and can be stampeded into doing something radical or into getting rid of the patient one way or the other. The second kind of pitfall is *impatience*. The therapist must be willing to sit for years with a borderline patient while he gradually catalyzes the rebuilding of the ego structure. Many therapists simply don't want to do this, and if they don't, it is probably unwise for them to attempt the psychotherapy of borderline patients. Every skilled therapist knows what kinds of patients he works well with and what kinds of patients he would prefer to stay away from.

CHAPTER 18

Transference in the Narcissistic Personality Disorder

From Kohut's theoretical structure it follows that the transferences that arise from the formal psychoanalysis of the narcissistic personality disturbance will come from the mobilization of the idealized parent imago—the "idealizing transference"—and from the mobilization of the grandiose self—the "mirror transference." This depends, of course, on "the appropriately attentive but unobtrusive and noninterfering behavior of the analyst" that Kohut calls "the analyst's analytic attitude."

In the borderline patient and psychotic, the danger of regression to the stage of the fragmented self corresponding to the stage of autoerotism makes mandatory the maintenance of a realistic, friendly relationship with the therapist and the provision of psychotherapeutic support, since a workable transference for a psychoanalysis cannot take place. But for the narcissistic personality disorder, Kohut (1971) writes:

> To assign to the patient's nonspecific, nontransference rapport with the analyst a position of primary significance in the analysis of these forms of psychopathology would, thus, in my opinion, be erroneous. Such an error would rest on an insufficient appreciation of the metapsychologically definable difference between unanalyzable disorders (psychoses and borderline states) and analyzable forms of psychopathology (transference neuroses and narcissistic personality disorders).

In the working through of the idealizing transference, regressive swings take place after each inevitable disappointment in the idealized analyst, but the patient returns to the basic idealizing transference with the aid of appropriate interpretation, providing these interpretations "are not given mechanically, but with correct empathy for the analysand's feelings." This leads to the emergence of meaningful memories that concern the dynamic prototypes of the present experience. This is the essential paradigm of the working-through process in the narcissistic personality with the patient that forms an idealizing transference. It seems clear-cut and clinically useful.

The therapeutic activation of the grandiose self occurs in the appearance of the mirror transference, which is more complicated because it is divided into several types. In its most archaic form the analyst is experienced as an extension of the grandiose self. In a less archaic form there is an alter-ego twinship transference in which the analyst is experienced as being very similar to the patient. In the most mature and more common form, the analyst is experienced as a separate person, important to the patient but accepted by him only in the framework of grandiose needs.

Thus, "the mirror transference is the therapeutic reinstatement of the normal phase of the development of the grandiose self in which the gleam in the mother's eye, which mirrors the child's exhibitionistic display, and other forms of maternal participation in the response to the child's narcissistic exhibitionistic enjoyment confirm the child's self-esteem and, by a gradually increasing selectivity of these responses, begins to channel it into realistic directions."

Which *type* of mirror transference appears is not as important as the establishment of a relatively stable transference by the activation of the grandiose self, for this enables the patient to mobilize and maintain a working-through process "in which the analyst serves as a therapeutic buffer and enhances the gradual harnessing of ego-alien narcissistic fantasies and impulses."

The therapeutic mobilization of the grandiose self may arise either (1) directly—a primary mirror transference, (2) as a temporary retreat from an idealizing transference—reactive remobilization of the grandiose self, or (3) in a transference repetition of a specific genetic sequence that Kohut calls "a secondary mirror transference." The regressive swings in the working through are desirable and cannot be avoided, since no analyst's empathy can be perfect, any more than a mother's empathy with the needs of her child could be. The understanding gained from therapeutic scrutiny of these swings is of great value to the patient.

In the treatment of these patients Kohut faces directly the technical problem of the extent to which the analyst must become "active." He feels that major forceful interference is necessary mainly in instances of borderline psychoses and in related instances of profound ego defect that result in unbridled impulsivity. The major approach to such disturbances or acting out is to alert the patient's ego that a change of behavior is indicated in the interest of self-preservation. No moral issue must be raised except that practically and realistically, in view of the prevailing mores, the patient is putting himself in jeopardy by his doings.

This leads to a crucial discussion of the so-called passivity of the psychoanalyst during the psychoanalytic treatment, which Kohut correctly observes has at times been mistakenly discussed as if it were a moral issue. The essential factors of the process in the psychoanalytic cure are outlined. A contrast is drawn between inspirational therapy and psychoanalysis: The former works through the active establishment of object relations and massive identifications. Psychoanalytic psychotherapy works through the spontaneous establishment of transferences and minute processes of "transmuting reinternalization." Kohut explains, "If the analyst assumes actively the role of 'prophet, saviour and redeemer' he actively encourages conflict solution by gross identification, but stands in the way of the patient's gradual integration of his own psychological structures and of the gradual building up of the new ones. In metapsychological terms the active assumption of a leadership role by the therapist leads either to the establishment of a relationship to an archaic (prestructural), narcissistically cathected object (the maintenance of the patient's improvement depends thereafter on the real or fantasied maintenance of this object relationship) or to massive identifications which are added to the existing psychological structures."

The formal psychoanalytic process attempts to keep the infantile need activated while simultaneously cutting off all roads except the one toward maturation and reality. "Only one way remains open to the infantile drive, wish, or need: its increasing integration into the mature and reality-adapted sectors and segments of the psyche, through the accretion of specific new psychological structures which master the drive, leads to its controlled use, or transforms it into a variety of mature and realistic thought and action patterns."

Kohut claims that *not* to make any active moves to foster the development of a realistic therapeutic bond may be the decisive factor on the road to therapeutic success; the endless ability to remain noninterfering while a narcissistic transference establishes itself is crucial. Furthermore, "the manifestations of the inability of such patients to form a *realistic* bond with the analyst must not be treated by the analyst through active interventions designed to establish an 'alliance!' " These manifestations also must be examined dispassionately.

Turning directly to the theories of Balint, Kohut believes that imputing to the very small child the capacity for even rudimentary forms of object love "rests on retrospective falsifications and on adultomorphic errors in empathy." More specifically, he argues that situations in which the analyst feels that he must step beyond the basic interpreting attitude and become the patient's leader, teacher and guide *are most likely to occur when the psychopathology under scrutiny is not understood metapsychologically.* "Since under these circumstances the analyst has to tolerate his therapeutic impotence and lack of success, he can hardly be blamed when he abandons the ineffective analytic armamentarium and turns to suggestion (offering himself to the patient as a model or an object to identify with, for example) in order to achieve therapeutic changes."

The calm, well-trained craftsman is held up as the ideal so that, "As our knowledge about the narcissistic disorders increases, the formerly so personally demanding treatment procedures will gradually become the skilled work of the insightful and understanding analysts who do not employ any special charisma of their personalities but restrict themselves to the use of the only tools that provide rational success: interpretations and reconstructions."

You can see why it is so important in the theories of Kohut to make a differentiation between borderline patients and narcissistic personality disorders. According to this theory, the essence of the therapy is the formation of a stable transference and the essence of the cure has to do with the calm, well-trained craftsman's interpretations and reconstructions. This requires from the patient a certain cohesive, stable self. Otherwise the therapy becomes completely immersed in just trying to pull the patient together in some kind of cohesiveness, and there is no atmosphere in which interpretation and reconstruction can be made.

However, it seems to me that many borderline patients provide a sufficiently cohesive self that a similar approach can be taken—that of a calm, well-trained craftsman based on what Giovacchini and others call the analyst's analytic attitude—a cool objective rational approach to the patient's material, without getting sucked into it and without having to save or rescue the patient. The skilled work of insightful and understanding psychotherapy can take place in certain borderline patients who have not at the same time formed these stable narcissistic types of transferences. They would not be characterized as narcissistic personality disorders, but they would not be so fragmented that all you could do with them was pacification and unification.

Psychotherapy of the borderline patient hinges on a consideration of narcissistic rage. Kohut (1972) explains, "I think that the overcoming of a hypocritical attitude toward narcissism is as much required today as was the overcoming of sexual hypocrisy a hundred years ago." That is to say, "We should not deny our ambitions, our wish to dominate, our wish to shine, and our yearning to merge into omnipotent figures, but we should learn instead to acknowledge the legitimacy of these narcissistic forces as we have learned to acknowledge the legitimacy of our object-instinctual strivings." Thus it must be carefully explained to the patient that *narcissism is not a dirty world.*

Narcissistic rage occurs in many forms, and it characteristically emerges during the intensive psychotherapy of the borderline patient when the defensive wall of a pseudotranquillity which has been maintained with the aid of social isolation, detachment and fantasied superiority—or chemicals—begins to give way. This rage must be tolerated and not retaliated against, even by sarcastic comments or "put-downs" by the therapist. It is vitally necessary for the patient to recognize how the rage emerges when his narcissistic needs are not totally and immediately fulfilled. These narcissistic needs come from the grandiose self, which expects absolute control over a narcissistical-ly experienced archaic environment and insists on boundless exhibitionism as well as the exercise of total control.

The dangers of fixed paranoid, depressive and psychosomatic

disorders developing in the borderline patient is always present because the persistence of *chronic* narcissistic rage particularly tends to take place. Kohut (1972) explains, "Conscious and preconscious ideation, in particular as it concerns the aims and goals of the personality, becomes more and more subservient to the pervasive rage. The ego, furthermore, increasingly surrenders its reasoning capacity to the task of rationalizing the persisting insistence on the limitlessness of the power of the grandiose self; it does not acknowledge the inherent limitations of the power of the self, but attributes its failures and weaknesses to the malevolence and corruption of the uncooperative archaic object." The danger of the insidious development of a paranoid state is thus evident.

In other patients, this chronic narcissistic rage may shift its focus from the self-object to the self or to the body self. "The result in the first instance is a self-destructive depression; the consequence in the second instance may be psychosomatic illness" (see Chessick 1972a, 1977b, 1977c). It is very important to be aware of the intensity and the dangers of this narcissistic rage, to watch as it develops in the patient's treatment, and to deal with it by appropriate interpretation rather than retaliative put-downs.

I agree with Kernberg (1974b) that it is important to differentiate cases where narcissistic rage appears as part of the initial clinical pathological narcissism at later stages of the treatment. Patients who show an early and open expression of narcissistic rage in the initial interviews represent "a serious risk for the treatment." Such patients usually do not do well with uncovering psychotherapy, and supportive help is the treatment of choice, characterized by confrontations about the narcissistic rage and the consequences of it as well as of the primitive tendency to deny it or rationalize it, and by firm limit setting where necessary. The therapist has to provide structure for the patient in these cases to help protect him against the consequences of narcissistic rage.

The therapist functions as an accessory ego to the patient in these cases, helping to protect him against the dangerous narcissistic rage which could result at worst in psychosomatic breakdown, depression and suicide and even at best in ruin to the patient's interpersonal relationships. This protection is provided by confrontation about the intensity of the rage, firm limit setting when matters are serious and a constant reminding and prodding of the patient about the dangerous consequences of this rage. At this point we have stepped away from intensive uncovering psychotherapy and moved to a very firm and structured supportive treatment which has a vital and life-saving function and is mandatory in order to help a patient who is in serious danger.

The therapist should not attempt to undertake the intensive psychotherapy of a borderline patient or a narcissistic personality disorder in uncovering fashion unless he is fairly confident that the narcissistic rage is within bounds that will not result in a catastrophic destruction to the patient of one form or another. He must be constantly aware of the dangers of the eruption of such rage, and when such eruption threatens he must be alert to it and help the patient to deal with it. That is one of the first priorities in the intensive psychotherapy of the borderline patient.

CHAPTER 19

Ambience of the Treatment

Primitive Anxiety. I wish to turn now to a greater refinement of our concepts, which will lead to a more sensitive concern with the ambience of the psychotherapy of the borderline patient. In the situation of the borderline patient the ambience of the treatment is extremely important. In fact, it probably constitutes the major nonverbal factor that determines the success or the failure of the therapy. One could distinguish between the characteristic affects that appear in the psychotherapy and the characteristic affects (Mahler and Gosslinger 1955) of the phase of regression or fixation that the patient is in at the current point. So for example, if the patient has regressed to or is fixated in the phase of separation-individuation, the characteristic affect that is experienced by the patient is an intense sadistic rage, which usually appears as sexual and anal sadism, often combined. For example, the patient may be much preoccupied with the tearing up of a person anally, in one way or another, as in Freud's famous case of the "rat man" (Freud 1909). The patient's preoccupation was with a story that he heard about a form of torture: a cage of rats was put on a man's buttocks and the rats burrowed their way or ate into his body. This enormous and primitive anal-sadistic and sexually sadistic rage is combined with profound separation anxiety. The kind of anxiety and upset that appears in these cases hinges on the issue of separation from the object, upon which the patient is extremely dependent and attached.

If we move a step backwards developmentally into the symbiotic phase, the rage tends to take more oral-sadistic form, with fantasies of cannibalism, biting and tearing and so on. The anxiety also becomes somewhat different and is expressed as a fear of literal annihilation, although it may be annihilation through abandonment. It doesn't have to be annihilation through abandonment; it also could be annihilation as retaliation for oral-sadistic destructive fantasies. Thus the patient may fantasy a kind of apocalyptic end of the world in which he is machine-gunning people right and left, tearing them to bits, and finally he is himself destroyed. Some psychotic patients have literally acted this out.

Then as we move towards a phase even farther backwards (whether we can really reach it or not is certainly moot), there appears a more autistic kind of situation. The patient displays a kind of pseudoserenity, which is based primarily on a sense of hallucinatory omnipotence. If this is disturbed in any way, what appears is a kind of massive undifferentiated rage discharge, and the anxiety appears to be of less consequence at this point than the rage, which, when it appears, is almost totally without overt psychic content, but rather appears as body expressions and behavior in a kind of an undifferentiated temper tantrum. Most psychotherapists do not work with this kind of patient in the office.

It is important to keep in mind the clinical fact that separation anxiety is not *synonymous* with the fear of annihilation. Separation anxiety is somewhat less abruptly overwhelming and is more complex. By paying careful attention to the kinds of rage and anxiety being expressed, one has extra diagnostic help as well as an extra indicator of just where the patient is at any given time in the psychotherapy.

It should be evident by this time that I consider the key to understanding the borderline patient to be our understanding of the intrapsychic contents of the symbiotic phase and the early separation-individuation phase. The aim and successful outcome of the separation-individuation process is, as is generally agreed, a stable or cohesive image of the self. Memory deposits within the inborn and autonomous perceptive faculty of the primitive ego tend to occur and coagulate into what Mahler calls little islands within the hitherto oceanic feeling of complete fusion and oneness with the mother in the infant's semiconscious state. These memory islands are not allocated either to the self or to the nonself. They are primitive memory deposits of *feeling*, either pleasurable-good or painful-bad.

Because the experience is repeated in psychotherapy, it is most important to keep in mind that the young infant is exposed to rhythmically and consistently repeated experiences of hunger and other need tensions arising inside the body that cannot be relieved beyond a certain degree unless relief is supplied from a source beyond the infant's own orbit. This repeated experience of a need-satisfying good outside source to relieve the infant from uncomfortable or "bad" inside tension eventually conveys to the infant a vague affective discrimination between self and nonself.

Arguments arise at this point; when the discrimination between self and nonself begins, do "good" or "bad" memory islands become vaguely allocated to self and nonself? Many authors think they do. The general trend of the authors assumes that confluence and primitive integration of scattered good and bad memory islands into two large good and bad images of the self, as well as into split good and bad part images of the mother, occurs somewhere around the end of the first year of life. Mahler feels that this is attested to be the normal emotional ambivalence that is clinically discernable during the second year of life.

We have, then, rapidly alternating primitive identification mechanisms, leading to what has been described by Klein and the modified Kleinian followers as projection and introjection, in which the infant attempts to deal with these images. As I have repeatedly pointed out, this appears to be too fanciful to me and assumes a greater cognitive capacity in the mind of the one-year-old than seems reasonable. It represents a kind of personification that we as adults make when we observe the clinical phenomena.

Projection. In the dialogue of the session, the patient talks of parents, friends, other people and the therapist without realizing that he is discussing aspects of himself. Through interpretation we hope that the patient eventually realizes his identification with the other and its connection with significant defenses against anxiety. The patient projects out certain unacceptable aspects of himself onto others around him, which enables him to become more comfortable. Then the patient reacts to others as if this projection was of the principle feature of the other person, utterly ignoring the true personality of the other individual.

Here is a clinical example: The patient at one point during her psychotherapy insisted that I was extremely harsh, critical and intolerant of her; this arose rather suddenly and in the context of a previously warm and strong therapeutic alliance. A considerable discussion took place of the patient's own harsh, critical and intolerant superego system, which really represented the internalized aggression that she had against her extremely disappointing parents. In the midst of this discussion the patient reported the following dream: "Dr. Chessick was giving a seminar and I was there with several other people. They became increasingly upset with what he was saying, and after the seminar we were discussing the content of his presentation. The others felt that he was very harsh and critical, but I reassured them he was not really that way at all—that actually he was warm and understanding—and after they get to know him they will see that they have made a mistake in their judgment of him. Thereupon they accused *me* of being very harsh and critical and they begin to argue with me bitterly."

Now of course, dreams can be interpreted out of context in many ways, but I have introduced this dream as an example of a critical working-through dream of a patient who had made a projection. My having done so presupposes that the therapist in this case was *not* in reality harsh and critical. For if he was, then the patient had a legitimate right to rupture the therapeutic alliance, since the therapist was showing a lack of empathy with the patient's difficulties.

In the psychotherapy of the borderline patient, one must be most careful not to fool oneself, when negative images of the therapist appear in dreams or overt material, into thinking that it is a projection, if there is solid reason for the patient's complaint! Patients are very intuitive and often present a picture of the therapist that he does not particularly want to know. Unfortunately, they tend to pick out the negative aspects of the therapist and emphasize these, while ignoring the positives. (I will discuss this in greater detail a little later when I bring up once more the concept of externalization.)

Adler (1973) utilizes projective identification (see Chapter 9) and splitting mechanisms to understand the behavior and the problems that staff members have with hospitalized borderline patients. He describes an approach to the treatment where the staff attempts to understand its own retaliatory fury toward these patients, a fury often aroused by their provocative behivior. The staff in the hospital has to be helped to set limits in a nonpunitive way, and the problem is essentially the same as the one that arises in the office treatment of the borderline, except that it is more acute.

Adler points out that because these patients exhibit so many areas of strength and even appear sometimes to be psychoneurotic when they are first seen, "behavioral regression," that is to say, provocative and manipulative behavior, is often interpreted by the staff as willful misbehavior. The patient is experienced as a bad child rather than as an overwhelmed patient under great stress. These patients are expert at devaluating and provoking staff members and making them feel helpless. The concept of projective identification is useful to understand the patient's attempts to get rid of a part of himself by placing it into an object, which may then really—out of retaliation— persecute the patient. Another aspect of projective identification is that the patient has to extend much effort and activity to control the person who is the recepient of the projective part of the patient, for if the patient does not control this person, he then feels in danger of being overwhelmed by the part projected onto that person. Adler also notes that on the psychiatric unit, different staff members may be the recipients of different split parts of the patient. The patient is actually like a chess player, as I see it; he splits off various aspects in the hospital and relates them to and projects them onto various staff members. Then he even manipulates the various staff members to act in a way which is essentially consistent with the role they are supposed to play in terms of their being the recipients of these split parts.

I cannot stress enough how important it is, in dealing with borderline patients, to be aware of their tendency to set up in external reality the kinds of situations they need to have occurring. Sometimes they are quite expert at this, and the therapist almost finds himself sucked into playing various kinds of roles, depending on the projection assigned to him. Please notice that the first reaction to this kind of maneuver is retaliation. Nobody likes to be used as an object, and nobody likes to be manipulated and forced into a role, especially a role that is negative and that they don't want to play. Therefore, in dealing with borderline patients it is almost invariably an error to take as a personal attack on oneself this kind of behavior; it is far more therapeutic to try to understand what is going on and to reflect it back to the patient. The worst possible approach is to become very defensive when one is accused of all sorts of negatives that are projected, even if a kernel of truth exists in the accusations. This in turn requires a thorough self-understanding from the therapist and a reasonably healthy therapist who is not thrown into an anxiety panic when his defects are pointed out to him.

The point is not that the therapist should have no defects, the point is (1) that the therapist should have only a normal amount of defects, and (2) that he should be reasonably aware of and comfortable with his defects, so that when the borderline patient seizes upon these or plays up to them, he doesn't fall into the trap of losing perspective on his own self—which is what the borderline patient wants him to do. The therapist recognizes that he has some of these defects but that that's not *all* there is to him, and therefore he doesn't feel that he has to make up to the patient or defend himself against the patient; he is aware that selective perception and projection are going on.

Obviously, it is impossible to argue a borderline patient out of the accusations that he makes against you. Only two possible roles are reasonable. First, if on objective assessment it turns out that the accusations are correct—and this sometimes happens—then the therapist needs to correct himself. If, as is hopefully the case, the therapist is reasonably healthy, we are dealing with projection. The proper approach to this is a calm, nonanxious and patient stand, with eventual interpretation of what is happening. It is this calm, nonanxious and patient stance that provides the basic ambience of the treatment. Any disruption of it interrupts the subliminal soothing that is always going on in a well-conducted treatment of a borderline patient. No matter how we wish to get away from this in our theoretical conceptions, the ambient subliminal soothing the therapist provides— in his habits of consistency, reliability and integrity; in the ambience of his office; in his personality; in his deep inner attitude towards his patients, which cannot be faked—provides the basic motor that permits the psychotherapy of the borderline patient to go forward.

CHAPTER 20

Rage and Externalization

From Kernberg's (1974b) point of view, borderline personality organizations which do not form the classical narcissistic transferences described by Kohut may still be amenable in many instances to a formal psychoanalytic approach "with parameters" as the treatment of choice. It should be noted that the Kernberg-Kohut debate is about the classical psychoanalysis of these patients; the minute one introduces so-called parameters, the debate shifts. I am at least fairly certain that Kohut considers himself to be talking *only* about classical formal psychoanalysis; Kernberg seems a little more prone to modifications of psychoanalytic technique when necessary because he is not concerned with fostering the development of Kohut's classical narcissistic transferences (Kohut also introduces the modification of not interpreting the idealization of the therapist, but this is relatively minor.)

Kernberg and I clearly differ on the optimal treatment for most borderline patients. He recommends attempting formal psychoanalysis with as few parameters as possible, whereas I feel that psychoanalytically informed psychotherapy twice or three times weekly is most effective. Still, we agree on one major aspect of the treatment, as he describes it (Kernberg, 1975a): ". . . the patient must come to terms at some point with very real, serious limitations of what life has given him in early years. . . . It is probably as difficult for borderline patients eventually to come to terms with the fact of failure in their early life as it is for patients with inborn or early determined physical defects to acknowledge, mourn, and come to terms with their defects. Borderline patients gradually have to become aware of how their parents failed them—not in the distorted, monstrous ways which existed in their fantasies when beginning treatment, but failed them in simple human ways of giving and receiving love, and providing consolation and understanding, and intuitively lending a helping hand when the baby, or the child, was in trouble."

It is questionable whether classical transference neuroses occur in uncovering psychotherapy (as opposed to a formal psychoanalysis) in a substantial enough form to be amenable to interpretation. Because of the mandatory increased activity of the therapist (H. Friedman 1975) especially in uncovering psychotherapy with borderline patients, other types of transference tend to predominate in many instances. I am inclined to agree with Kernberg that, on the one hand, numerous borderline patients placed in the modified psychoanalytic situation do not regress and fragment into an open psychotic state; on the other hand, they do not form the classical narcissistic transferences of Kohut.

This may be a function of the personality of the therapist or of his entire approach. As described in my books (1969, 1974b) such patients *can* form workable transferences which are amenable to interpretation. Often they cannot, however, and so they can respond only to some form of supportive psychotherapy which aims at giving the patient a better structure in dealing with internal and external adaptations and conflicts.

Clinically speaking, the big problem with many of these patients boils down to helping them deal with their paranoid feelings and their tremendous rage. Actually the explosions of rage, as painful as they are for both patient and therapist, are not as serious to deal with as calculated (conscious or unconscious) retaliatory attacks over a long period by the patient on the narcissistic defects in the therapist, as discussed in the next chapter.

Sometimes the rage of the borderline patient is stirred up directly by frustrations of his need for omnipotent control of everything; sometimes the rage is a secondary phenomenon to a paranoid projection or a transference projection in which, if someone criticizes the patient or interferes with one of his plans, the instant reaction is that someone *hates* the patient. The patient then reacts as anyone would to someone who hates him. The recipient of the patient's reaction is often surprised and stunned and finally goaded into retaliatory behavior by the patient's clearly hostile and provocative action.

Thus in a sense these patients are correct when they predict that all human relationships will end up badly for them, with disappointment and dislike coming from everyone around them. I have spoken of this in another context (Chessick 1972b) as externalization in the borderline patient, a phenomenon in which the patient responds selectively to the negative aspects of the people around him and develops a case based on selective negative perceptions for expecting attack from all sides. The chronic calculated attacks on the therapist's defects, if not interpreted, can lead easily to countertransference acting out on the part of the therapist, even to the point of getting rid of the patient. This is quickly worked into "proof" by the patient of his expectation of apparently unprovoked betrayal and abandonment.

Credit for coining the term *externalization* is usually given to Anna Freud (1965). She described externalization as a subspecies of transference and separated it from the transference. Her main experience with externalization is, of course, in the analysis of children, and she sees externalization in child analysis as a process in which the person of the analyst is used to represent one or another part of the patient's personality structure.

The concept of externalization was made a great deal more precise with respect to the psychotherapy of borderline patients with deep narcissistic problems in a paper by Brodey (1965). Brodey points out that in his experience working with family units, externalization appeared as a mechanism of defense defined by the following characteristics: (1) Projection is combined with the manipulation of reality selected for the purpose of verifying the projection. (2) The reality that cannot be used to verify the projection is not perceived. (3) Information known by the externalizing person is not transmitted to others except as it is useful to train or manipulate them into validating what will then become the realization of the projection. In other words, externalization makes possible: "A way of life based on relationships with unseparated but distant aspects of the self. What is perceived as reality is an *as-if* reality, a projection of inner expectation. The senses are trained to validate; the intense searching for what is expected dominates and enforces validation. It is difficult not to validate an unquestionable conclusion. Each validation makes the conclusion even less questionable. The restricted reality perceived is experienced as if it were the total world."

The psychotherapist feels the intensity of his patient's effort to manipulate him into validating projections. He feels the conflict as he struggles against this manipulation, but behavior that will be used as validation seems the only way to gain relationship with the patient.

Thus, the manipulation of the therapist into behavior that is symmetrical with the projection is different from the simple transfer of feelings to a therapist.

"Even if the therapist does not wish to conform, he still finds himself conforming to the narcissistic image. For no matter what he does, pieces of the therapist's actual behavior irrelevant to the therapist's self-identity are seized on by the patient, to whom they are predominant *as-if* characteristics. The identity that the patient sees may be unknown to the therapist (although it holds a kernel of truth which usually is disturbing to the therapist)" (Brodey 1965). Even the therapist's active denial of the patient's presumption is used by the patient in the service of proving to himself that the therapist actually is congruent with his projective image.

Brodey points out that the therapist of the ego-disturbed patient must become skilled at managing his congruence with the patient's projected image. This management is often intuitive and usually very demanding emotionally. "Being a distorted object is much easier than being nonexistent."

Fundamentally, externalization is projection combined with and followed by selective perception and manipulation of other people for the purpose of verifying the initial projection. Other people are experienced wholly in terms of their value in verifying the initial projection, and only those aspects of other people which have this value are perceived at all. Thus, the most benign therapist approaching the borderline patient finds himself transformed into a horrible monster very quickly by the patient's selective perception, and unless he is aware of this danger he is inclined either to retaliate or to quarrel with the patient's extremely unflattering image of him, which usually contains a kernel of truth and is a direct assault on the therapist's narcissistic conception of himself as a benevolent physician.

Giovacchini (1967b) emphasizes paradoxical self-defeating behavior with a defensive purpose, which is usually the result of externalization. This must be distinguished from self-defeating behavior resulting from a breakdown of the personality. Patients of the former type cannot cope with a warm and nonthreatening environment: "They react to a benign situation as if it were beyond their level of comprehension. These patients do not have the adjustive techniques to interact with a reasonable environment. Their formative years were irrational and violent. They internalize this chaos and their inner excitement clashes with their surroundings. When the world becomes benign and generous, the patient withdraws in panic and confusion."

Giovacchini points out that the patient expects and brings about his failure and adapts himself to life by feeling beaten in an unpredictable and ungiving world. He distinguishes this from a masochistic adjustment and points out the relationship of externalization to the repetition compulsion upon which it is based.

Thus, when the therapist presents the patient with a consistently benign environment, one which Winnicott (1958) has described as being parallel to the healthy maternal environment, the patient cannot trust the lack of frustration. To risking the inevitable disappointment that he expects, the patient prefers relating "in a setting in which he has learned to adjust. If the analyst does not frustrate him, the patient's psychic balance is upset. To reinstitute ego equilibrium the patient attempts to make the analyst representative of the world that is familiar to him."

Externalization is not simply a projection of internal aspects of the personality onto the therapist; it contains also a mode of adaptation or adjustment that makes any other interaction between ego and the outer world impossible. As Giovacchini (1967) points out, "Externalization provides the patient with a setting that enables him to use adjustive techniques that he has acquired during his early development."

Such patients, therefore, are often in a rage for one reason or another, and techniques must be found to help them calm down, for such rages directly interfere with their functioning and provoke retaliation from those around them. When the patient is unable to gain insight into this crucial problem, the psychotherapist may have to be satisfied with the development of tranquilizing techniques that the patient must learn. One way to do this is to help him regard his rages as a fever that comes upon him, which demands treatment as an illness rather than viewing his rage as justifiable and appropriate.

In a few cases I have seen, severe obsessive rumination appears instead of these rages. The net result is the same in that the patient is functionally paralyzed, although less retaliation is provoked by the rumination.

In all of these cases, helping the patient in psychotherapy to become acquainted with his grandiose self, his search for an idealized parent, his tendency to regard others as self-objects, his paranoid projections and the continual rages that ensue, and his chronic and self-damaging narcissistic rage forms the core of the psychotherapy.

As Kernberg (1974a) explains, the problem of rage poses the greatest danger to the psychotherapy of the borderline patient: "The relentless nature of this rage, however, the depreciatory quality that seems to contaminate the entire relationship with the therapist, and what evolves as a complete devaluation and deterioration of all the potentially good aspects of the relationship for extended periods of time so that the very continuity of treatment is threatened, are characteristics of narcissistic patients functioning on a borderline level." To put it another way, the autonomous ego of the patient must form an alliance with the therapist if the therapy is to proceed successfully; the outbursts of such narcissistic rage tend to submerge the autonomous ego and rupture the therapeutic alliance either directly or by the production of acting-out or serious symptomatology or psychosomatic disorders that make treatment impossible in an analytic setting.

Loewenstein (1972) points out that psychoanalytic treatment requires the patient to have "some degree" of integrity of the ego: "This means intactness not alone of some defenses, but also of autonomous functions," for "the autonomous ego is the medium through which patients communicate to the analyst what they observe in themselves." The analytic setting, with its frequent sessions and use of the couch encourages the relative increase of primary-process thinking and the mechanisms of displacement and projection, "and yet the basic rule also requires the patient to communicate all his resulting self-observations in a way that is intelligible, as only secondary process allows it." More precisely, the autonomous ego must ally itself with the analyst. This requires "relatively intact memory, thinking, perceptions, reality testing, capacity for self-observation and for verbal expressions."

The autonomous ego must be available for the patient to become aware through appropriate interpretation how each minor empathic failure by the therapist or each inevitable frustration in the psychotherapy (such as the therapist's changing an appointment or taking a vacation) produces narcissistic rage and tends to produce in addition a psychic switch from searching for the idealized parent-therapist to withdrawal into the grandiose self (Kohut, 1971). Clinical manifestations of this switch, along with overt narcissistic rage, are: coldness toward the therapist, a tendency to primitivization of thought and speech (from stilted speech to neologisms and grammatical peculiarities), attitudes of superiority, a tendency toward increased self-consciousness and shame propensity (due to increased exhibitionistic tendencies of the grandiose self) and hypochondriacal preoccupations. It is necessary for the clinician to be exceptionally alert for the occurrence of these manifestations.

If narcissistic rage shatters the therapeutic alliance, of course achievement of insight cannot occur. Similarly, if the therapist reacts to these manifestations with rage of his own, a complete metapsychological misunderstanding, usually based on countertransference, has taken place and the therapy is destroyed.

CHAPTER 21

Countertransference

Clearly, countertransference is of great importance in the psychotherapy of both the borderline patient and the patient with a narcissistic personality disorder, regardless of how one metapsychologically separates these two kinds of patients. The difficulties in the path of therapeutic dealing with such patients are enormous. Even Anna Freud (1969) in her famous discussion of difficulties in the path of psychoanalysis has mentioned the problems and divided them into difficulties coming from the external world, difficulties within the patient and difficulties within the analyst. For instance, the external-world difficulties include the fact that psychoanalysis has to compete with other therapeutic modalities; the patient is often under tremendous pressure from friends and relatives not to come so long and to beware of the therapist—the news media are filled with discussions of the exploitation of innocent patients by unethical therapists, and even some young people today tend to see psychoanalysis as a conservative force, designed to adjust people to society as it is. There are similar pejorative implications toward psychoanalytic psychotherapy. To this we have to add the stigma, the expense, the stress, the time loss and so on, all of which create external-reality problems for the patient who is involved in any long-term psychotherapeutic efforts.

The difficulties within the patient are probably even more important. Anna Freud labels such factors "constitutional," involving adhesiveness or rigidity—a "weakness" of the ego on a constitutional basis.

Psychological sources working against the cure within the patient include the need for punishment, intolerance to anxiety, the innate incapacity to accept substitute gratifications and find suitable sublimations for the drives and the inevitable inner conflict between the wish to develop or grow up versus the desire to hold on to the past.

Although some authors speak of this as "the adhesiveness to the past," we also have to realize that no matter how poor and inadequate the patient's solutions are, they are his production, they are his creation, they were formed by him as a child during the highly narcissistic phase, and they are extremely invested with narcissistic libido. Therefore, there is a certain unconscious pride in these solutions no matter how poor they may be on a realistic basis, and it is always a narcissistic blow to the patient to give up long-standing patterns of adaptation that he has developed under hardships and with much effort, even though he is giving up these patterns for something better. There is also a risk involved, because sometimes the patient has to depend at least to some extent on the faith of the therapist that the new patterns of adaptation *are* going to be better. The patient may know it intellectually, he may see that it works for those around him, he may hear the faith of the therapist, but he himself has not experienced it. So there is unquestionably an unknown-risk factor that tends to cause a conservative tendency in the patient and a tendency to fall back on tried and tested patterns, no matter how poor they may be.

In addition to this, the factors within the patient have to do with the developmental phase during which the crucial difficulties began. When you are dealing with disasters in the first year or two of life, you are making an assumption that the damage such archaic events have caused in a patient's psyche can be reversed or at least ameliorated by psychotherapy. This is as yet an assumption not generally agreed upon. In addition, the role of constitutional factors becomes especially crucial in the very early months of life. Rates of development of the nervous system, constitutional endowment and so on have a great deal to do with how the very young infant deals with stimuli. Thus the farther back you go in patients with early developmental disorders, the more vagueness, confusion, and disagreement there is about what happened and how to make it better.

Finally, there are the difficulties in the therapist himself. This is the source of difficulty for which we have the most direct responsibility. It is important to realize that we have an ethical obligation to develop the maximum understanding of the limitations of our technique and of the countertransferences that arise when we work with borderline patients, and we also have to realize that the two are connected. When you work with patients of this type, and you begin to bump up against these limiting factors, a typical and specific variety of countertransference is produced.

Grinker (1955) claims, "What is not treatable and not analysable are the effects and results of the first vital non-conditioned reflexes when mother-child ego-non-ego are not differentiated. This is the non-reducible residue like the amorphous dust of a ground-up object of art. . . . The effect is 'in the tissue' and analysis cannot modify it. . . ." What we *can* do is to ". . . loosen, decrease, or modify the learned function; to get as close as possible to the primary, narcissistic, depressive, or psychosomatic core; then to help rebuild and reconstitute more adaptive assemblages of defenses and syntonic expressions."

In this task, new technical problems confront the therapist. The closer he approaches to the basic core functions, the more difficult and dangerous are his problems. Grinker explains, "He is confronted with primary processes and an ego which seems unable to perform its functions of self-discrimination, reality-testing, or synthesis." At this point the alert analyst then questions himself "as to whether he is pursuing a harmful procedure which could destroy the defensive capacity of the ego against the development of a psychosis or the liberation of serious suicidal trends or the acting-out of asocial or anti-social behavior." It is at this point that we restudy our material of the first interviews and our diagnostic workup to determine whether we have overlooked latent psychosis of some kind that is now threatening to become active and dangerous. These are the kinds of anxieties that must be stirred up in the alert and conscientious therapist even in a well-conducted treatment of the borderline patient.

Borderline patients and narcissistic patients are especially vulnerable to acting out manipulations, exploitations, retaliations and seductions from psychotherapists who are untrained and untreated. But even well-trained therapists tend to fall into some of these countertransference problems. For example, Grinker (1955) mentions,

"The countertransference may be maternally seductive towards deep or rapid regression and a high value placed on therapeutic, hopefully temporary, dependency. Sometimes countertransference attitudes may consist of firmness and *tacit* urging towards growth and change either at the onset or too soon after regression has developed. Some analysts may vacillate between these two attitudes as many parents do, seducing dependency and urging growth at the same time." It is very important for the psychotherapist to keep in mind, as I have stressed in my books on psychotherapy (Chessick 1969, 1971c, 1974b), that every patient has a kind of internal timetable, an internal unfolding program that must not be hurried regardless of the need of the therapist or the external pressures on the patient! Attempts to hurry it simply result in failure.

Probably the best analogy is to the timetable of a young teenager trying to catch on to algebra. The development and the unfolding of the cognitive apparatus determines the point at which even the reasonably motivated teenager grasps the concepts of algebra—of substituting letters for numbers. This is consistent with Piaget's discussion (See Evans 1973) of the developmental phases of cognition and thought. Time is required to work these things through, and the therapist must not hurry them or push them on the one hand or hold them back on the other. A well-conducted psychotherapy implies that the therapist gradually gets the picture of how the patient's internal timetable works and gradually understands the specific patient's techniques of learning, cognition and assimilation, which differ biologically from individual to individual. This is the greatest protection against countertransference pushing and shoving of the patient.

As our knowledge of psychotherapy with the borderline patient increases, it is apparent that the attitude and reaction of the therapist are of much greater importance in the treatment situation than is the case in the treatment of neurotics. Therapists who work with borderline patients cannot avoid from time to time experiencing extreme and intense anxiety and suffering the indignities of being ridiculed, scorned, ignored, disarranged and verbally assaulted. Physical assault is a very unusual event and has diagnostic considerations for psychosis involved in it, but verbal assault is ubiquitous in the treatment of such patients.

Furthermore, borderline patients often note the anxiety of the therapist and seize on it for externalization. Although we advocate an objective, analytic and nonanxious approach, we realize that from time to time such patients are bound to make the therapist anxious. One of the most important factors in the treatment of the borderline patient is how the therapist deals with his own anxiety. This forms an adaptational model that the patient can incorporate, or introject, or identify with, depending on what terminology you wish to use. It is unavoidable in psychotherapy, and I think the subliminal observation that the patient makes about such things as how the therapist deals with his own anxieties in the treatment has an important effect in terms of whether the treatment moves forward or not.

You cannot teach this to a therapist; you can only tell him to get an intensive, thorough psychotherapy of his own, so that his ego mechanisms and adaptational techniques are as healthy as possible; then you have a psychic field to offer the patient that is as healthy as possible. Most authors agree today that the goal of the therapist's personal analysis and training is not to eliminate countertransference problems, but to shorten the time required for their recognition and resolution. It is impossible not to develop countertransference reactions.

It is well known that borderline patients frequently threaten suicide and even make desperate gestures. This produces a special kind of countertransference. Maltsberger and Buie (1974) point out, "The countertransference hatred (feelings of malice and aversion) that suicidal patients arouse in the psychotherapist is a major obstacle in treatment; its management through full awareness and self-restraint is essential for successful results. The therapist's repression, turning against himself, reaction formation, projection, distortion, and denial of countertransference hatred increase the danger of suicide." I think in all fairness and honesty we have to report that the psychotherapist who wishes to work over many years with a large practice of borderline patients has to be prepared for the eventuality that from time to time, a patient will either directly or even by accident successfully destroy himself. When this happens it is always a terrible experience for everybody concerned, and dealing with this kind of experience is a test of the psychotherapist's personality.

It is remarkable, in my own clinical experience, to observe the reaction other psychiatrists have when they discover that a psychiatrist's patient has committed suicide. The most striking reaction I have seen is omnipotent denial: "I cannot understand why it happened; it never happens to me." A therapist dealing with borderline patients will have such a crisis from time to time, but it will be a rare occurrence. A therapist may practice for many years without any borderline patient successfully committing suicide. (If it appears that a large number of the therapist's patients are attempting or successfully committing suicide, then obviously we have a different problem.)

When suicide happens, as it does from time to time, it stirs up tremendous problems, both realistic and internal, for the psychotherapist. One of these problems is the narcissistic blow to the therapist. We all know that the normal mourning process includes with it a rage at the person who has left us. No matter how fine that person may have been, we have suffered a narcissistic loss and we rage about it.

Therapists with narcissistic problems tend to ward off anxiety over the very passivity of the psychotherapy situation and certainly over the helplessness a therapist feels when his patient has treatened suicide. They usually tend to ward it off by such behavior as excessive verbal activity, prescription writing or overaggressiveness. Murphy (1973) explains how such therapists may misuse and overcharge patients considerably, and sometimes they undercharge them for the same reason. Patients find it is easier to entice narcissistic therapists into playing roles assigned to them via projective identification and even attempt to seduce such therapists, who are flattered by the affectionate attention of patients.

It is almost superfluous to add that when a borderline patient or a patient with a narcissistic personality disorder is being treated by a psychotherapist who is himself a borderline patient or a patient with a narcissistic personality disorder, the situation is bound to end up in something destructive or, at worst, suicide. Most commonly it ends up with acting out, sometimes individually, sometimes mutually and together. I have to add this because although it seems obvious, it is not so rare. I have run into a variety of cases in many years of practice with borderline patients or patients with narcissistic personality disorders who have been treated by psychotherapists (and the variety of these is endless, including social workers, psychologists, ministers and psychiatrists) who are clearly borderline patients or are at best patients with narcissistic personality disorders themselves; there has occurred a mutual seduction, a mutual acting out, and the events that follow are often cataclysmic and always destructive in one way or another.

I must sadly record that at the present time there are absolutely no standards in the United States that license or don't license a person to practice psychotherapy. Since there are far more borderline patients desparately in need of help than there are skilled psychotherapists, the unskilled, the sick, and the acting out, enticed by money and gratification, are rushing in to breach the gap. It remains the ethical duty of anyone who practices psychotherapy to press for social legislation to deal with the training and licensing of psychotherapists. That is the very least we can do about this present and dangerous problem, which at times is absolutely life-destroying for a patient.

A special remark about countertransference belongs in the hazy area of rationalization. The theoretical model one uses in the treatment of the borderline patient or the narcissistic personality disorder has to be adopted on the basis of a choice, for a variety of theoretical models of all sorts is available. To be perfectly consistent with the psychoanalytic orientation, we have to assume that the choice of theoretical model, whether it be behavioral, supportive, medical, whether it be based on the work of Kernberg, Kohut, Zetzel, Klein or whomever, is multiply determined or overdetermined by both the therapist's autonomous rational ego function and his conflictual needs. As long as a reasonable model is chosen which has some justification in practice, this by itself does not produce any difficulty.

The trouble is that a theoretical model can be chosen to justify a series of acting-out techniques in the treatment, and that is why one must be very careful in evaluating the choice of theoretical models and in evaluating a therapist's work with borderline patients. *Look at the clinical phenomena to see what the therapist is doing with his patient, regardless of his theoretical model.* Remember Freud's (1914a) admonition: "I learnt to restrain speculative tendencies and to follow the unforgotten advice of my master, Charcot: To look at the same things again and again until they themselves begin to speak".

For example, the technique of Kohut, in which the idealization of the therapist is permitted over a long period of time so that the full transference involving the search for the idealized parent imago is permitted to develop, can easily be used by an untrained or untreated therapist as an excuse to permit a flattering kind of worship and to massage the narcissism of the therapist. Conversely, the technique of Kernberg, in which a lot of confrontation goes on with the patient's rage, can be used to act out hostility and aggressiveness and to produce chaos, either to "take it out on" the patient, to discharge one's own rage on the patient or to deliberately create a therapeutic situation in which chaos and rage reign supreme. This would be an example of externalization on the part of a *therapist* who is more comfortable with situations of chaos and rage. Thus good, sound theoretical models which have been carefully thought out and worked over by highly respected and very excellent authors, psychoanalysts and thinkers can be used by the untrained and untreated to rationalize just about anything they want to do!

Remember, much of the negative countertransference that arises in the psychotherapy of the borderline patient comes from therapist discouragement (Wilie 1972), which is sometimes concealed by phony optimism. We are dealing with a long, slow procedure. Therapists have a narcissistic need to cure, and there is much social pressure on them to cure. Furthermore, we are confronted with the powerful needs and the emptiness of the patient day in and day out. We are drained, and our own needs and emptiness, wherever they may be in our deep unconscious, are stirred up. On the one hand we have to avoid primary process, the tangible and the touchable, and on the other hand we must genuinely care for the patient.

We are in a situation where we have to be an auxiliary ego in terms of the atmosphere we provide. We have to be very patient, consistent and reasonable. We must not exploit the patient or retaliate against the patient. Our ethics are constantly on the table. There is a tendency to identify with the patient out of hatred, the hatred having been stirred up by suicide threats or attempts and various other provocative acting-out behavior, and sometimes then—if we are overidentified with the patient—we feel depressed, we feel as if we are empty like the patient is empty. The typical behavior at this point is to come with the prescription pad and to fill us both up. How many prescriptions are written for borderline patients because they stir up emptiness in therapists who then want to fill the patients and vicariously fill themselves?

A similar problem causes us to look for gratification from the patient. To sit with provocation, rage and emptiness for long periods of time and to inevitably have our own problems and emptiness stirred up causes an almost reflex searching for gratification from the patient. The patient is not there to gratify us, so we withdraw our affect in revenge or conversely we make a seductive assault on the patient to try to seduce him into loving us and so on. It is usually a good rule of thumb to remember that in the deep unconscious somewhere, the intense wish to rescue the patient is the other side of the coin from the wish to kill the patient. If the therapist finds himself flooded with intense rescue fantasies, he better beware that underneath is a very negative countertransference!

Countertransference crises often have their origin in whatever *role* the patient has put the therapist in. Sometimes he has unwittingly accepted this role is insufficiently understood by the therapist. For example, the most simple, common and obvious cause of counter-transference crises is the repeated threat of suicide. Every therapist becomes uneasy when a patient threatens suicide. He anticipates all kinds of problems, complications, disappointments and terrible publicity, and of course it reverberates into the very depths of his own being to see someone with whom he has a relationship threaten to kill himself. Often threats of suicide are used by patients to manipulate or maneuver the therapist, to disrupt the treatment and in many ways to punish the therapist and the patient's family.

Dealing with suicide is not as big a problem if the therapist is willing to be very straightforward about it and is very carefully aware of his limitations. If a borderline patient (or any patient) threatens suicide in a manner that seems on clinical judgment to be serious, it is necessary to bring family members into the therapy if at all possible and to inform the patient and the patient's family that hospitalization is necessary. This is usually straightforward. If the patient refuses hospitalization when the therapist feels that it is appropriate, then the therapist has to insist that either hospitalization take place or the patient and family have to find another therapist. Otherwise the patient has the therapist over a barrel, raising the therapist's anxiety level and leaving him helpless and impotent to do anything about it.

A bigger problem is the borderline patient who repeatedly threatens suicide but demonstrates little clear clinical evidence of suicidal intent. We obviously cannot have patients going in and out of the hospital every other weekend, because it has a totally disruptive effect. In such situations the patient and the patient's family have to be told straight out that there is a suicide risk with any patient who threatens suicide, even if it seems to be essentially a maneuver of one kind or another. It is often necessary to point out to the patient and the family that they have to make a choice whether or not to take the risk of having such a patient in out-patient therapy and that they have to be aware that there is such a risk. They also have to be told that the therapy cannot be optimally continued if it is going to be continually disrupted by such threats, and the therapist has to make it plain that his anxiety level is also at stake. An anxious therapist cannot hear his (or her) patient.

One can see from this simple discussion of suicide how borderline patients can torment his therapist if the therapist is not clearly aware both of the level at which the patient is functioning and of the psychodynamic meaning of the patient's suicidal threats and gestures.

The exact same thing is true about the use of drugs. Drugs have a very appropriate place in the office psychotherapy of any patient in terms of relieving intense suffering for brief periods when it occurs. The therapist tends to get into trouble in two areas. These are: first, when he uses drugs as a substitute for understanding what is going on with the patient; and second, when he uses drugs out of his need to cure the patient.

The ambition to forcibly cure a patient by some magical gesture is a particularly lethal form of countertransference, especially in therapy of borderline and schizophrenic patients (Chessick 1969). Any therapist using drugs with patients should have a clear notion of why he is doing it at the time and should continuously on a weekly basis review to himself whether the drugs ought to be continued and why. In psychotherapy of borderline patients who are not chronic or institutional patients, prescriptions for drugs should be written for small quantities and rewritten on a weekly or fortnightly basis. They should be marked Not Refillable, which will ensure that the matter is constantly brought up and reviewed by the pharmacist, if by nobody else.

A similar situation occurs in another common problem, that of missed sessions (Chessick 1974b). Patients use missed sessions just suicidal threats or the abuse of drugs to torment the therapist. It is important for the therapist to recognize that payment for sessions is for the needs of the therapist and that therefore patients must pay for missed sessions unless in the therapist's judgment there is a good and fair reason for the session being missed. This always leaves an option for discussion. The therapist should never be rigid. One should not in psychotherapy try to force a patient to pay for sessions missed for a good reason, such as acute illness, or even in typical situations where a patient is married and the spouse has a vacation and it is the only vacation time available for them together. A benign attitude toward the patient is more important than anything else. In psychotherapy it is better to err in the direction of being taken advantage of than to err in the direction of being too strict, but missed sessions and also lack of payment of the bill should not be allowed to be used as a way of manipulating or tormenting or punishing the therapist. As one gains experience, the judgment of what is legitimate and what is a manipulation becomes easier; in the meantime, consultation is often helpful.

In general, patients use overt rage, the creation of "uproar," acting out in the transference through erotization and seduction involving others or other forms of acting out as sensory-motor patterns (Piaget) of communication. It is relatively easy for the well-trained and well-treated therapist to deal calmly with this uproar, as long as he doesn't have too many narcissistic ambitions of his own. The principle is, of course, to point out to the patient that the uproar, rage attacks, etc. disrupt the treatment, make it impossible for the patient to listen to what the therapist is saying and in some cases—given the mores of the society in which the patient lives—get the patient in trouble with the law and even get him jailed. A great deal of the uproar and acting out can be stopped by pointing out to the patient that you don't make calls to the jail or, if the patient is riding a motorcycle and not paying attention to the street signs, even to the hospital's fracture ward. The goal is calling the patient's attention to the vital recognition that he is disrupting his own treatment.

Two of the most difficult problems are the erotization and seduction of the therapist on the one hand, (Chessick 1966) and chronic rage (Kohut 1972), aimed at the narcissism of the therapist, on the other. Both of these are more difficult because they are often, in an unconscious fashion, calculated and parceled out in small amounts so they are not obvious and overt! Thus, for example, if a patient comes in, sits on the chair and pulls up her dress, that is obvious and overt, and any therapist who deserves the name of therapist would tell her to pull her skirt down and then discuss the meaning. But what about the patient who sits in just such a way that at just a certain angle a young male therapist can see up her dress and who in a thousand little ways indicates to the therapist how wonderful he is and how romantic she feels about him?

The well-trained therapist can relatively easily accept, confront, and interpret overt narcissistic rage attacks, and each therapist has pretty much his own style of doing so. If the patient is amenable to insight, the psychotherapy can then proceed. The expression of narcissistic rage actually gives relief to the patient. In addition, if the therapist can stand his ground and not be steamrollered by this narcissistic rage, the patient becomes able to gradually incorporate the therapist's way of dealing with the patient's rage.

Much more difficult to manage is the chronic rage that patients have because they are unable to get from the therapist all the gratification of their wishes for the ideal parent—the constant little pricklings that the patient produces hour after hour when he spots the minor narcissistic weaknesses of the therapist. The clever patient who has especially calculated intuitively the therapist's narcissistic weakness, who complains in little ways of the expense of the treatment, of the idea of the treatment, of how little he is getting out of the treatment, gradually wounds the vanity of the therapist. I believe it is this kind of atmosphere that gradually shifts the therapist's benign attitude toward the patient to an increasingly aggressive and sadistic one.

This is often the point at which the therapist begins either to badger the patient, to force interpretations, to exhort, to advise, to sermonize or to come out with a prescription pad to give the patient drugs. It can have a more lethal outcome if the therapist actually begins to manipulate things to get rid of the patient. For example, a patient with considerable narcissistic rage and years of experience in psychotherapy was gradually able to make a therapist feel that he was not doing a good job and was not sufficiently responsive to the patient's needs. One day the therapist had to miss a session and rescheduled the patient for a different day at a different time. When the patient arrived, he found that the therapist had also scheduled another patient for that time. This was discussed at some length but not in depth, and the issue was passed over until a similar incident took place again a few months later! In giving his vacation dates to the patient, the therapist gave the wrong date of return, so that the patient came down to the office a day early and found an empty, closed office. At this point a consultation became necessary, because the therapy went into a complete standstill.

Another typical maneuver at this point is for the therapist to decide that the patient is not amenable to psychotherapy and thus should have a less frequent "supportive" treatment, say, for example, once every two weeks or once a month, or perhaps a group therapy; this is duly recommended to the patient. A related countertransference maneuver arises when the patient begins to miss sessions and the therapist decides that this means that the patient is getting too intensive a treatment, and he then allows the patient to determine the frequency of the psychotherapy. This is acceptable technique with very anxious patients who cannot stand too much frequency, and of course the therapist has to titrate the frequency of the sessions according to the anxiety level of, for example, adolescents or patients who have a homosexual-panic problem. To do this with a patient who is obviously manipulating or who has found that the therapist gets irritated or enraged when the session is missed is losing sight of what psychotherapy is all about.

The most useful indicator that something has gone wrong in the psychotherapy is when decisions by the therapist such as changing the frequency of hours, what to do about threats of suicide, the giving of drugs, or the handling of missed sessions produce further uproar and chaos which last for a substantial time and lead to further such destructive decisions. It is evident that a transformation has taken place from a healthy and therapeutic relationship to one in which both parties are trying to protect themselves from the consequences of their own anger and the frustration of their own narcissistic needs. This is the time when consultation is extremely useful, and it can often put the therapy back on the right track.

This is also often the time when consultation does *not* take place, because the therapist is too angry and may even be ashamed of his anger. Unless he is aware of what is happening, he tends to simply act out to get rid of the patient.

The erotized transference and countertransference and the raging transference and countertransference are furthermore *related* to each other in a very important and complicated way. Blum (1973) explains, for example, how a therapy can be silently stalemated by an unconscious conspiracy of mutual admiration and endearment. He sees this as a subtle repetition of the parents' use of the child for their own narcissistic needs. Thus, countertransference can divert the tensions of transference into shared erotic fantasies or frightened flight. Confronted with the calculated narcissistic rage of the patient, this tension can be diverted by the therapist into his "falling in love" with the patient, becoming preoccupied with erotic fantasies about the patient, or taking flight from the patient. At the same time countertransference behavior can anchor the patient's fantasies into transference reactions in a reality of actual seductive responses by the therapist. This similarly leads to a deadlock.

Every therapist must arrange in advance (1) that he has a good consultant available and (2) that if he finds himself falling in love with a patient he is determined to go to that consultant. The reason for this vital advance program is that when the therapist actually begins to experience the feeling of falling in love with the patient, the greatest temptation by far is to do nothing. Often it is a very pleasant sensation; it is often ego syntonic, and having been rationalized, it even seems to make sense sometimes! The patient is invested with a certain beatific and erotic radiance which is characteristic of all falling in love. Because that radiance appears or is perceived by the therapist, it seems to justify his falling in love.

The proof that this is countertransference is that if consultation takes place and correct analysis of the countertransference occurs, the "radiance" will (often suddenly) disappear and the therapist will find himself wondering, "Why on earth this particular patient?" It will be almost as if a sheen or a halo or a background light has suddenly been put out in back of the patient.

When we find highly erotized transference or countertransferences or highly raging transferences or countertransferences, we must examine the material meticulously to see what is a defense against what. Careful examination and understanding of the patient and the psychodynamics will again and again clarify the situation and lead directly to the solution. This cannot help but be therapeutic, because direct confrontation and honest discussion is the exact opposite of what the patient has experienced as a child. In those situations everything was hypocrisy, everything was covert; everything was usually distorted to make the parents look good and the child look as if he were at fault. Even reality testing and reality perception were deliberately distorted! The parents manipulated so that the child was made to feel that the parents were good and he was bad, and the child was used for the narcissistic needs of the parents.

Most of the maneuvers patients use that lead to these deadlocks are attempts to find out how the therapist is going to relate to the patient. Will he deal with these things in a straightforward, honest way, thus providing a new model, or will he be a repetition of the disappointing and destructive model that the patient experienced from the parent? Giovacchini (1975b) reminds us, "The patient's defenses attempt to create a situation in treatment designed to force the analyst to abandon the analytic role. ... The patient has suffered all of his life. Is it surprising, then, that he wants us to suffer for him? Gradually we learn to absorb the patient's suffering without feeling too uncomfortable, a discomfort which is mitigated by our witnessing the release of the patient's developmental potential and the gradual emergence of his autonomy."

Countertransference does not have to be a problem in psychotherapy. It is the therapist's attitude toward countertransference and what he does with it that determines whether it will be a tremendous hindrance, even destroying the psychotherapy, or it can even be helpful in obtaining more insight about the patient and oneself. Furthermore, one may argue that an affirmative or therapeutic form of countertransference is a necessity if psychotherapy is to succeed. Spitz (Gitelson 1962) introduced the phrase "diatrophic function of the analyst—his healing intention to 'maintain and support' the patient." Thus, in response to the patient's need for help the analyst offers an empathic imbrication with his patient's emotions that "provides a sustaining grid of 'understanding' (or 'resonance')." The result is a certain rapport or alliance, which leads the patient to a new beginning.

The diatrophic position of the therapist arises as a response to the patient's anaclitic regression and represents a regression by the therapist in the service of the ego. The difference from active therapy with direct intent to cure is that in the latter, direct libidinal gratification is deliberately provided; the active therapist suggests himself as a substitutive "good object." In contrast to this, the psychoanalytically informed attitude operates as "an auxiliary to the patient's ego with its own intrinsic potentialities for reality testing, synthesis, and adaptation" (Gitelson 1962).

CHAPTER 22

Helpful Clinical Suggestions

The "emptiness" of the therapeutic relation is a very important problem in the treatment of borderline patients. For example, those with the narcissistic personality disorder who are using the therapist as a self-object don't really relate to the therapist as a human being with a self of his own. This is bound to stir up countertransference.

Treatment of most borderline patients, whether a couch is being used or whether it is a face-to-face treatment, is almost always a psychoanalytically informed psychotherapy. Parameters have to be introduced; for example, the therapist has to be somewhat more active and cannot tolerate many long silences. A borderline patient's silently lying on the couch for a long period of time indicates something is seriously wrong, and it is very dangerous to sit passively while this happens.

One must *actively* inquire, when one is dealing with a borderline patient, about what is going on outside of therapy hours. We have to ask! We don't wait patiently to find out, because by the time we do find out, irreversible disasters may have taken place. After a while the patient gets the idea that the therapist is interested in what's going on in his real life. This by itself constitutes a salutory form of limit setting. Conversely, if no questions are ever asked about the reality of the patient's life and if one concentrates solely on dreams, fantasies and free associations, the road is paved for a disaster in the patient's external life.

It is debatable in the psychotherapy of the borderline patient whether a true classical transference neurosis forms. There is no doubt that a workable transference relationship often does form, but one gets into sticky metapsychological terminology when one tries to distinguish between a workable transference and a true transference neurosis. The therapist must have a great deal of flexibility if he works with borderline patients. *He must learn to suit the treatment to the patient, not the patient to the treatment.* If a borderline patient is advised to lie on the couch four times a week, sometimes the therapy will go forward and will work, but sometimes the patient can't stand it. The deprivation of not seeing the therapist or even the lack of structure is absolutely intolerable. To insist that the patient use one rigid procedure, regardless of what it is, is a great mistake in the psychotherapy of the borderline patient (or any patient).

We want as smooth and workable a relationship as possible. We meet the patient's needs tacitly by being able to listen and by demonstrating that we have empathy with the patient's fears and anxieties. This is the sharpest contrast we can personally present to the parents of the patient, who could not listen to the patient and who could not empathically grasp the patient's needs.

The way we structure the psychotherapy is especially important to the borderline patient. Paradoxically he always fights the structure, because all structures and all limitations remind him of irrational authority and his own sense of helplessness. Therefore the structure has to be flexible and reasonable and it has to make sense to the patient. He doesn't take it on faith.

If one works with borderline patients, it is important either to have medical training or to be very closely in touch with a consultant who has it. This is because borderline patients are in serious ever-present danger of developing psychosomatic disorders (Chessick 1972b, 1977b, 1977c). Either these appear as a result of the regressive processes that are taking place in the patient anyway or they are stirred up by therapeutic regression or the patient engages in medically dangerous acting out, which can be another type of behavior that requires medical knowledge. If the patient doesn't take his digitalis or his insulin and gets wobbly and dizzy, the therapist has to know that he may not have taken his insulin or (if he has cardiac symptoms) his digitalis.

As a general rule of thumb one should never, never, never disregard physical complaints made by a borderline patient. They should always be taken seriously. They should not be brushed aside as "psychosomatic." They should be medically checked out, because the therapist often does not know the source of these complaints; there could be organic changes regardless of whether the etiology is psychic or not. The method of checking out these complaints is to have at hand a thorough and reliable and understanding internist to whom the patient is referred, as well as a coterie of specialists available for referral, such as gynecologists and neurologists that you are used to working with and to whom you can send the patient.

It is invariably an error in the psychotherapy of borderline patients or patients with narcissistic personality disorders to do physical examinations on them yourself. This produces an entirely different kind of primary-process interchange and gratification that will encourage the development of more psychosomatic symptoms in order to produce more physical examinations.

Borderline patients often present life-and-death issues dramatically and quickly, including even such issues as whether to kill or be killed. Sometimes their regression is disruptive and it is up to the skill of the therapist to deal with it, to know how much of it to encourage in the psychotherapy or how to vigorously oppose it if he possibly can. Obviously, if a patient is inevitably going to regress, he is going to regress, no matter how hard the therapist works against it.

Therapists who are puritannical, extremely overconventional, and prone to sermonize about ethics and sexuality do poorly with borderline patients. Rigid morality, rule giving, or condemnation of patient implies a grandiosity and omnipotence on the part of the therapist that borderline patients cannot tolerate. Furthermore, because of their wobbly ego function, borderline patients get into many kinds of bizarre scrapes and indulge in all kinds of sexual behavior which an overconventional or puritanical therapist may find repulsive, disgusting and unacceptable.

It is important to keep in mind that the therapist's countertransference should *not* be "confessed" to a patient. There are some papers and books in the literature which advise one to share countertransference with the patient. This is a beginner's mistake. The patient does not come to therapy and pay to listen to the therapist's problems! When one has countertransference problems, as everyone does, one resolves them, after promptly identifying them, either by oneself, through supervision, or through more therapy for oneself. One uses the countertransference problem as much as possible to understand more about the patient. If one gains any understanding of the patient, one reflects that back to him without having to discuss with him one's own problems—this is exploitation!

It is important to keep in mind that the use of medication with borderline patients has a similar kind of danger to doing physical examinations with them. There are times when it is inhumane in this day and age not to give a patient tranquillizers or even help with sleep, and it can be a manifestation of countertransference to withhold medication in emergency situations as well as to give it out all over the place. If one is reasonable and humane and very careful, there is a place for both the neuroleptic and the anxiolitic as well as the soporific drugs in the treatment of the borderline patient. It is incumbent on the therapist to be knowledgeable about these classes of drugs and to know how to use them when they are indicated. A good rule of thumb is that for the majority of borderline patients it is not necessary to write prescriptions except on rare occasions. The number of prescriptions the therapist writes per week for his total borderline practice should be small. If it is large, he is not doing a good job of psychoanalytically informed psychotherapy with borderline patients. Very few prescriptions for borderline patients are written each week even in full-time practice, but one must be willing to write a prescription if it is indicated.

The same applies to hospitalization. These patients do not do well with hospitalization, especially of a long-term nature. They tend to interact in the hospital with other patients with other diagnoses, and they act out, make trouble and get themselves hated by the personnel. Any hospitalization should be used the same way medications are used—for emergencies, for brief periods of time when it seems to the therapist either that the patient must be protected from destroying himself or from creating social or economic ruin of some kind, or that he is a danger to others.

On the one hand, the family should not be allowed to pressure the therapist into hospitalizing the patient, but on the other hand, it is necessary to listen carefully and without prejudice or hostility to what the family has to say, because they will give the therapist information about the patient's reality which the patient may not provide, and it may greatly help the therapist in judging what problem he is dealing with. A certain percentage of borderline patients must have medication and a certain percent of these patients, not necessarily the same patients, must be hospitalized from time to time. In fact, failure in psychotherapy with certain patients is prevented by appropriate medication and at times by appropriate hospitalization.

The basic clinical question has to do with the therapist's feeling about whether these patients are immutably damaged and defective or they can be approached and cured by psychoanalytically informed psychotherapy. Here one must make a choice with each patient. It is clearly a tragedy either way if we make the wrong choice. A patient who is immutably damaged and defective who is subjected to several years of intensive long-term psychotherapy has experienced something very unfortunate in terms of loss of time, money, energy and so on, and vice versa. A patient who could respond to long-term psychoanalytically informed psychotherapy who is given just a periodic brief visit and a medication is also being terribly hurt and shortchanged.

In psychoanalytically informed psychotherapy of these patients, one tends away from analyzing dreams and phantasies too exclusively or thoroughly. Thus, although we listen to the patient's dream material, we tend to concentrate more on reactions to everyday living, job, and family rather than going deeply into interpretations of dream material. We stay with where the patient is more than in a classical psychoanalysis, and we proceed more slowly in most cases.

The word *change* is often a turning point in the psychotherapy of the borderline patient or the patient with a narcissistic personality. This word often brings forth an amazing and violent reaction of rage. The patient does not want to change and cannot change "ever." The way the therapist reacts to the challenge that he gives the patient to change is often one of those unwritten—even nonverbal at times—turning points that decide the success or failure of the psychotherapy of a borderline patient. We all live in a constantly changing environment, and change is the normal adaptation of all beings. When the patient doesn't want to change, there is going to be a confrontation between the therapist and the patient. If the therapist is hesitant to bring up change after that, there is going to be trouble in the psychotherapy. On the contrary, the concept of change has to be brought up again and again and has to be employed as a focal point for the study of the patient's life.

Why should talk of change produce such a response in these patients? First of all there is the narcissism; why should some one who secretly imagines himself to be perfect change? Second, there is the great anxiety that is involved in the risk of change with a weak ego structure. Finally, to change means to accept and recognize someone beside oneself as a functioning personality. That is the beginning of a healthy relation to another human being, in this case the therapist.

It takes infinite patience and a great deal of empathy on the part of the therapist to work on the reconstruction of a very defective ego for a long time, even after the first breakthrough on such matters as narcissistic facades has been achieved. The reward of such patience is to help some sick but often very valuable people, at least to sometimes avoid a functional collapse or psychotic breakdown in their personalities. Also our own insights grow about ourselves, and our depth of understanding and technique in dealing with emotional illness in general is greatly enlarged.

I believe that in the psychotherapy of the borderline patient, there is always a corrective experience. There is a counteracting of the deception and frustration the patient experienced in early infancy or childhood, especially in the area of empathy. After the patient's confidence has been gained, there is a concentration by the therapist, on the reality of the patient's life, and the therapist has to be very careful not to be fooled by lack of affect or obscure dreams, which may mask terrific fears and terrific anxieties. After the therapy is off the ground, concentration on change is very important.

One searches for the repressed grandiose self as it shows itself first in the vertical split (Kohut 1971) and later behind the repression barrier itself. The core of narcissistic fantasy around which the patient bases his life always represents a weakening of the ego by delusionary-type thinking, and it is very important to get at these narcissistic configurations. This is true regardless of what theory of narcissism one wishes to hold. Dealing with narcissistic configurations is one of the central issues in the psychotherapy of borderline patients, both in terms of helping the patient and in terms of what is stirred up in the countertransference of the psychotherapist.

Certainly this discussion should demonstrate that many therapists ought *not* to work with borderline patients and patients with narcissistic character disorders. The kind of work involved has been described, and if one does not care to do it, one should not do it! It is an awesome responsibility to take on the long term psychotherapy of any patient. One should know what one wishes to handle and get involved in, but one must also know what one should avoid. This is the mark of any skilled and experienced psychotherapist, and it is a basic sign of his integrity, because the results of the treatment wholly determine the patient's prognosis and hope for a decent life. As Karl Jaspers wrote, "The doctor is the patient's fate."

CHAPTER 23

Improvement and Repair

Clearly, the initial and basic repair that has to go on in patients of this nature is the correction of a preverbal disaster. How does this take place? Modell (1968) writes, "A successful psychoanalytic treatment can provide in part the experience of 'good enough' parental care, and an identification with the analyst can become a permanent part of the patient's ego, thus permitting further ego maturation. In some cases the faulty, negative, or defective sense of identity of borderline and psychotic patients can be repaired. If such a process is successful, it leads to the development of a more definitive self-image and the capacity to form mature love relations. In others this does not occur. It is as if the failure of the environment at a critical phase has proved to be decisive." Modell points out that we have not been able to account fully for why in some cases we fail and in some cases we succeed.

Modell has the "impression" that "the degree of sadism and consequently the need for talion punishment may prove to be a determinant factor." This view is similar to Kernberg's. Patients whose sadism is overwhelming and who do not possess some capacity for love or for tender regard for others seem to remain unable to take in something good from the environment. Modell explains, "They are unable to form new identifications and in a larger sense are unable to profit from experience. To learn from others and the capacity to love others are at bottom similar; both are based on the capacity to identify. Without this capacity there is no possibility of psychic growth."

This initial basic repair proceeds extremely slowly and is character-ized by often taking place in spite of what is verbally going on between the patient and the therapist. Signs that it is taking place can be watched for in the psychotherapy. For example, a most characteristic sign is increase of ego span. A patient who would explode into a variety of symptoms upon frustration shows a longer and longer period of frustration tolerance. Sometimes the patient or those around him will notice this and report it. It is frequently spoken of as a softening or mellowing. Thus, if the frustration tolerance has previously been a day, now the patient can wait a week for an important letter or a misplaced salary check or the like without developing the characteristic explosive symptoms.

When questioned closely as to why this sort of improvement has taken place, the patients disappoint us. At best they usually can give only vague answers that seem to relate to being "wrapped up in the therapist," although sometimes they even vigorously deny that therapy has had anything to do with their improvement at all. A therapist-patient symbiosis gradually is tacitly established in which the patient develops an almost "animal faith" (in the sense that this term is used by Santayana) in the consistency, honesty, determination and, above all, the reliability of the therapist.

Now this introduces a somewhat different and rather hazy aspect of the psychotherapist—the psychotherapist as a human being. I have already hinted at this in my discussion of what happens when the therapist confronts a patient with the need to change. Such crucial moments can be considered points in time when the therapist's existence is shared with the heretofore isolated patient. The shared moments represent a significant intrusion of the therapist into the patient's private world. This is very tricky. From time to time in a well-conducted psychotherapy there is a moment of true communication or contact between the two parties, even though such contact may not necessarily be a loving contact. For example, it can be during a debate—a sharing not based on projective identification, but on contact between two relatively autonomous egos. Of course, the therapist then has to be unconditionally ready to recognize the other person and to share his world with him.

This begins to get vague, and it is the point at which I like to introduce residents to the concepts of existentialism. My experience with this has been uniformly negative. The resistance to these concepts among people with medical training in the United States is very powerful. It is very difficult to explain what exactly is meant by existential concepts of "being there" or of "being with" the patient in the patient's existence. Meaning is hard to point to, and unless one is fairly steeped in the existential literature, even the words are rather different—"I-Thou" relationships and so on.

Buber, for example, talks about "swinging into the life of the other" (Havens 1974). Other existentialists talk about caring, staying, presence and so on. A lot of this is close to empathy and the capacity to really be there with the patient, and it does have some similarity to a healthy mother's interaction with her infant. In my experience, the expositions of existential technique in the literature have been very unpopular with residents in psychiatry and have been rather unclear. It is difficult to see exactly where the difference is between an existential psychoanalyst and an ordinary psychoanalyst.

What is definitely recommended and what is important in the psychotherapy of the borderline patient is the mental attitude that Havens (1974) calls a keeping looking—a pushing away of every temptation the patient offers or the therapist finds to make definite conclusions—which is comparable to the state of empathic listening or free-floating attention. I would suggest that anyone who wishes to work in therapy with borderline patients carefully familiarize himself with existential philosophy and concepts to see if the suggestions given by the existentialists about direct grasp of the Being or the Existence of the patient afford a further dimension of understanding the patient and of offering him something. Some therapists seem to intuitively grasp the concepts of existentialism and use them; to others they simply make no sense at all.

One must be very careful not to use the existential approach as a rationalization for engaging in all kinds of primary-process acting out with the patients. This is a common error and it is unreasonable. Unfortunately, existential terminology is vague because the subject of Existence that existentialism tries to study is also vague. Therefore existential philosophy and terminology can be used to justify just about anything from Christian faith on the one hand to seducing and having sexual relations with the patient on the other hand. It does not follow from this, however, that the existentialist has nothing to tell us.

Especially in the psychotherapy of the borderline patient, who is so preoccupied with problems of life and death, it is necessary for the therapist to have some knowledge of this field. I will return to existentialism in the final part of this book.

It almost goes without saying that the demands made on the therapist by borderline patients are tremendous. They force a great deal of thought and introspection and brooding and reflection on the data, and they require time for the therapist to reflect on this data. If a therapist is trying to do intensive psychotherapy of borderline patients, he cannot carry a tremendous practice. It's too much. They require the therapist to avoid acting out over years of intensive therapy during which the utmost tests are put to him to see if he can withstand what the patient has to offer. Such incidents as the therapist's canceling or getting ill or coming late to appointments, mistakes in the time of appointments, broken promises, vacations, even scientific meetings, become major items for discussion in the therapy.

There is a continuous scrutiny by the patient to see whether these everyday matters cannot be attributed to a basic dislike assumed to be in the therapist for the patient. Now if there *is* a basic dislike, obviously the therapy will fail. It is impossible to hide this from any patient over the years of treatment.

Hopefully, after some months or even some years of this kind of relationship, the patient gradually swings around from oscillating psychiatric and psychosomatic symptoms and various kinds of bizarre acting out to behavior resembling more and more what we see in ordinary psychotherapy situations. The therapist at that point begins to shift roles bit by bit toward a more neutral stance, with the aim of eliciting the basic early narcissistic fantasies that the patient has lived around. However, this can be done only after there has been sufficient locking in of the symbiosis between therapist and patient, so that the patient can withstand the frustrations and anxieties involved in the uncovering of such items as his pet and secret narcissistic consolation fantasies and so on.

Thus, in the successful psychotherapy of the borderline patient we utilize the transitional-object type of transference that tends to form. If we become a transitional object to the patient, then that forms a kind of glue that holds the patient in the treatment in spite of the profound anxieties and the profound rages that take place during it. Meanwhile we can uncover important material, help the patient's ego to deal with it and consequently build in defenses and mechanisms that will promote better adaptation and better integration of such material. The transitional-object type of transference holds the patient in the treatment during this extremely painful process. The therapist's dedication and understanding of the importance and the seriousness of what he is doing also holds the *therapist* in the treatment during this painful process.

In those cases where a classical narcissistic transference forms, we don't find such a primitive type of transitional object transference, but the principle is the same. The narcissistic transferences actually become something of a transference neurosis, depending on how you define that term; at any rate they become important enough to the patient that if the therapist behaves himself and conducts the therapy properly they hold him in the therapy. Obviously the great problem with the borderline patient is to get him to stay in therapy and locked into treatment, because it is so painful and generates so much anxiety and so much frightening rage that the patient has to deal with the tendency to run away from it or to act out massively and destroy it.

It is very important to look more technically at what we mean when we talk about *basic change* accomplished by the process of psychotherapy with the borderline patient. An intrapsychic structural change is hopefully an ongoing process throughout the course of the psychotherapy. It has to be considered on a continuum involving the degree of change which is occurring and also the rate of change.

DeWald (1972) points out that change may be manifest in a specific microstructure, such as a defense mechanism, or manifested in a macrostructure by change in broader groups of functions simultaneously. Structural change may involve the progressive dissolution and ultimate elimination of specific pathological structures. For example, one observes the dissolution of specific defensive responses to an archaic fantasy, or further, the subsequent establishment of new structures to replace the previous pathological ones, such as the development of the capacity for sublimation of a drive which has been previously dealt with by mechanisms of defense such as reaction formation and so on.

How do we measure structural change? Clearly, two general approaches can be employed (DeWald 1972). We can use the patient as his own control, comparing his psychic structures at the present moment with previous levels and types of function and even with his status prior to the beginning of the treatment. Again, we can look at microstructures or macrostructures. We look for changes in "the intensity, frequency, and stereotyped nature of the automatic (structured) responses" that have existed, and we look to see whether new automatic patterns of functioning have emerged.

Another approach, which can be taken essentially at the same time, is to assess how closely the patient's various psychic functions approach a theoretical ideal or composite image of psychic structure regarding particular issues that are at hand. Here we compare the changes in a particular patient against a kind of hypothetical composite image of modes of functioning in a theoretically healthy individual. This is very tricky, because we should not introduce our own personal standards and values in this kind of comparison, but it is appropriate, since we do have some notions of the general way that a healthy individual functions as compared with an unhealthy individual.

An alert psychotherapist uses both of these approaches simultaneously, observing the rate and extent of changes occurring in his patient and comparing them to the patient as the patient was and, at the same time, comparing and contrasting them to the therapist's own concept and understanding of the potential degree, range and rate of change that the patient could undergo. DeWald (1972) mentions certain key indicators or signs of structural change. One such sign is the increasing richness in the recovery of infantile and childhood fantasies and memories and, obviously, the undoing of infantile repression. Such memories and fantasies as they are uncovered have a quality of immediacy for the patient. They carry a sense of conviction and personal experience and frequently occur unexpectedly, often accompanied by the concurrent childhood affective experience. When this happens, it is an indication of structural change. Another indicator of core structural change is that once basic nuclear conflicts have been resolved, their various derivative manifestations will change spontaneously, even without specific scrutiny in the psychotherapy and sometimes even without conscious effort by the patient. This may even include behavior which is recognized as having been symptomatic only after it is modified and disappears. In my clinical experience, the patient will report this with a sense of delight.

Another indicator to look for is the patient's reaction to previously traumatic or anxiety-provoking material. Now he is capable of remembering, accepting and understanding the traumatic experiences that previously evoked intense affect. Still another indicator of structural change is the nature of the patient's dream work. We watch for the increasing freedom and directness with which the underlying dream thoughts and wishes can be expressed as well as for the patient's increasing ability to interpret his own dreams. The work the therapist has to do on the patient's dream material diminishes as the patient undergoes strengthening of the ego and structural change. "Such a change reflects an ego and superego acceptance of unconscious infantile drives and drive derivatives, and an increasing confidence in conscious integrative processes for the control of such drives."

Still another indicator is the changed nature of the patient's relationships with people outside the psychotherapy. The patient begins to manifest more realistic expectations and responses toward them and is increasingly capable of tolerating and adapting to realistic stress and frustration in such relationships. Much of Strupp's (1973) writing about psychotherapy has to do with this indicator, which he feels is essentially obtained through conditioning and learning in psychotherapy, but it is also possible to see this as having been made possible by a structural change in the ego.

Similarly, another indicator is the patient's growing dissatisfaction with previously gratifying infantile relationships or objects and the replacement of these by age-appropriate, realistically satisfying objects. A significant enhancement or deepening of the patient's affective life and responses occurs, particularly when his previous patterns of behavior in this regard have been inhibited and restricted. The implication is a change in the defensive ego structures, a modification of superego attitudes in regard to affective life, and an increasing confidence manifested in self-esteem and the capacity to tolerate and manage the affects.

Genuine improvement in object relations can only begin with such patients when narcissistic fantasies have been uncovered and given up and the patients recognize that they can get on in the world without them, but to get to this point sometimes requires a very long period of intensive psychotherapy. Clinical evidence of improvement appears in such areas as showing greater ability to empathize with others, showing greater consideration for the feelings of others, developing closer and more mature relationships with family and friends, and manifesting interest in and concern for community problems.

In addition, we aim at transformations of narcissism, as described by Kohut (1966). Depending on one's theoretical orientation, this is an additional indicator for structural change. If we believe that narcissism has a separate line of development from that of object libido, as does Kohut, then we aim in our psychotherapy with the borderline patient at what he calls transformations of narcissism. According to this theory we are less hopeful that there will be a tremendous outpouring of improved object relationships because of the fundamental defect in the patient, and we are more willing to settle for what Kohut would call healthy narcissism.

Technically speaking, we hope that the grandiose self will become gradually integrated "into the web of our ego as a healthy enjoyment of our own activities and successes and as an adaptatively useful sense of disappointment charged with anger and shame over our failures and shortcomings." Similarly, the ego ideal "may come to form a continuum with the ego, as a focus for our ego syntonic values, as a healthy sense of direction and beacon for our activities and pursuits, and as an adaptively useful object of longing disappointment, when we cannot reach it" (Kohut 1966).

Clinically speaking, we assess the healthy transformations of infantile narcissism through the process of psychotherapy and watch for evidence of the ego's capacity to harness the narcissistic energies and transform the narcissistic constellations into more highly differentiated new psychological configurations. We look for creativity, the ability to be empathic, the capacity to contemplate one's own impermanence, a sense of humor and, finally, the attainment of what Kohut calls wisdom. Kohut defines wisdom "as a stable attitude of the personality toward life and the world, an attitude which is formed through the integration of the cognitive function with humor, acceptance of transience and a firmly cathected system of values."

Tolstoy's *War and Peace,* which is not mentioned to my knowledge anywhere in Kohut's writing, is an enormous novel. If you study and read it closely, in many ways it is the story of the transformations of narcissism in all the important characters, five of them; Pierre, Prince

Andrew, Nicholas, Natasha and Marie, exactly along the lines described by Kohut. The suffering and vicissitudes all five have to go through as they mature through these transformations of narcissism present a magnificent literary description of what Kohut is talking about.

Thus we hope in the psychotherapy of the borderline patient that narcissism will be transformed and reshaped into aspects of wisdom as a result of the therapy. This hope stands in contrast to the classical expectation of a more dramatic change from narcissism to object love. We would certainly welcome the development of greater and greater capacity for object love also, but we are assuming in this theory separate developmental pathways for narcissism and the object libido. Ideally, we would hope to see in the borderline patient *both* narcissism and the capacity for object-love appropriately transformed through the process of psychotherapy. The more metapsychological understanding we have of the given borderline patient, the more hopeful we become for change and improvement and health in that patient, and the more capable we are of caring and patiently staying with the patient over a long period of intensive uncovering psychotherapy.

Part VI
METAPSYCHIATRY

CHAPTER 24

Concepts of Cure in
Intensive Psychotherapy

If one looks in standard textbooks on the subject of psychotherapy, one finds an amazing lack of discussion of the patient's basic cognitive capacity to understand what the therapist is talking about. It seems almost incredible that so little attention has been paid to the fact that many patients are developmentally arrested or have regressed to earlier phases of cognitive development and therefore they are literally either unable to find the words to describe their feelings or to communicate their feelings to another person, or they are simply unable to understand communications that one would expect, if given from one adult to another, they ought to be able to understand.

Piaget (Pulaski 1971; Evans 1973; Piaget and Inhelder 1966) describes phases of cognitive development very carefully. The basic developmental division is between what he calls the Sensorimotor Period and the appearance of what he calls thinking operations. The Sensorimotor Period lasts for about the first two years of life. At that period of life the infant is locked into egocentrism, the lack of awareness of anything outside the realm of his immediate experience. Piaget describes psychic "adualism" as prevailing at this time—that is to say, there is no boundary between the self and objects. Even object permanence, the notion that something exists when you can't see it, doesn't occur until about eight to twelve months. However, logical structures *do* display themselves in the Sensorimotor Period, but they don't display themselves through words and symbols. This, by the way, is one of the strongest arguments that adult logic and mathematics are not simply derived from language, but rather come from something prelinguistic.

It is only around eighteen months of age that what Piaget calls the Period of Representational Intelligence begins. The first early beginning of thinking, or symbolization, or concept formation, begins to occur around the middle of the second year of life, and with it is brought a tremendous hunger for names. To put this another way which is pertinent to psychotherapy, the child of eighteen months already has a number of perceptual concepts but doesn't have the names for them yet. This is in contrast to what was originally thought, namely that first the child learns the name and then he gets the concept. "Reality," as we understand it then, consists of various conceptual patterns that we build up. It is not a given; it is something that is constantly being created every minute of our lives, and it depends on the people we interact with.

Before the child is one-and-a-half to two years old, a form of cognition or intelligence goes on without representation, concepts, or symbols. From about the second to the seventh year of age occurs what Piaget calls the Preoperational Period of Representational Intelligence. Here begins the use of language and mental images, and thus instead of a sensorimotor activity such as grasping, the infant can ask for things. The mental level is still that of egocentrism and rests on the notion that everything is made for man and for children. It is the phase of magical omnipotence and animism.

During this phase something else very important to psychotherapy occurs, what Piaget calls "interiorized imitation." The child is able to imitate significant adults without the significant adults being present and actually doing something in front of him. Before two years of age, the adult in the presence of the baby may scratch his head and the child may imitatively do that, but after two years of age the adult doesn't have to be right there doing it. This indicates that an evocative or representational memory is present *after* eighteen months to two years of age.

This phase is followed by what Piaget calls the Period of Concrete Operations, from about seven to twelve years of age. These, of course, are the grade school years, in which the child can operate on and talk about concrete objects or their representations. Finally, something else extremely important, the Period of Formal Operations, begins from about eleven or twelve years and does not finish until about fourteen or fifteen. If this cognitive period is not completed, the child cannot go through adolescent development. This cognitive period consists of the capacity to make abstractions, to find laws, to think about thoughts; operations of the second order are involved here. It enables the subject to free himself from the concrete, and it is a very important task of preadolescence or early adolescence to reach this point. I think one of the best ways to test whether the adolescent has reached this point is to see how he deals with basic algebra. Can he jump for example from the concept of number to the concept of a letter representing a number? Then can he operate with the letters and convert the solution back into numbers?

Whether Piaget is describing the developmental stages as they occur in the organic maturation of the central nervous system or not is really a different discussion. The movement from one phase to the next is a combination of innate maturity and social stimulus in some way, and the self-image of an individual has a lot to do with how much success he has in getting through these cognitive phases!

Piaget's own words are also interesting here on the subject of behaviorism. His research indicates the relative unimportance of outside stimuli in development and change in individuals and the very great importance of what he calls internal reinforcement. Self-regulation and internal reinforcement as they develop through these cognitive stages become increasingly more important than external stimulation. In general, the factors in cognitive and affective development, according to Piaget, are a combination of organic growth, exercise and acquired experience in the actions performed on objects, social interaction and transmission, and equilibrium involving self-regulation.

Now this is no simple academic matter for psychotherapists, because we would expect in many conditions where there has been developmental arrest to see these phases gone through as therapy moves forward. Thus we expect to see the period of equilibration and then a period of puzzling, of searching for new and better adjustments, and of striving to achieve a balance between past experience and present stress. As Piaget explains, when equilibrium is established in one area the restless organism begins to explore in another. Notice then that far from being black boxes or *tabulae rasae* or empty organisms reacting passively to stimuli, human beings are active explorers adjusting to the world as they find it and modifying the world and their perception of the world to meet their needs. Rather than passive reaction, the process is much more what Piaget calls "assimilation." Stimuli and responses interact with each other; action schemes or thought operations are modified and enriched by the stimuli, which at the same time are filtered through previously formed conceptual patterns. At the very early stage of life, the sensorimotor stage, this leads to a construction of reality in the child that is lasting. This is the foundation of Piaget's notion of "genetic epistemology."

It is interesting that dreaming for Piaget is thought of as falling back on preoperational thought and as resembling play. Unfortunately he uses the term *operation* to mean thinking in the usual sense, and thus the term *preoperational thought* has to do with conceptual operations before the age of reason, before around seven years old or school age.

Thus it is not surprising to find a patient's entire perception of reality changing and shifting over a period of successful psychotherapy. The most obvious example of this is the quasi-paranoid patient or the patient who externalizes, as I have described it in my (1972b) paper on externalization and existential anguish. The patient may begin therapy with the feeling that everyone around him is out to take advantage of him, to cheat him, gyp him, rip him off, and if the patient is paranoid enough he may even believe that everyone is out to hurt him or knife him. The patient sustains his beliefs by selectively picking out aspects of the external environment which fit the predetermined conception and by forcing the perceptions into a pattern that fits a predetermined schema.

Of course, the purposes of this schema may be multiple. For example, it may protect the patient against a surprise attack which he has come to fear more than anything else. It may represent a projection of the patient's own hatred, which he then has to rationalize by pointing to what he thinks he sees in the outside world, etc. The point is that argument with the patient about what he is perceiving gets nowhere because he only perceives what fits into the preexisting map and this map is necessary for defensive purposes. It can't be expected to drop away until something has happened in the relationship between the patient and the therapist so that the patient is more comfortable and doesn't need the map anymore. I can't think of any better proof of how completely dependent our concepts of reality and what we think we perceive are upon our preexisting psychodynamic and affectual states. What a gross error it is to think that cognition is a kind of autonomous independent function not substantially affected by emotional factors, conflicts, etc. To think that the individual is a blank slate that experiences can then shape in an operant-conditioning manner is impossible, for its converse is easy to observe clinically.

It is most important for the psychotherapist to have this all in mind. We must always ask ourselves, At what level of cognition is the patient and where do we hope to bring him cognitively? Otherwise we will find ourselves speaking to a patient who does not exist, talking to a level he does not have and thereby simply being either completely ignored or misunderstood.

Langer (1942) points out how much more complicated our thinking and language really are than we tend to assume. Mental life is much more than simply discursive reason. She distinguishes between discursive symbolism or language, the usual notion of thought and ideas in the intellectual sense, and what she calls presentational symbolism. Presentational symbolism includes the nonverbal representations, the connotations, the inflections, the voice emphasis, etc., and forms a very important vehicle of meaning, much widening our conception of communication and having an important influence on what the patient really gets from the therapist in the way of communication.

If we are not aware of this we may not realize, for example, that we are saying one thing and communicating another. This is well known, but what is sometimes not so well known is that when we are talking, what the patient is really listening to or looking for is something on an entirely different level, for instance the inflection of our voice, or the look in our eye, or what have you, and that is really what is affecting the psychotherapy—not our fancy formulations or what we have to say! This is why for many patients the therapist may think he is following a pure psychoanalytic model, but what the patient is really responding to is something entirely different. It doesn't matter that the therapist is pleased that he has made a correct interpretation; what matters and what the patient is responding to depends on what level the patient is at and what is he perceiving.

To put it another way, what does the therapist mean to the patient? Goldberg (1975) points out that no therapist should fail to ask just what role or relationship he or she has been assigned and is performing at various points throughout treatment. "More often than not the answer will be that of a narcissistic object (a functional part of the self) and the issues will revolve around handling of grandiose ambitions or the yearning for powerful ideals." It is very important for the therapist to be aware of what role he is playing for the patient (whether he wants to play the role or not) and how the patient perceives him. This perception in turn is based on what cognitive level the patient is at.

Very often the relationship between the patient and therapist gives us crucial information on the patient's self-esteem and narcissistic problems, and clues in the patient's behavior are used as communications and help the patient to see why he is disappointed in relationships elsewhere. This is utterly lost if the psychotherapist attempts from some fuzzy-minded notion of the "psychoanalytic model" to play the role of the impassive neutral withdrawn psychoanalyst who is unresponsive to the patient's behavior—a role that no experienced psychoanalyst would present either.

This discussion also shows why it is so exceptionally destructive to psychotherapy if the therapist practices hypocrisy. The therapist who says, for example, that there is something therapeutic for the ordinary patient in paying the fee, implying that paying the fee is primarily for the patient and not for the therapist's needs, is already starting with hypocrisy. Similarly, any kind of deals that one makes with the patient, getting anything *sub rosa* beside the fee, begins to set up this hypocrisy with double messages. One cannot then know what the patient is responding to. Therefore one cannot understand what to correct.

The patient comes (out of the transference) into psychotherapy seeking another chance and looking for all the love and the gratification of infantile wishes that he never had. He is actually putting these wishes onto an unsuitable object. The therapist is not going to be the patient's mother and gratify all the patient's needs. The way the therapist deals with the transference, especially with the patient's attempt to get all the things he didn't get as a child, will either help the patient to integrate and mature or set up a hypocritical situation in which the patient will be doomed to experience another bitter disappointment.

In psychotherapy we actually have to apply our knowledge of cognitive development into helping the patient put these vague wishes and desires from infancy into words and concepts. Similarly we help the patient put sensorimotor patterns into words and concepts. The purpose of all this conceptual elaboration is to describe what one is doing in order to gain more control over it, to refine it and to teach it to others. In psychotherapy we try to carry the patient up from the sensorimotor level—from the level of behavior that caused him all kinds of difficulties. Such behavior is essentially communication but not verbal communication, for it is not conceptualized yet. It therefore is very important to urge and to help the patients to describe their feelings, to label their feelings and to think about their feelings, rather than to allow them to act out the feelings or communicate the feelings in sensorimotor patterns.

By closely watching the relationship and the behavior of the patient during the therapy, one can point these things out to the patient and put them into concepts and words. This has the important effect of allowing the normal developmental trends which were arrested to take over again. Similarly, during periods of regression in psychotherapy, the alert psychotherapist watches for the cognitive level the patient is at and tries to gear the interpretations to that level of vocal tone and of concreteness in speech. Otherwise, in a sense his interpretation falls on an unreceptive brain, and no matter how correct it may be, it is rendered inappropriate by the communication level he uses.

The way the therapist spots these problems is by constantly asking himself, How does the patient perceive his own behavior? What needs is the patient trying to fulfill? How does the patient perceive the problem, and why? It is permissible and even desirable, if the patient is at the appropriate level, to allow the patient to cling to the perception of the therapist as need-fulfilling—providing the therapist does not actually make an attempt to force such a perception by acting out and trying to fulfill the needs! In due time, as the patient proceeds in development, the perception of the therapist as the need-fulfilling, gratifying, all-powerful giving parent will drop away by itself.

One of the ways this perception drops away is when the therapist begins to be belittled and laughed at by the patient. A perceptive therapist learns to accept this belittlement at the appropriate time. It is very much the way that an adolescent in early adolescence separates away from the longing for the ideal parent by finding various little weaknesses of the parents, caricaturing them and snickering at them and teasing the parents, etc. This is an important form of evaluation and separation, and the therapist should not respond to it as a narcissistic blow.

Our task in psychotherapy, very often especially at the beginning, is to get the patient to give conceptualization to nonsymbolized affectual or sensorimotor experiences. The way this is done is very simple. The therapist has to do it for the patient. Very often he has to give a verbal description to the patient of the patient's behavior in order to provide the patient with the words and concepts to talk about, rather than allowing the patient to act out or to present communications in a sensorimotor form. The patient in a sense, then, is literally dragged up from a sensorimotor level by the therapist's insistence on labeling and talking about feelings and communication.

Notice that this leads to a certain model of the psychotherapist which is different than the model of the classical psychoanalyst sitting neutrally behind the patient. Please notice that I am discussing intensive psychotherapy, *not* classical formal psychoanalysis.

The psychotherapist has a model-building function for the patient. In treatment we find out what the previous maps and schemas have been or what models the patient has used. Often these are self-defeating. We try to help the patient build new ones. In terms of their "inner speech," patients often talk to our presence as if they were talking to us when they are not even in a session. They internalize us first. They ask what would we say. Gradually this inner speech and these models become unconscious, and they come to function something like the program of a computer.

The model of us as the therapist, if it is correct, cannot hurt the patient even if we make many mistakes. It is what we are like that is really most important. If we are basically not destructive toward the patient and don't want to see him hurt, this attitude will be internalized by the patient, who then will not want to see himself hurt.

No matter how ridiculous or idealizing the transferences may be, we must present a tone of acceptance of these transferences—recognize where the patient is at rather than trying to push or force him to be somewhere else. For example, if the patient says, "You know it's amazing how we look alike!" it is not clever to point out to him, "Oh, that's not true!" This is experienced by the patient as a straight-arm which in a sense keeps him from psychologically taking from the therapist what he needs and causes the patient to withdraw, to become arrogant and to show a grandiose self. Thus the therapist waits until the patient no longer needs to feel that he looks like him and this drops by itself.

When the therapist finds himself feeling that he has to push and correct the patient, especially to correct the transference distortion rather than wait for the patient to grow up on his own time, we are getting into the area of countertransference. In general, the patient gets better in psychotherapy if you don't dc too many wrong things. If you say some right things, that also helps. Generally speaking, thc more ambitious you are in most cases, the more counterproductive the therapy will be.

What we are hoping is that the patient will take on the therapist's way of looking at things, especially a more benign way of looking at himself. The patient often hates himself. After he has experienced your benign attitude toward him, not your ambitious pushing of him, the patient then is able to modify this attitude. Thus, in psychotherapy the therapist participates more to bring about an existential encounter between two persons. The individual style is not as important as the *basic humane attitude that the therapist has on the basis of his own thorough psychotherapy* in working through his own narcissistic problems.

One might say that with the psychotic patient, the matter reaches an extreme point. Here a real relation is absolutely necessary. The psychotic patient actually needs a real person out there to help him in his real life, and this cannot be avoided.

As a general rule of thumb, remember that soothing rather than raging at a child produces a better self-image. The benign competent parent is gradually microinternalized, leaving an accumulation of experiences to fall back on. A therapist can often tell when he has put down or straight-armed the patient; one must not forget that many interpretations are not heard by the patient—rather they are experienced or felt as a put-down. In those situations one observes a developing affectual coldness; a tendency to primitivization of thought and speech—from stilted speech to gross use of neologisms and so on—attitudes of aloof superiority, an increased tendency to self-

consciousness and shame propensity, and hypochondriacal preoccupations. I am of course echoing Kohut (1971).

In psychotherapy we see the patient proceed from a first phase of
early anaclitic object choice (Gitelson 1962) to a narcissistic type of
object choice, in which he wants to be like you or who you are or who
you were or who he thinks you are, etc. Then occurs a more or less
sexualized choice, in which what is really important to the patient is
relating, not to the therapist, but to the idea that he has someone to
relate to, and finally there occurs a real object choice in which other
persons are perceived as having an existence and needs of their own.
Thus we see that before the later phase of real object love, the patient is
literally unable to perceive a therapist as a separate person with needs.
This greatly colors the way the patient behaves with the therapist and
again reverts to a problem of cognition.

To put it another way, the fabric of the ego consists of numerous
experiences that help tell the patient what to do or what not to do in
certain situations. A library of tapes of past experiences to call on is
present in everybody. Competence in human affairs has a lot to do with
this tape library. With benign early experiences a good library exists;
with bad experiences, the person is basing his decisions on a shredded
or disrupted fabric. It is our first task in psychotherapy to build into the
patient a series of benign experiences that he can fall back on later. This
is more important than deep interpretations or bringing the patient's
attention to long-repressed infantile wishes, etc.

This also explains why sometimes we find patients boring. Falling
asleep on a patient is a sign of countertransference and often has to do
with our response to highly narcissistic patients who are using us as
self-objects and show no investment in us as humans. the reaction to
this is to sense the lack of investment in us and feel as bored as if we
were listening over and over to a phonograph record. What we have to
keep in mind is that our benign presence—allowing the patient to do
this—is therapeutic, and in due time the patient can gradually give it
up. Arguing with the patient or confronting the patient repeatedly or
condemning the patient for this behavior is useless, because the patient
simply does not understand what we are talking about. He cannot
perceive things any other way.

Strupp (1973, 1975), as already discussed tries to reformulate
therapeutic factors. The important factors according to him are: "a

solid, reliable, and trusting relationship with his therapist," and "learning experiences in constructive living" which constitute a meaningful emotional experience.

More controversial is "moral suasion implicit in the therapist's seemingly neutral, task-oriented and 'clinical' stance." As the bedrock of all forms of psychotherapy, the therapist establishes himself as a "good" authority figure or parent and creates conditions that maximize the chance of being listened to. He "seeks to neutralize or undercut roadblocks the patient places in the way of his teachings; he points out maladaptive patterns of behavior and their underlying infantile assumptions; he sets an example by remaining calm, unruffled, reasonable and rational; he refuses to get entangled in the patient's neurotic machinations; he conveys the message that the patient must learn to accept *personal responsibility* for his own actions" instead of blaming everybody else for his predicament, etc. He teaches the patient to be less demanding and grandiose, to scale down his expectations and to accept a more active role in managing his life, and he conveys the philosophy of reasonableness, rationality, moderation, mutuality and fairness as the guideposts of a good life. He is a good kindly parent figure in some ways, and given strong motivation to seek change (chiefly suffering) and adequate personality resources, the idea is to win the patient over to these new ways of living.

To put this another and less pleasant way, for Strupp the essence of psychotherapy is manipulation in the transference, a sophisticated technology for persuasion and influence. By taking advantage of the positive transference, we persuade the patient to adopt better ways of living, based on following the "golden rule" in interpersonal relations. Sadder and wiser, he has been influenced to renounce his infantile greed.

The trouble with Strupp's approach is that it mixes too many things together. How important interpretations are and how important lessons in constructive living are depends on the kind of patient we are dealing with. The healthier the patient, the more intense the workable transference that forms, the more the transference is amenable to interpretation, and the more important, obviously, interpretations are going to be. In many borderline patients, schizophrenic patients and patients with character disorders, the utter lack of benign investment in the patient by anybody makes the investment by the therapist—even his not falling asleep—and his attempt to reeducate the patient an extremely important aspect of the treatment.

Strupp does us a service by pointing out that to try to do a formal psychoanalysis on profoundly disturbed patients misses the whole point of where the patient is at the time. The patient who is that sick, who has no solid repression barrier, who cannot form a transference neurosis, is not a patient who is amenable to a formal psychoanalytic treatment. Saying that interpretations with such patients are the main therapeutic influence runs the risk of an attack by such meticulous and careful authors as Strupp. To conclude that interpretation generally or usually is a minimally important matter, however, is a swing to the extreme of gross oversimplification.

A variant of all this is the existential approach to psychotherapy. Here too there is an attempt to directly influence or heal the patient. The method used, as well as the descriptive terminology, however, is different than either the various behavioral therapeutic techniques or what Strupp called "moral suasion." Trying to educate and persuade, as Havens (1974) has pointed out, we find ourselves trying to use "the self." It is very unfortunate that Havens's article is entitled "The Existential Use of Self," because the term "self" has come to mean something entirely different in metapsychology, and this is not the "self" that Havens is talking about. A better phrase would be "the use of the therapist's presence."

Havens takes off from a much more extreme author, R. D. Laing, who is among the pioneers in emphasizing the indispensability of the therapist's human presence as the essential factor in whatever good he may do his patient. The therapist who acts as a detached technician only reinforces his patients's problem by becoming one more in a chain of powerful individuals who have pretended to take an interest in the patient. What is worse is the demand that the patient too must pretend this interest is real, while all the while they both know that the therapist's response is determined by his definition of himself as a psychiatrist, rather than by the feelings his patient as a person arouses in him. Laing feels that faced with this clinical detachment, the patient can only respond to what he cleverly calls "the absence of the therapist's presence or, still more destructively, the presence of the therapist's absence" (Friedenberg 1974). That is very important and is a good starting point to understanding what the existentialists are talking about.

Existential therapists approach the gathering of data in psychology by the "phenomenologic" method. The term *phenomenologic approach* is really a very tricky one, because it is in psychology and philosophy allegedly related to Husserl's (1965) phenomenology. Husserl's phenomenology was an attempt in epistemology to find *absolute certainty in reality*. That is *not* what the psychological phenomenologists are interested in. The classical example of phenomenological psychology is from Jaspers (1963), who wrote an enormous textbook from that point of view entitled *General Psychopathology*. Jaspers was attempting to directly present to us "the mental states which our patients really experience, observing them with respect to their kind and species, carefully delimiting them, and differentiating them by well-defined terms." A better phrase would have been "descriptive psychology"—the equation with Husserl's phenomenology is unjustified (See Chessick 1977a).

Phenomenology from the point of view of psychoanalytic psychology is just a *beginning point* of clinical work, whereas from the point of view of phenomenological psychology (Jaspers), it is the whole of psychological work. Hartmann (1964) points out, "But we must recall that at the outset of our investigation into the scientific status of psychoanalysis we came to the conclusion that no scientific psychology is capable of preserving in its concepts the lived immediacy of its primary material, and that any psychology has to sacrifice to its scientific goal the illusion of that 'deeper penetration' into its subject which belongs to immediate experience. ... In its place we gain definitive systematic knowledge."

As soon as one moves away from recording the phenomenology of the interaction, one sacrifices vivid immediacy, or "being there," as the existentialists like to call it, and finds oneself involved in theoretical concepts and explanations at more or less of a remove from the immediacy of the data.

How far is removal from the immediate data justifiable? Grinker (1975) and his co-workers feel that this removal is permissible only to the point of forming hypotheses about the observations which are essentially laws, descriptions, representations and models. Hartmann and Freud did not think so. They moved even farther from the clinical data in terms of presenting what they considered to be *causal* descriptions, and in trying to do that they introduced aspects of the mental apparatus which they conceived to be of a causal explanatory nature. A simple example of this is the statement that because certain thoughts appear to be either conscious or unconscious, it follows that there is such an apparatus in the mind as a *system* conscious or a *system* unconscious. This is the point at which the question arises whether such concepts represent an overextension of the evidence.

There is no way one can answer this question, because it rests on a metapsychiatric, or philosophy-of-science, or epistemological, premise upon which there is simply no agreement. The attempt to abstract from the data of empathy and introspection certain metapsychological conceptions and the postulation of concepts about the mental apparatus such as changes and shifts of energy, etc., represent an attempt to bring psychology of a psychoanalytic nature as close as possible to Newtonian physics.

The behaviorist psychotherapist rules out all methods of gathering data except the usual "empirical" procedures of measurement. The existential psychotherapist begins from a descriptive psychology or a "phenomenologic psychology" and attempts to preserve the vivid lived immediacy of the data. He becomes engrossed in descriptions, using the language of the humanistic imagination, that try to preserve this lived immediacy, and he approaches psychotherapy by trying to "be there" with the patient in this immediacy.

The point of the existential technique is to *keep looking* and listening in a "phenomenologic" sense, staying right with the material of the patient and taking everything the patient has to say at face value rather than searching for hidden processes. This is by itself therapeutic and is labeled the practice of phenomenological reduction. Appearances are accepted and one tries to stay with where the patient is, for example with how it feels to be paranoid, manic, or simply awake. To see things as the patient sees them and experience them as the patient experiences them is supposed to lead to a breakdown of the doctor's objectivity and authority and to the production of spontaneous reactions which are appropriate to the situation and are highly therapeutic, e.g. losing one's temper with a whining, irascible, repetitious patient.

This is to be thought of, *not* as just opening the door to wild behavior, but as an invitation to free expressiveness, as long as this expressiveness serves being with and staying with the patient. Remaining with the patient, or reaching the patient, becomes very, very important—"swinging into the life of the other," as Buber called it. This avoids the problem of the patient suffering from the presence of the therapist's absence or the absence of the therapist's presence.

The argument of the existentialist is that a distance is opened between the doctor and the patient by the analytic technique of free association, a gap which is unproductively filled by abundant verbal material and abundant analytic ideas, conceptions and theories rather than by an emotional interchange based on staying strictly with the phenomena and the appearances that the patient presents. Phenomenological reduction of the emotional distance between patient and therapist is the crucial procedure, leading to a "true meeting" or encounter.

It is extremely difficult to grasp exactly what the existentialists are talking about, but I think it is well worth having a look at and considering using, especially in those situations where there seems to be a stalemate or a draw in the psychotherapy. I have found it useful in such situations to sit back and to try and feel myself into how the patient is phenomenologically feeling *right then.* Having done that, I go deeper to try to find *why* the patient is feeling that way. This often leads to an explanation that has been missed or even to something in the rest of the patient's real life that has been overlooked.

I think that the existentialist approach of trying to identify or empathize with the superficial conscious feeling state of the patient at the time is useful, but I would greatly question whether one could call this process or the results of it a curative influence on the patient! It is reasonable to alternatively argue that the real proof of the therapist's presence comes when he makes an interpretation. If it is a proper, correctly phrased and correctly timed interpretation, it indicates that the therapist has indeed been listening and doing his work of empathy and introspection and then correctly communicating what he has learned back to the patient. A proper interpretation at the proper time in the proper way often is responded to with a feeling on the part of the patient of the very strong presence of the therapist.

Carrying this discussion to a more difficult level, we may begin with Strupp's concept that the therapeutic process rests on the development of trust in the therapist's integrity. In fact the whole procedure of psychotherapy is contingent on the development of this trust. According to Strupp, psychotherapy can be viewed as a *technology* eliminating the barriers against openness, honesty and trust. If psychotherapy is a lesson in the development of basic trust that unfortunately has not developed in a patient because of faulty mother-child symbiosis, the question is *What else is there?* How far can we go?

In psychotherapy what happens next is an integration, a greater sense of identity and cohesiveness of the self, and this is marked by generativity, as Erikson would call it—an interest in establishing and guiding the next generation, progress in the ability to love and work, a greater expansiveness in generosity, probably a greater optimism, altruism and creativity—the "transformations of narcissism" that Kohut (1971) describes. We contrast this to despair, in which the untreated individual is always feeling his life time is too short and feels disgust, misanthropy, contemptuous displeasure and so forth.

This is obviously far more complex an intrapsychic change than any simplistic conceptions of behavior modification would permit. By just looking at the goals of therapy one can see the enormous difference between behavior-modification techniques and psychotherapeutic techniques. The therapist in many ways launches the patient on a different course of life, and he has to inculcate some of his own values. He fosters self-examination and self-knowledge and honesty, and he fully participates in the patient's personality and personal development.

To what extent is the psychotherapy simply an identification with the wisdom and insight of the therapist as a model, and to what extent are there limitations on what the therapy can do by such modeling? I feel that there is in human life a forward force, and that this is built into the human organism. We are limited because all we can do as therapists is to repair and enhance ego function in the patient by freeing the ego from internal conflicts and providing an atmosphere in which this forward developmental force can take over (Chessick 1974b).

This takes psychotherapy away from the realm of education, suggestion and manipulation and places it back primarily into the realm of evoking the patient's constructive potentials. Psychotherapy then emerges as a practice based on the assumption that many patients have the inner motivating force to get well and heal if given the opportunity to do so and even to go forward beyond that and reach phisolosophical faith and transcendence—which is beyond what a therapist can do for a patient. If I am correct, then any idea of psychotherapy as primarily a modeling or educational process in which somehow the therapist influences and makes the patient do something is a severely restricted idea, because there is a profound unpredictability about the outcome of psychotherapy.

In the stages of life there are phases that begin with a hedonistic or pleasure-principle orientation and then move to an ethical or reality type of orientation. This is normally followed by the development of a sense of identity and a sense of self, self-authentication and self-esteem or inner sustainment, depending upon which author's phrases you wish to employ. As we move along in psychotherapy, taking the patient through these developmental phases, the creative or generative capacities of the ego take over the treatment, the therapist drops into the background, and the patient takes over. As this happens, the therapist can no longer determine the course to be taken. Thus, it is not possible to predict or to mold a genuine movement to specific individual self-authentication. It is the built-in unfolding-forward pattern in people which is their most important healing force and also drives them on an unpredictable course. The therapist clears away the obstacles that are present in the patient at the level of developing basic trust and moving from the pleasure principle to the reality principle, but if he has done his work he should be able to observe the taking over of the creative or generative forces that are built into the patient and carry the patient forward into the search for self-authentication. The therapist is not able to predict in any mechanistic or deterministic or stimulus-response manner what form the self-authentication will take. In a way the therapist can only withdraw and wonder at this point and watch the unfolding of the patient's personality.

Furthermore, we are really unable to predict how far the patient will continue to unfold. I suggest that the search for transcendence (Chessick 1974b, Chapter 15) is an even further step in this unfolding, but this is speculative and I cannot prove it. It is fascinating to watch this unfolding as it takes hold in our patients. We often do not get a chance to see how far it will go, because as the generative and forward force takes over, the patient really needs us less and less and usually leaves us *before* the complete course of the therapy is finished. I am firmly convinced that an enormous amount of very important therapeutic change takes place after the termination of psychotherapy, change in which the forward force simply carries forward the development through an internal generation. There is remarkably little research on this subject.

The crucial difference between psychoanalytically informed psychotherapy and other forms of psychotherapy is that the former does not *directly* attempt to cure, heal or influence the patient. It works indirectly, although it recognizes that direct influences are also at work. The degree of importance of the direct influences, whether they be induced by therapist-presence, or education, or what have you, is related to the state of the patient's ego. The poorer the ego function or the more fragmented the self of the patient, the more direct pacification, unification and optimal disillusion is necessary. As the self coheres and the ego gets stronger, a shift takes place in the psychotherapy, allowing the patient to take over and allowing the patient's ego to pick up the psychotherapy and move forward. This is the crucial difference between other forms of psychotherapy and psychoanalytically informed psychotherapy, in my opinion.

Now, how do we do this? We use a special mode of observation of which introspection and empathy are essential constituents (Kohut 1959). The limits of introspection and empathy are the limits of psychoanalytically informed psychotherapy. This is our data gathering, and "this observational method defines the contents and the limits of the observed field." It is not the way we try to cure anybody.

As the patient's sense of self coheres and his identity becomes solid and his ego function improves, we shift away from direct influencing by pacification, unification, education or optimal disillusion (Gedo and Goldberg 1973), and we begin to listen more and more with free-floating attention. We use empathy. We try to understand what is going on inside the head of the patient and use introspective self-observation as we resonate with the patient's unconscious.

In the very sick patient—the schizophrenic or the borderline patient—the problem is different, because the therapist is experienced as actually being the whole object which has caused the trouble, and the patient is somehow attempting to simultaneously separate, cling and protect himself from intrusion. As Kohut (1959) puts it, "In the analysis of the psychoses and borderline states, archaic interpersonal conflicts occupy a central position of strategic importance that corresponds to the place of structural conflicts in the psychoneuroses." In these situations the real relationship, the so-called therapeutic alliance, is extremely important, and the benign therapist's attitude or his presence (if you insist on approaching it that way) has a major direct influence on allowing the fragmented ego of the patient to cohere and to develop a sense of self, which is then followed by improved ego function in many areas even without the benefits of interpretation.

Now if that is as far as we want to go with a patient, fine, but we may wish to try to go farther. If we do, then we begin to shift over into a stance that enables us to reflect back to the patient what we have learned about him from empathy and introspection. If the patient now has a sufficiently coherent sense of self and ego strength to hear us, this is followed by increased strength in the ego, until gradually the internal generative force of the patient takes over more and more, which is what we are after.

There is a long-standing feud between those who think that there is no difference between psychoanalysis and psychotherapy on the one hand, and those who think there is only one genuine psychotherapy—psychoanalysis—on the other. There is no way to resolve this issue because it is so overloaded with status considerations, etc., but there *are* certain basic clinical and practical differences that we should be aware of. The most obvious difference between classical psychoanalysis and psychotherapy stems from the development of a workable transference neurosis in psychoanalysis. If a workable transference neurosis develops and the focus of the therapy is the analysis of this transference neurosis, then you have by definition a formal psychoanalysis. Only a limited number of patients are in a sufficient state psychologically, economically and sociologically to allow this to happen.

Ticho (1970) mentions certain indicators of dangerous transference difficulties, for example intense early transference fantasies where the patient cannot completely distinguish between the treatment reality and the fantasy. Beware of a lack of containment of the regression to the therapy hours, with the transference behavior spilling over into the outside world, and of the early appearance of intense oral demands and masochistic wishes. Any therapist who attempts to do formal psychoanalysis with patients while these things develop is taking a terrible risk, requiring much special skill and experience; switching to a less frequent face-to-face psychotherapy is the obvious practical solution.

A variety of techniques for reducing the intensity of the psychotic or unworkable transference are described in DeWald's (1964) book on psychotherapy. Most important is that the therapist must realize what is happening before it gets out of hand. I take an essentially psychoanalytic stance with many patients at the beginning to see how things develop. For the minority of patients who show the potential to develop a substantial transference neurosis and who have the social and economic capacities to undergo a formal psychoanalysis, that is certainly the treatment of choice. Most patients do not have this capacity, at least in the ordinary private practice of psychotherapy, and thus most patients are seen once or in my opinion preferably twice a week. Even this often is more than many patients can afford.

Another important difference is in the analyst's "neutrality" compared to the psychotherapist's. This is a much more controversial issue. There is no doubt that the psychotherapist is a more real figure to the patient, a reality usually facilitated by the face-to-face relationship. In fact, one can easily argue, as I have already done, that the psychotherapist's real interest in the patient and efforts at reeducation are tremendously important to the patient—far more important in many phases of therapy than interpretations. There is no agreement as to whether this is true of psychoanalysis or not, but in general the psychoanalyst makes an effort to avoid being a real object to the patient. Whether that is really possible or not over frequent sessions and long periods of time is a matter of great debate.

Finally, Ticho (1970) explains that the interventions in psychoanalysis are almost exclusively insight-producing, such as interpretation, confrontation and clarification, whereas in psychotherapy, interventions are also supportive or noninsight producing, such as suggestion, advice, reassurance, persuasion, setting examples, proving points, giving recommendations and giving prohibitions—all of which also imply a much greater personal involvement on the part of the therapist. The danger of this increased personal involvement is an increased expectation of immediate improvement.

It follows that the danger of uncontrolled countertransference is much greater in psychotherapy than in psychoanalysis. This is a very difficult concept and is more of a theoretical difference or one of degree in many instances than a real and substantial one. The psychoanalyst often attempts deliberately to keep his interpretations as free of direct educational influence as he can, but it is really impossible to do this in a total way, especially when the patient is coming four or five times a week, whereas the psychotherapist feels much more free to assert direct educational pressures, because many patients simply need that. The techniques of pacification, unification and optimal disillusion (Gedo and Goldberg 1973) are essentially educational techniques which the psychotherapy patient must have to develop a coherent sense of self.

The picture of a novice psychotherapist trying to model himself on the neutral psychoanalyst, sitting with a schizophrenic patient or with a schizoid or borderline patient in silence trying to listen to free associations and make interpretations with such patients at a deep unconscious level, represents a complete misunderstanding of psychotherapy. In teaching residents I have tried to compare this to a situation in which two people are sitting in a burning house. The obvious thing to do is to get out of the house and then put the fire out. If instead the two people simply sit around the table and discuss the chemical nature of the process of fire, in my opinion somebody is going to get hurt badly. It may seem strange that I belabor this subject, but it is a fact that in many training programs today the model of the neutral psychoanalyst is still used as the ideal model in *psychotherapy*.

CHAPTER 25

Philosophy of Science

What are the philosophical foundations of psychotherapy? In a field in which there is so much disagreement, it is absolutely necessary to review the fundamental premises behind various forms of therapeutic endeavors, for whether we like it or not we are forced in the practice of psychotherapy to make certain philosophical assumptions and conceptions and even forced to make philosophical choices.

The field examining the highest or first principles that underlie or form the "ground" of all scientific investigation and all thinking is classical metaphysics, usually containing epistemology—*how* we get our knowledge—and ontology—the search for Being, or the *ground* of all knowledge.

Assumptions about epistemology and ontology are at the basis of all scientific endeavor, and since these assumptions differ from individual to individual, they greatly influence the kind of thinking and scientific work that takes place. From the point of view of the psychotherapist, the most important aspects of classical metaphysics are the assumptions behind scientific work and thought, an area which is usually known as philosophy of science. We might characterize these assumptions as second order principles, because philosophy of science is based in turn on certain first assumptions from metaphysics, ontology and epistemology.

Getting more specific, from the point of view of the psychotherapist we have also a third order of principles, which I call metapsychiatry (Chessick 1974b, 1977). Metapsychiatry, to be discussed in more detail later, simply represents those aspects of the philosophy of science that are specifically important to psychotherapy.

From philosophy of science and me apsychiatry there is then a jump to scientific research in areas such as physiology, brain study, psychology and—if one is willing to accept them—the research methods of psychoanalytic psychology, utilizing data gathered by empathy and introspection. At the very bottom of the theoretical ladder, but closest to the actual empirical material, we have the clinical application of these various orders of principles and of basic research—the disciplines of clinical neurology, clinical psychology, clinical psychiatry and psychotherapy.

The task of philosophy differs from that of science, for unlike science, philosophy examines not our conclusions but the basic conceptual models we employ—the kind of concepts and ordering patterns that we use. Philosophy concerns not the explanation of this or that but questions such as "What really is an explanation?" or "What really is change? or "What really is a cure?"

For example, Is something explained when it is divided into parts and if we can tell how the parts behave? This is but one type of explanation. It works fairly well for a car, although it does not tell us what makes it run, and less well for a biological cell, the "parts" of which are not alive; certainly it does not explain life, and it works very poorly to explain personality—what are the parts of a person? Or, choosing another of the many types of explanations, has something been explained when we feel that we "understand" it because we have been shown how it fits into some larger context or broader organization?

These questions, which are essentially philosophical questions, are not designed to determine the explanation of this or that, but to discover what an explanation is. Yet as we have seen, there are many different kinds of explanations. In any one case, what shall we use? Or should we try to use them all, and, if so, when and to what advantages and pitfalls? How is our choice among these varied explanations to be made? Should it depend on the feeling with which we work, on what we want an explanation for, or on the style of the times?

When we ask questions of this sort we seem to be talking about nothing in particular—such philosophic issues at first seem to be empty. Yet they very basically affect whatever we study, for depending upon which mode of approach we use, different questions and hypotheses will be formulated, different experiments set up, different illustrations cited, different arguments held to be sound, and different conclusions reached! *Much in our conclusions about anything comes not from the study of the things, but from the philosophical decisions—the prior philosophical decisions—implicit in the way we start!*

The whole matter is even incredibly more confused because a number of generally held classical assumptions about scientific method and science are clearly by this time known to be wrong. For example, there are inductive and deductive theories, but these are not the same as inductive and deductive inferences. A deductive theory is not solely the product of deductive inference and inductive theory is not solely the product of inductive inference. Bacon's classical notion that the method of inductive inference leads to the generalizations of the inductive sciences is simply not correct!

Let us turn to classifying the various possible kinds of scientific theories and see where the theories of psychotherapy fit appropriately into the classification and where they have been incorrectly placed in the past. What are various kinds of theories that scientists work with? First come the well-known deductive theories (which do not proceed only by deduction) in mathematics and logic. We will not go into technical details about mathematics and logic because we are obviously not dealing with that kind of a science when we talk about psychotherapy.

Clearly theories of psychotherapy based on clinical empirical material belong under the rubric of inductive theories. The inductive theories can be further subdivided (Basch 1973) into *classificatory* and *explanatory* theories. The classificatory theories are formed by abstractions from observations. These are the natural sciences in which, for example, one looks at all the birds one can find and tries to make classificatory abstractions to divide them into groups, species, etc. This activity forms a very important aspect of the natural sciences. We assume that classificatory inductive theories are based on empirical data and that the empirical work was done by a trained observer who knows what methods to use and how to examine the various materials. Then the trained observer has to make abstractions from those observations.

More complicated are the so-called explanatory inductive theories. These theories generate *hypotheses* about the observations, not simply abstractions from the observations. Basically, two kinds of hypotheses are made. First of all come laws or descriptions: *How* do things take place and along what general laws or principles do they occur? The second kind of hypothesis might be said to consist of the causal types of inductive explanatory theories: *Why* do things take place? Answers to the latter questions imply that something causes something else.

If we look at the various forms of psychotherapy we find a good deal of confusion about which kind of theory the author is using. For example, take the trained observer in psychoanalysis or psychoanalytic research. His method of observation, empathy and introspection, is his stethoscope, his microscope, his telescope. If he is properly free of his own problems, then he is able to listen with free-floating attention, as Freud describes it, to the free associations of the patient. Through the method of empathy he is then able to identify temporarily with what is going on in the patient's mind, and by introspection into his own mind he is able to come up with information about the patient. This is considered to be an empirical science *providing* empathy and introspection are acceptable as a method of observation. If they are not, then psychotherapy must be dealt with strictly in terms of behavior descriptions. Introspection and empathy are essential constitutents of psychoanalytic fact-finding, and this observational method defines the contents and the limits of the observable field.

Grinker (1975), Basch (1973, 1975) and other authors claim that among the inductive explanatory theories the *how* type of theory (laws or descriptions) is *all* that is really necessary. These authors emphasize transactions, and they use the language of general systems theory to describe the transactions or interactions that go on between the patient and the therapist; psychotherapy is conceived in terms of error-correcting feedback systems. For example, much of psychotherapy for these authors has to do with self-esteem problems and with situations in which a patient pushes away someone whose esteem he wants over and over again. The therapist asks, "What is the patient looking for? What is the patient doing to me? What kind of messages is he sending?" Then he confronts the patient with the here-and-now in the transference, and in so doing he breaks up a system which has led to great trouble for the patient.

It is *not* necessary in this approach to postulate concepts like psychic energy or the mental apparatus (ego, id and superego). The implication of this metapsychiatric or philosophy-of-science premise is that the experienced relationship between the therapist and the patient is the crucial aspect of the treatment in *psychotherapy*. We do not interest ourselves as much, from this point of view, with interpretations of the infantile roots of the transference. The transference is there as a given and is utilized in getting the patient to listen to our error-correcting feedback. In this view, formal psychoanalysis and psychotherapy are fundamentally different.

Toulmin (1960) proposes asking for any science, "What are the methods of representation? What are the models employed in doing so?" He proposes that we look for the *form* of given regularities and do not ask what is the *purpose* of these regularities. According to Toulmin, science tells *how* things happen, not *why* they happen. It consists of descriptive methods of representation. The most interesting corollary to this, Toulmin points out, is that when two scientists do not agree on *what* is to be explained, there is no hope for their agreement on a description. Again, if the epistemological premises with which two scientists approach the data are not the same, it is impossible for them to agree. They will come up with entirely different methods of representation which seem to conflict with each other, although actually they are different because they start from different premises. They may indeed be complementary, and no one set of premises in the philosophy of science can be said to be the only truth.

One has to remember that at the time Freud was writing, the prevailing scientific attitude was quite different. Newtonian dynamics were considered to be *the* answer. It was felt that the scientific method in terms of cause and effect, with laws as described by Newton and others, had a tremendous success and was *the* method. General systems theories and other alternative paradigms did not exist, and it was of the utmost importance to Freud, who was founding what he hoped was to be a new science—which unfortunately psychoanalysts tend to refer to as "our science"—that methods of representation be employed which sounded as scientific as possible and as closely related to the concepts of Newtonian physics as possible. Such terms as "energy" became very very important, and if one looks at Freud's (1895) early unpublished work, *Project for a Scientific Psychology,* one sees a kind of transition between Newtonian science and psychoanalysis in which every effort is made to describe the data in as physicalistic-sounding terminology as possible. These efforts did not succeed, because the data obtained by empathy and introspection cannot be forced into the mold of Newtonian physics.

Freud soon gave up this approach, but his basic bias, the basic epistemologic or metapsychiatric premise that "science" implies classical mechanics, remains and is only recently being challenged. Today it is mainly the behaviorists who are trying to adhere to as close to a model of Newtonian science as is possible. And it *is* possible to do this if one throws out all data obtained through empathy and introspection and concentrates strictly on precise observable phenomena of behavior.

Psychologists can further be divided into (a) those who attempt to find descriptions or laws that describe the transactions between the therapist and the patient in terms of the here-now relationship and the meaning the therapist has to the patient and the patient has to the therapist, and (b) those who make a further step—a generalization or removal from the evidence that is even farther away from the lived immediacy—and postulate metapsychological conceptions such as the mental apparatus, energy, instincts, genetic-dynamic formulations, etc., which they believe provide a causal explanation of what has happened.

These differences in basic epistemological premises explain why it is when you get a group of psychotherapists together and present them with the same phenomena, you can't get agreement, for there is no agreement on what the phenomena are that are supposed to be explained or even on what an explanation is in science or in psychotherapy! The way out of this predicament as I see it is to use the principle of complementarity. It is not necessary that any one epistemological approach be the only right approach. It *is* clear that if we have explanatory concepts of various abstract orders we *will* move away from the vivid immediacy of the data.

Bohr's great principle of complementarity was developed in the discipline of physics in order to meet a similar apparent paradox. What Bohr (1934) was pointing to when he introduced his principle of complementarity was the curious realization that in the atomic-particle domain the only way the observer (including his equipment) can be uninvolved as if he observed nothing at all. As soon as he sets up the observation tools on his workbench, the system he has chosen to put under observation and his measuring instruments for doing the job and the observer himself form one inseparable whole. Therefore, the results depend heavily on the observer and his apparatus.

Bohr was able to show that on the level of atomic particles any apparatus designed to measure position with ideal precision cannot provide any information about momentum and vice versa. Thus two mutually exclusive experiments are usually needed to obtain full information about the mechanical state, each complementing the other. He expressed this conclusion as a general principle of complementarity, and in developing this principle he asserted that it is neither possible nor necessary to make a choice between waves and particles, as indeed both are essential for complete comprehension of reality.

The uncertainty principle of Heisenberg has sometimes been misconstrued to mean a particle actually *has* both a precise position and momentum until it is disturbed by the experimenter and that the act of observing the position precisely destroys the precise momentum. In other words it is assumed that nature is involved in a bizarre conspiracy to prevent the discovery of something that has a real existence. It is nearer to the truth to assert that a particle in itself has *neither* a position nor a momentum and that the act of observation *creates* its mechanical state.

Bohr's point of view was criticized because it seemed to treat particles and waves as equal whereas particles are a mode of *existence* while waves are a mode of *behavior*. But the choice is a matter of the temperament and taste of the observer! The apparent paradox between describing psychotherapeutic interaction in terms of existential psychiatry or in terms of interpersonal psychodynamics presents an identical dilemma to a participant observer. Thus, some choose to characterize the interaction as an investigation of and an intrusion into the patient's mode of existence, whereas others are more comfortable using Freud's psychodynamics. The point is that both are essential for a complete comprehension of reality and it is not a matter of one descriptive language being right and one descriptive language being wrong.

Bohr hoped that the principle of complementarity would come to be applied to many other areas of knowledge beside atomic physics. As explained, for example, by Holton (1973), Bohr's real ambition for the complementarity conception went far beyond dealing with the paradox of physics in the 1920s: "From this point of view we realize that Bohr's proposal of a complementarity principle was nothing less than an attempt to make it the cornerstone of a new epistemology. . . . It was the universal significance of the role of complementarity which Bohr came to emphasize."

In place of a precisely defined conceptual model, the principle of complementarity states that we are restricted to complementary pairs of inherently imprecisely defined concepts, and the maximum degree of precision of either member of such a pair is reciprocally related to that of the opposite member. The specific experimental conditions, then, determine how precisely each member of a complementary pair of concepts should be defined in any given case. But no single overall concept is ever possible which represents precisely all significant aspects of the behavior of an individual, for example. The principle of complementarity renounces the notion of the neat and precisely defined conceptual models in favor of that of complementary pairs of imprecisely defined models and represents an absolute and final limitation of our investigation and understanding of every domain of knowledge.

Only those who have attended international psychotherapy congresses can be aware of the intensity of the debate in the western world today between the proponents of the Freudian deterministic metapsychology and the proponents of the existentialist and phenomenological approaches to psychotherapy. To see these as complementary descriptions that are related to whatever critical nuclear aspects of the psychotherapist's mind being employed on the data at the time is a way out of the dilemma. The two maps of the reality of psychotherapeutic interaction and the two descriptions of what is going on are not fundamentally opposed—they may be used successfully to complement each other providing the therapist is carefully aware of when he is using each complementary map.

Furthermore, as is the case with physical experiments, the kind of approach, attitude and personality that the observor or psychotherapist brings into the psychotherapeutic interaction will determine the kind of descriptions or language that he uses to describe the process and results of psychotherapeutic interaction. Thus, for example, Freud, who was extremely concerned to make psychoanalysis scientific, describes all psychotherapeutic interaction in strict, classical scientific terminology; Buber, who bordered on the existential mystique, uses an entirely different language in describing the same kind of confrontation that takes place in a meaningful or therapeutic interaction.

This notion of complementarity also explains why there is actually not a great deal of difference between the practical technique of psychotherapy employed by the analytically oriented psychotherapists and that employed by the existential psychotherapists; the enormous differences appear far more in the language employed in describing the phenomena than in the techniques used. Perhaps the only way to characterize this is by describing the analagous study of a neon sign. An expert physicist from another planet could probably describe in great detail the electronic working of the sign, but he could never explain why people were throwing rocks at the sign unless he knew the language of the insulting message the sign was sending out. Similarly, in psychotherapeutic interaction we can experience the rigid determination of the repetition compulsion and use it in understanding our patient's behavior in one way, or we can experience the patient's freedom for existential choices and leaps into life styles if we approach the psychotherapeutic interaction from an entirely different standpoint.

In his famous essay *The Structure of Scientific Revolutions,* Kuhn (1972) has described this shifting back and forth between paradigms as a "Gestalt switch", and what I am recommending for the psychotherapist is clearly a similar capacity to switch back and forth in the interest of complete understanding of the patient. I have been surprised by the resistance to this recommendation, which usually springs from a naive or inadequate understanding of the philosophy of science or, more ominously, from an almost religious fervor for one or the other paradigm. As Kuhn explains, "Philosophers of science have repeatedly demonstrated that more than one theoretical construction can always be placed upon a given collection of data. History of science indicates that, particularly in the early developmental stages of a new paradigm, it is not even very difficult to invent such alternates. But that invention of alternates is just what scientists seldom undertake except during the pre-paradigm stage of their science's development and at very special occasions during its subsequent evolution. . . . The reason is clear. As in manufacture so in science—retooling is an extravagance to be reserved for the occasion that demands it."

The difficulty of resistance to other paradigms is apparent. In fact, ". . . the proponents of competing paradigms practice their trades in different worlds. . . . Practicing in different worlds, the two groups of scientists see different things when they look from the same point in the same direction. . . . That is why a law that cannot even be demonstrated to one group of scientists may occasionally seem intuitively obvious to another. Equally, it is why, before they can hope to communicate fully, one group or the other must experience the conversion that we have been calling a paradigm shift. Just because it is a transition between incommensurables, the transition between competing paradigms cannot be made a step at a time, forced by logic and neutral experience. Like the Gestalt switch, it must occur all at once (although not necessarily in an instant) or not at all."

The principle of complementarity leads us into an overall consideration of basic unresolved problems and limitations in our general seeking after knowledge. The particular work of Aristotle that was inserted by some unknown commentator after his treatise on physics deals with these problems, or "first principles" as he called them, and has come to be known as "metaphysics", which means literally "after physics." The basic problems dealt with by metaphysics are of two sorts. (1) How do we know anything?—the discipline of epistemology, and (2) What is there to know?—the discipline of ontology, or study of Being or Reality. A moment's reflection will convince you that our convictions about "What is there to know?" depend on our theory of "How do we know anything?"

For example, the continental rationalists in the seventeenth century—Descartes, Spinoza, Leibniz—attempted to arrive at knowledge from reasoning or from the mind alone, and they subsequently developed an essentially theological point of view about what there is to know where God played a vital role. On the other hand, the British empiricists in the seventeenth and eighteenth centuries— Locke, Berkeley, Hume—believed the arrival of knowledge comes from sense experience alone and our mind is a *tabula rasa* on which all knowledge is brought in from the outside. This viewpoint leads to scepticism about whether there is anything that we can know at all and to a more or less deterministic and behavioristic approach to psychology.

The existentialists of today present a somewhat modified version of the continental rationalist philosophy; they attempt to gain knowledge about Reality or Being by a study of our kind of Being, that is the Being of man as thrown into the world. For example, Heidegger claims that the inner voice of Being can be heard in solitude if we are authentic and do not live a life of essentially falling away from Being. Sartre argues that crucial ethical actions and choices represent the essence or Being of man. Husserl grounds Being in the phenomenology of the consciousness, and Jaspers maintains that certain "boundary situations" reveal man to be free to make crucial choices. These are examples of what Jaspers calls "ciphers," which offer a chance for man to get in touch with Being.

It still seems that the best starting point is Kant's combination of (a) the sensory manifold with (b) space and time added by the synthesis of the imagination and finally (c) the activity of the synthesis of the understanding in producing the awareness of objects of physics. Phenomena and noumena as described by Kant mark the boundaries of the knowable and the unknowable. At the same time we must constantly recognize the human tendency to try to transgress this boundary. This human tendency could be defined as the discipline of metaphysics, which, according to Kant's philosophy, cannot ever actually succeed in this endeavor.

Thus, human reason is ineradicably metaphysical. It is haunted by questions which, though springing from its very nature, nevertheless transcend its powers. We might call this viewpoint a form of metaphysical agnosticism.

I began this section by showing how certain apparent paradoxes arising from the clinical practice of psychotherapy of borderline patients could not be resolved without appeal to a "higher" level of theoretical discourse, namely, the philosophy of science. Thus toward a general principle, we may state that problems apparently insoluble and paradoxical at level L_0 may be resolved at level L_1; the level L_x refers to the language employed, which always includes all the language parts of the previous level (L_{x-1}) and also introduces more abstract and "meta+" language concepts.

Thus any language level L_x is a metalanguage for L_{x-1} and so forth. Generalizing, we may say that problems insoluble at level L_n should be appealed to level L_{n+1} in order to make them soluble. In fact we may have to *invent* a special language L_{n+1} in order to do so. This commonly occurs; the most famous example is modern "metamathematics."

However, as one ascends from L_n to L_{n+1}, one gets farther and farther removed from the immediate empirical and clinical data and closer to inborn expectations, intuitive grasps and other such methodologies to establish principles, and so proof by empirical methods becomes increasingly impossible. Here again, the principle of complementarity is at work. The price we pay for resolving problems by using ascending levels of abstract discourse is to reduce the empirical certainty of our solutions!

For example, let us return to my argument (Chessick 1971) that science and art are separate by their very nature and cannot be thought of as "coming together" as our knowledge increases. Meyer (1974) gives further detailed evidence for this view and then concludes: "Stern and Snow are "on the side of the angels" in that both want to bring the various kinds of human activities and pursuits together. So do we all. But mistaken analogies, however commendable the motive behind their advocacy, will not unite disparate disciplines or join non-comparable ways of knowing. Like crossing a horse with an ass, they will only beget mulish recalcitrance and sterile dispute. One way of comprehending all knowledge is through meta-disciplines such as history and philosophy. The difficulty with these modes of integration, at least for me, is that the more encompassing they are, the more obscure and vaporous they become. Instead of the clarity and concreteness of scrupulous observation and the precision of rigorous argument, we are given elusive 'spirits' and untestable speculations clothed in abstruse language."

CHAPTER 26

Metapsychiatry and Beyond

The concepts of science and of being a scientist have all kinds of cultural overtones. Suppose one therapist says that another's approach is "not scientific"; that phrase has come to have a derogatory or pejorative meaning, and therefore, each investigator tends to insist that his method is *the* scientific one. This has other overtones in terms of prestige, getting money for research, etc., but it is very destructive to the field of psychotherapy.

Psychotherapy in general is much more complicated than classical Freudian psychoanalysis. If one stays strictly with the writings of Freud, and perhaps some of the extensions by Hartmann of Freud, psychoanalysis is a very specific clear-cut method, a subdivision of psychotherapy. If one agrees with the premises and the metapsychological conceptions and is well trained, one knows exactly what one is supposed to be doing. Psychotherapy, on the other hand, is far vaguer, and many more vital factors are recognized to be at work. This permits a far greater amount of argument and disagreement. With psychoanalysis, one either accepts the premises or rejects them, and that determines what follows. With psychotherapy there are so many factors involved, so many different kinds of patients involved, that the situation is much more complicated.

Psychoanalysis tends to get into trouble when it attempts to use its methods on patients for which it was not intended. Let us not forget that Freud conceived of psychoanalysis as a method of treatment for certain specific types of neurotics, and as far as I can see from the literature, the only theoretically legitimate extension of formal psychoanalysis from the treatment of the transference neuroses has been Kohut's (1971) effort to establish the psychoanalysis of narcissistic personality disorders as he defines them. Even in making this effort, Kohut had to make a major modification in psychoanalytic metapsychology.

Those who would attempt to use a classical psychoanalysis on disorders such as the borderline state or overt schizophrenia run the risk of introducing a tremendous confusion into the meanings of the terms in the field, or contrary-wise they will have to make a complete revision of psychoanalytic principles. The closest to the latter, of course, is in the work of Melanie Klein and her followers. It is only after one has completely revised Freud's psychoanalytic theory that there is some theoretical justification (whether it is right or not is a different discussion) for approaching borderline patients or patients with overt schizophrenia by classical psychoanalysis.

In evaluating presentations of psychotherapy from various schools, it is now absolutely mandatory for the reader to keep in mind the basic epistemological premises of each school. If they differ from his, he must try to evaluate the presentation in terms of the implicit premises and not expect that the presentation will follow the lines of his own epistemological premises. Irreducible philosophical differences rather than "right or wrong" or "scientific or unscientific" are at the basis of the acrimony and controversy that contaminate the field of psycho-therapy.

Because of this, we cannot avoid the subject of metapsychiatry, whether we like it or not. Only a theoretical understanding of psychotherapy promises to help disengage us from some of the unnecessary and acrimonious controversy in our field. The founder of the subject was Freud, who defined metapsychology as the study of the assumptions on which the system of psychoanalytic theory is based. This is an unfinished study.

Although in a jocular vein Freud spoke of metapsychology as the "witch" of psychoanalysis, he was insistent about the need for it as a stable theoretical foundation for his empirical findings. Waelder (1960) defined metapsychology as that level of abstract concepts which lies between inductively constructed clinical theory and the philosophical assumptions upon which the entire science is based. The crucial scientific test of clinical theory is that of truth or validity; for metapsychology, it is that of usefulness and internal consistency. New empirical finds that do not fit into existing metapsychology should lead to its revision. Such changes should be made, however, so as not to disturb the internal consistency of the whole system. The entire set of theories must not be treated as a rigid and fixed system; on the other hand, it is equally sterile for a science to regard its theories in an offhand or amorphous manner.

A more general epistemological question regarding the relationship of metapsychology to reality and to scientific method has been repeatedly raised, sometimes seriously and sometimes in a pejorative manner. This kind of study I have defined as the subject of metapsychiatry in previous publications (Chessick 1969, 1974b). We ask the following questions in this discipline: (1) What is the position of psychotherapy in the western philosophical tradition? (2) To what extent can psychotherapy be said to be a science and to yield scientific knowledge? (3) To what extent is psychotherapy a philosophy or an art? Thus we might ask, "Do generalizations based on the clinical data of psychotherapy represent scientific knowledge? Where do such propositions stand with respect to knowledge by intuition, knowledge by philosophy, or knowledge obtained through the method of science?" The three kinds of propositions are often mixed together as "knowledge." *All* propositions are matters of opinion regarding truth or reality, and there are *no* absolutely true propositions that are not at the same time tautological.

Through a rigorous use of scientific method we approach certainty with the greatest probability. However, many areas of study simply do not lend themselves to scientific experimentation in the rigid sense but must depend on the common accumulated historical experience of mankind; for example, "Slavery is always undesirable," or "Participatory democracy is the most advanced form of government." I call such propositions philosophical, and they are arrived at by the method of philosophy and suffer from a lesser certainty. Propositions with the least certainty, such as insights or religious intuitions, are arrived at by the method of intuition. These are sometimes believed but never testable.

Generalizations from the clinical data of psychotherapy are on the borderline between philosophical knowledge and scientific knowledge because, although some experimental manipulation is possible in restricted situations, no crucial experiments can be devised that could lead to the definitive acceptance or rejection of a system of generalizations from the clinical data of psychotherapy.

An outstanding example of metapsychiatry is provided by Kohut (1971). How does one decide whether a specific form of psychotherapy is primarily scientific or primarily inspirational? He suggests asking three important questions: (1) Do we have a systematical theoretical grasp of the processes involved in therapy? (2) Can the treatment method be communicated to others, learned and practiced without the presence of its originator? (3) Does the treatment method remain successful after the death of its creator? This latter question frequently separates out therapies that primarily depend on the charisma of their originators.

One of the most important areas of metapsychiatry to have generated much controversy and needless acrimony lies in the understanding of what goes on in psychotherapy between the patient and the therapist, often labeled psychotherapeutic interaction. The basic trend in intensive psychotherapy since the time of Freud has been to increasingly emphasize and understand the therapeutic aspects of the relationship between the psychotherapist and the patient, and we know that in the psychotherapy of the borderline patient the psychic field and the deep inner attitude (Nacht 1963) of the psychotherapist are absolutely crucial. We know that the psychotherapist must have inborn talent, close supervision and thorough knowledge of psychodynamics and therapeutic technique. Furthermore, it is clear that an optimal psychic field must be presented to the patient by the psychotherapist.

The traditional models of intensive psychotherapy have often been based on the chess model first suggested by Freud (1913). It is common knowledge that the opening and ending rules in a chess game can be exhaustively analyzed but the middle game moves offer innumerable creative possibilities; only general guidelines can be taught, followed by careful analysis of the games of master players. In chess each player influences the other continuously. Thus the same player plays differently against different opponents, even though he may have a persistent style of his own.

In a previous paper (Chessick 1971b) in which the parallel between learning difficulties in chess and learning problems in psychotherapy has been presented, I have emphasized the parallel between "chess blindness" and the inherent difficulties in "seeing" what the patient is trying to communicate in the myriad of material. I have in a book (Chessick 1971c) presented a special theory of psychotherapeutic interaction which attempts to minimize this loss of understanding by better focus on and improved descriptions of the mutual interaction between patient and therapist. Let me review this briefly.

Just as the special theory of relativity holds only for certain special situations (observers in uniform relative motion), I use the phrase "special theory" (maintaining the analogy to physics) because my theory also holds only for certain special situations—individual psychotherapy using the definitions, settings and techniques generally accepted as constituting psychoanalytically oriented psychotherapy (1969, 1974b).

A second analogy to the special theory of relativity is that my theory can be reduced to Freudian psychodynamics for everyday practical use if certain limitations are observed (similarly the special theory of relativity can be reduced to Newtonian physics for practical terrestial use).

Whitaker and Malone (1953) developed a preliminary concept to the special theory of psychotherapeutic interaction which they labeled "symbolic synchronization and complimentary articulation." It rests on the belief that in all psychotherapy both participants have both therapist and patient vectors within them. Their concept received very little attention of a technical nature in the literature. According to these authors, therapist vectors are defined as responses to the needs of the immature part of the other person. Usually a therapist's responses are therapist-vector responses to the patient; at times, however, the patient will respond with therapist-vector responses to the relatively small (we hope), residual immature part of the therapist. Patient vectors are demands for the expression of feelings from the other person comparable to the demands of the hungry child for a response from his parents. It is obvious that the patient will get well only if the precondition is met that the therapist's patient vectors do not make excessive demands on the patient's therapist vectors.

Although Whitaker and Malone politely draw a contrast between the "gross pathological patient vectors of the immature therapist," and the "minimal, residual patient vectors in the mature therapist," their main point is that successful psychotherapy requires the therapist to bring along both his therapist and his patient vectors and to engage in a total participation with the patient. The therapist expands the frontier of his own emotional growth through the therapy; if he refuses to participate totally in this fashion, the patient experiences a rejection and therapy is a failure. Neither therapist nor patient may even be aware of what is happening. Many experienced psychotherapists seem to be able to confirm this by pointing out that in each successful psychotherapy they experience some aspect of further emotional growth, ego integration or maturation—often called "learning from the patient."

It is usually assumed that psychotherapy is in part an art merely because of our ignorance about the field. This assumption implies that as we gain more knowledge—or more precisely scientific understanding—of psychology and psychotherapy, the practice of psychotherapy will become more and more scientific, thereby approaching the ideal doctor-patient model in medicine.

I maintain that this generally held fundamental assumption is completely wrong and it accounts for much of the confusion and acrimony in our field as well as for unfair and invidious comparisons with other "more scientific" branches of medicine. For this assumption is based on a misconception about the nature of knowledge—notice that we are again back to the subject of metapsychiatry. This misconception, which has prevailed for centuries, currently appears as a squabble between the proponents of science and the proponents of the humanities, often defined as the two cultures. The usual answer to this squabble is that with understanding and time and patience the two cultures can become one.

Some authors have challenged this popular answer directly. For example, Levi (1963) bases the challenge on a study of the philosophy of Kant. He argues that the disagreements and differences between scientists and humanists are based upon ignoring the distinction already found in Kant. Science focuses on facts and basically relies upon a mechanistic formulation of the principles of causation. The humanities are teleological, dramatic and emotional, and they are oriented to human purposes in a manner that cannot be allowed by the impersonality and objectivity of science. Levi writes, "The avowed and willing anthropocentrism of the humanities is far removed from the neutral 'causation' of science." Scientists and humanists think differently and use different languages.

The language of science stresses true and false propositions, error, causality, law, prediction, fact and equilibrium of systems. The language of the humanistic imagination focuses upon destiny and human purpose, fate and fortune, tragedy and illusion. It is certainly possible to argue that depending on which critical faculty of the mind—imagination or understanding—is being employed, an entirely different map of what appears to be reality will emerge. One map will be sober and factual, claiming to be the custodian of literal truth, mechanistic and objective. The second will be mythical, teleological and dramatic and will deal more with concepts of creativity, destiny and human purpose. According to Levi the first will be based on Kant's synthetic *a priori* principles of the understanding, and the second will be based on Kant's concept of reproductive imagination from the *Critique of Pure Reason.*

It is not possible to carry this argument from Kant's philosophy much further. Actually, in Levi's interpretation there is considerable debatable extrapolation from Kant. At any rate, as Levi conceives of it, imagination is the human faculty from the active functioning of which the humanities stem, whereas science is based on the faculty that employs principles of cognitive understanding. The basic point is that scientific understanding and humanistic imagination are fundamentally different, utilize different languages, provide different maps of reality, and are grounded on different nuclear operations of the mind.

To construct objective, factual mechanistic chains of casual explanations, as well as to construct heuristic, often dramatic and anthropomorphic explanatory fictions, are both fundamental human cognitive needs. The great physicist Bohr (Heisenberg 1971) similarly distinguished among the languages of religion, science and art and suggested, "We ought to look upon these different forms as complementary descriptions, which though they exclude one another, are needed to convey the rich possibilities flowing from man's relationship with the central order." Thus the language of the imagination and the language of the understanding represent different ways of looking at the same sensory manifold (of course, *sensory manifold* is a term borrowed from Kant, although this argument is no longer being presented in Kantian terminology).

The special theory of psychotherapeutic interaction takes into account the different nuclear operations of the mind which may be used in organizing the sensory manifold and makes it more understandable how differences and arguments arise among observers of the sensory manifold depending on what operations they apply to it. We thus provide four roots of psychotherapeutic interactions instead of the usual two. This is because maps of the psychic fields interacting between the therapist and the patient must be described in a bilingual fashion and the languages must not be confused with each other. Each language selects a center for the psychic field of the therapist and another analogous center for that of the patient.

In the language of scientific understanding, the *therapist* may be described in terms of his ego operations, countertransference structure, therapist and patient vectors, and training in therapeutic technique. In this language the *patient* may be described in terms of his ego operations, a genetic-dynamic formulation, the structural theory of Freud, transference, and patient and therapist vectors. Thus a scientific understanding of the process of psychotherapy would have to examine the study of mutual influencing throughout the psychotherapy on both unconscious and conscious levels of the psychic fields of the therapist and the patient, using the descriptive terminology just outlined.

In the language of the humanistic imagination, which is much more dramatic and emotional and is oriented to human purposes, the two psychic fields would be described quite differently. Here we find terminologies such as the I-Thou relationship, self-actualization, the authentic life, the encounter, basic anxiety, the will to power, caring, presence, the capacity for trust, life-style, career line, and even Freud's famous statement that psychotherapy is a labor of love.

The quarrel between so-called opposing schools of psychotherapy will arise in the contrast that naturally emerges when the method of science or the method of the humanistic imagination is applied to the same sense data. The two maps of reality and descriptions of what is going on are not fundamentally opposed and may be used successfully to complement each other, provided the therapist is carefully aware when and why he is using each competing map. If this is possible, then a greater understanding of patient material and patient problems can be achieved and we can have greater depth or conception of how to present the most effective psychic field to the patient.

Obviously if this basic theoretical orientation is correct, a corresponding education in the language of the humanistic imagination will have to be provided for the psychotherapist so he may move comfortably from one map of the sensory manifold to the other—from the language of science to the language of creative imagination. Kinzie and Jurgensen (1976) have made an effort to apply this to the improvement of psychiatric education. The genius of Freud was often expressed in his remarkable capacity to move back and forth from the faculty of scientific investigation to the faculty of creative and humanistic imagination. Because of his unusually wide erudition and genius he often tended to switch back and forth between these languages in order to present as immediate and complete a description of the clinical phenomena as he could, and in addition his contemporary readers had a significantly broader background in the humanities than the average physician does today. What subsequently happened, of course, is that the two languages became confused in the minds of his less erudite followers and even more in the minds of general readers, so that a number of pseudoproblems arose, leading to various animosities that still exist.

An education strictly confined to the technique and practice of scientific psychotherapy tends toward a stability and a withdrawal from participation with the patient at a truly human level. On the other hand, an education too heavily weighted in the humanities and without the firm anchor of both scientific methodology and dedication to the medical physicianly vocation causes a profound loss of the scientific grounding and the objective observation aspects of psychotherapy, with a consequent serious tendency to misunderstand and even to go off the deep end and engage in bizarre and unjustifiable procedures with patients. Neither of these extremes is fair to the patient. *Both of them are exploitation and they represent a serious and inexcusable defect in the psychic field of the therapist.*

Furthermore, it is clear that psychotherapists will be more inclined to fail if all aspects of the psychotherapeutic interaction are not taken into account or not understood. The best insurance against failure in such cases would be the ability of the therapist to describe the interaction in both languages and to visualize maps of both psychic fields. Because of the limits of our knowledge or of our capacities, we can sometimes express success or failure in psychotherapy in one language, but not in the other. Thus a failure that seems inexplicable from the point of view of scientific understanding can sometimes be explained in the language of humanistic imagination and vice versa.

The highest, most abstract and least empirically verifiable level is of course that of metaphysics and metaphysical propositions—about Being, etc. Besides the powerful human tendency to push to the limits and transgress the boundaries of what can be known by reason, is there any other justification for our interest as psychotherapists in metaphysics? I believe there is. Just as appeal to the philosophy of science resolves some apparent paradoxes in the psychotherapy of borderline patients, certain aspects of metaphysics explain some of the clinical phenomena of borderline patients. This is forced upon us whether we like it or not, because these patients often present their complaints in the language level of metaphysics. They complain of innumerable "existential crises" and difficulties in their sense of Being and sense of aliveness; of alienation and isolation from the world, from man and from God; of preoccupation with nothingness and so on. It is wise not to just brush off such complaints—they are very meaningful to the patient and positively are *not* merely ways of expressing depression.

Let us appeal, then, to the level of discourse of metaphysics in an attempt to understand these complaints, which appear so strange and vague at the level of empirical clinical examination.

The rock bottom of the entire theory of Kant is founded on our inner awareness in time. All commentators on Kant agree with this. It is from this inner awareness that he deduces his whole architectonic. There is a parallel between Kant and Freud in that both agree that the phenomena of the conscious are knowable and that from these phenomena we have to deduce the existence of the stimuli from the unconscious or noumena, which are basically unknowable. Thus the id is knowable only through its derivatives in the ego. There are many difficulties in this view, but for our purposes what is very important to focus upon is the concept of the ego experience itself, which Kant called our inner awareness of ourselves in time.

Winnicott (1968) writes, "Good enough holding . . . facilitates the formation of a psychosomatic partnership in the infant. This contributes to the sense of 'real' as opposed to 'unreal.' Faulty handling militates against the development of muscle tone, and that which is called "coordination," and against the capacity of the infant to enjoy the experience of body functioning, and of Being. ... If the environment behaves well, the infant has a chance to maintain *a sense of continuity of Being;* perhaps this may go right back to the first stirrings in the womb. When this exists the individual has a stability that can be gained in no other way." What in psychodynamic terms is this sense of Being and the continuity of Being which is called a function of good enough holding in infants?

To answer, I (see also Chessick 1974b) am going to refer to Federn (1952) as translated by Weiss. It is not always clear where Federn is talking and where the translating, editing and introducing by Weiss is presenting Federn or Weiss. At any rate these authors present a difficult concept of the ego as a subjective experience. They label this subjective experience the ego experience *(Icherlebnis).*

This phenomenon of the ego's experience of itself cannot be clearly explained. As long as the ego functions normally one may ignore or be unaware of its functioning. As Federn says, normally there is no more awareness of the ego than of the air one breathes; only when respiration becomes burdensome is the lack of air recognized. The subjective ego experience includes the feeling of unity, continuity, contiguity and causality in the experiences of the individual. In waking life the sensation of one's own ego is omnipresent, and it undergoes continuous changes in quality and intensity.

Federn sometimes distinguishes clearly and very carefully between ego consciousness *(Ichbewüsstsein)* and ego feeling *(Ichgefühl).* He writes, "Ego feeling is the sensation, constantly present, of one's own person—the ego's own perception of itself . . . we can distinguish, often accurately, between ego *feeling* and ego *consciousness.* Ego consciousness, in the pure state, remains only when there is a deficiency in ego feeling. And the mere empty knowledge of one's self is already a pathological state, known as estrangement or depersonalization."

Ego consciousness represents an enduring feeling in our knowledge that our ego is continuous and persistent despite interruptions by sleep or unconsciousness. We feel that the processes within us, even though they be interrupted by forgetting or unconsciousness, have a persistent origin within us and that our body and our psyche belong permanently to our ego. Ego consciousness is an entity involving the continuity of a person in respect to time, space and causality, and the sense of ego consciousness plays a central role in the argument of Kant's *Critique of Pure Reason.*

Ego feeling, however, is the "totality of feeling which one has in one's own living person. It is the residual experience which persists after all the subtraction of all ideational contents—a state which, in practice, occurs only for a very brief time. ... Ego feeling, therefore, is the simplest and yet the most comprehensive psychic state which is produced in the personality by the fact of its own existence even in the absence of internal stimuli."

To say the least, this is an extremely important and neglected concept for both philosophers and psychotherapists. Federn explains that ego feeling is quite different than new knowledge of one's self or of consciousness of the ego at work—it is primarily a *feeling* or *sensation* normally taken for granted. This is parallel to Heidegger's (1954) explanation that "The Being of beings is the most apparent; and yet, we normally do not see it—and if we do, only with difficulty." Furthermore, both Heidegger and Federn would agree that ". . . even the clearest *knowledge* of one's ego is experienced as something insufficient, uncomfortable, incomplete, and unsatisfying, even akin to fear. . ."

Freud (1917) used the same term ego feeling (*Ichgefühl*) in *Mourning and Melancholia,* but he used it to mean something akin to self-esteem, which is of course quite different. Also, notice that I am not discussing or advocating Federn's theory that schizophrenia represents a deficiency of ego libido at all—for this is a different discussion and a much more controversial concept. In general, Federn's thinking is ingenious and original but semantically confused, as others have noticed.

The notion of ego feeling *is* extremely important to our modern work with borderline patients. The capacity to develop mature and secure relationships with other individuals and a strong sense of inner sustainment is grounded on a healthy ego feeling. The ego defect so frequently talked about in vague terms in describing the borderline patient to a great extent is a defect in ego feeling. The cause of this defect, or, as we may call it philosophically, disturbance in the sense of

Being, can be traced clinically in the borderline patient to a lack of good enough holding in infancy. The result of such a falling away from Being is that relationships become more "uncherishing" and come to partake of the quality Buber calls I-It; the individual often becomes immersed in an obsessive search for something he intuitively knows is missing but cannot describe clearly in words.

Heidegger spent his life in an obsessive intellectual search for Being, which he projects at least in part outside himself and which he can never find. In this, he is like the typical borderline patient, who is able to function very well in business and mundane matters, but, for example, finds herself obsessed with the need for holding as in the series of women described by Hollender (1970; Hollender et al. 1969, 1970) and a search for the magical sensation this produces. At an extremely primitive level, these patients are searching for a temporary sense of relatedness and ego feeling that is basically missing in them and cannot be replaced with any kind of intellectual or verbal exchange.

Those who have not experienced such problems clinically have an extremely hard time understanding this set of concepts. The patients have to teach us. As Heidegger (1953) put it, "But an age which regards as real only what goes fast and can be clutched with both hands looks on questioning as 'remote from reality' and as something that does not pay, whose benefits cannot be numbered. But the essential is not number; the essential is right time, i.e. the right moment, and the right perseverance."

We have come a long distance in our discussion of the borderline patient in this book, from Kraepelinean descriptive psychiatry all the way to metaphysics. If a therapist has thoroughly grasped all the concepts discussed in this book and has accumulated twenty years of experience in working with borderline patients, he may feel secure that he has acquired 10 percent of the preparation necessary to practice psychotherapy. The other 90 percent can only be acquired by a thorough intensive personal psychotherapy of the psychotherapist.

References

Adler, G. 1973. Hospital treatment of patients with borderline personality organization. *International Journal of Psyco-Analysis* 49: 600-619.

Appelbaum, A. 1975. Transactions of the Topeka Psychoanalytic Society. *Bulletin of the Menninger Clinic* 19: 384-390.

Arieti, S. 1974. *Interpretation of Schizophrenia.* New York: Basic Books.

Balint, M. 1953. *Primary Love and Psychoanalytic Technique.* New York: Liveright.

———. 1968. *The Basic Fault: Therapeutic Aspects of Regression.* London: Tavistock.

Basch, M. 1973. Psychoanalysis and theory formation. In *Annual of Psychoanalysis* 1: 39-52.

———. 1975. Toward a theory that encompasses depression: A revision of existing casual hypotheses in psychoanalysis. In *Depression and Human Existence,* ed. E. Anthony and T. Benedeck. Boston: Little, Brown.

Blum, H. 1973. The concept of erotized transference. *Journal of the American Psychoanalytic Association* 21: 61-76.

Bohr, N. 1934. *Atomic Theory and the Description of Nature.* Cambridge, Mass.: Cambridge University Press.

Breuer, J., and Freud, S. 1895. Studies on Hysteria, *Standard Edition.* 2: 1-305 (1955).

Brodey, W. 1965. On the dynamics of narcissism. Externalization and early ego development. *Psychoanalytic Study of the Child* 20: 165-193.

Cary, G. 1972. The borderline condition. *Psychoanalytic Review* 59: 33-54.

Chessick, R. 1966. Office psychotherapy of borderline patients. *American Journal of Psychotherapy* 20: 600-614.

————. 1968. Crucial dilemma of the therapist in psychotherapy of borderline patients. *American Journal of Psychotherapy* 22: 655-666.

————. 1969. *How Psychotherapy Heals.* New York: Jason Aronson.

————. 1971a. Amaurosis schacchistica. *American Journal of Psychotherapy* 25: 309-311.

————. 1971b. The use of the couch in psychotherapy of borderline patients. *Archives of Psychiatry* 25: 306-313.

————. 1972a. Angiopastic retinopathy. *Archives of Psychiatry* 27: 241-244.

————. 1972b. Externational and existential anguish. *Archives of Psychiatry* 27: 764-770.

————. 1971c. *Why Psychotherapists Fail.* New York: Jason Aronson.

————. 1973. Contributions to ego psychology from the treatment of borderline patients. *Medikon* 2: 20-21.

————. 1974a. Defective ego feeling and the quest for Being in the borderline patient. *International Journal of Psychoanalytic Psychotherapy* 3: 73-89.

————. 1974b. *The Technique and Practice of Intensive Psychotherapy.* New York: Jason Aronson.

————. 1975. The borderline patient. In *American Handbook of Psychiatry,* 2nd ed., ed. S. Arieti. New York: Basic Books.

————. 1977a. *Great Ideas in Psychotherapy* New York: Jason Aronson.

————. 1977b. *Agonie: Diary of a Twentieth Century Man* Ghent, Belgium: European Press.

————. 1977c. The coronary-prone personality. *Medikon International* 6: 17-20.

Deutsch, H. 1965. Some forms of emotional disturbances and their relationship to schizophrenia. In *Neuroses and Character Types.* New York: International Universities Press.

DeWald, P. (1964). *Psychotherapy.* New York: Basic Books.

————. 1972. The clinical assessment of structural change. *Journal of the American Psychoanalytic Association* 20: 302-324.

Erikson, E. 1959. *Identity and the Life Cycle.* New York: International Universities Press.

Evans, R. 1973. *Jean Piaget.* New York: Dutton.

Federn, P. 1952. *Ego Psychology and the Psychoses.* New York: Basic Books.

Ferenczi, S. 1950. Stages in the development of the sense of reality. In *Selected Papers,* vol. 1. New York: Basic Books.

Fairbairn, R. 1952. *Object Relations Theory of the Personality.* New York: Basic Books.

Freud, A. 1965. *Normality and Pathology in Childhood.* New York: International Universities Press.

References   289

———. 1969. Difficulties in the path of psychoanalysis. In *Writings of Anna Freud,* vol. 7. New York: International Universities Press.

Freud, S. 1895. Project for a scientific psychology. *Standard Edition* 1: 283-387 (1966).

———. 1909. Notes upon a case of obsessional neurosis. *Standard Edition* 10: 153-318 (1957).

———. 1913. On beginning the treatment. *Standard Edition* 12: 121-144 (1958).

———. 1914a. On narcissism. *Standard Edition* 14: 67-104 (1957).

———. 1914b. On the history of the psychoanalytic movement. *Standard Edition* 14: 3-66 (1957).

———. 1915. Observations on transference love. *Standard Edition* 12: 157-171 (1958).

———. 1917. Mourning and melancholia. *Standard Edition* 14: 237-258 (1957).

———. 1923. The ego and the id. *Standard Edition* 19: 3-68 (1961).

———. 1924. Economic problems of masochism. *Standard Edition* 19: 157-172 (1961).

———. 1927. Fetishism. *Standard Edition* 21: 149-158 (1961).

———. 1938. An outline of psycho-analysis. *Standard Edition* 23: 141-208 (1964).

———. 1940. Splitting of the ego in the process of defense. *Standard Edition* 23: 271-278 (1964).

Friedenberg, E. 1974. *R. D. Laing.* New York: Viking Press.

Friedman, H. 1975. Psychotherapy of borderline patients. *American Journal of Psychiatry* 132: 1048-1051.

Friedman, L. 1975. Current psychoanalytic object relations theory and its clinical implications. *International Journal of Psychoanalysis* 56: 137-146.

Frosch, J. 1971. Technique in regard to some specific ego defects in the treatment of borderline patients. *Psychiatry Quarterly* 35: 216-220.

Gedo, H., and Goldberg, A. 1973. *Models of the Mind.* Chicago: University of Chicago Press.

Giovacchini, P. 1965. Transference, incorporation, and synthesis. *International Journal of Psychoanalysis* 46: 287-296.

———. 1967a. The frozen introject. *International Journal of Psychoanalysis* 48: 61-67.

———. 1967b. Frustration and externalization. *Psychoanalytic Quarterly* 36: 571-583.

———. 1972. *Tactics and Techniques in Psychoanalytic Therapy.* New York: Jason Aronson.

————. 1973. Character disorders: with special reference to the borderline state. *International Journal of Psychoanalytic Psychotherapy* 2: 7-20.

————. 1975a. *Psychoanalysis of Character Disorders.* New York: Jason Aronson.

————. 1975b. *Tactics and Techniques in Psychoanalytic Therapy II: Countertransference.* New York: Jason Aronson.

Gitelson, M. 1962. On the curative factors in the first phase of analysis. In *Psychoanalysis.* New York: International Universities Press.

————. 1963. The problem of character neurosis. *Journal of the Hillside Hospital* 12: 3-17.

————. 1973. *Psychoanalysis: Science and Profession.* New York: International Universities Press.

Goldberg, A. 1975. Narcissism and the readiness for psychotherapy termination. *Archives of Psychiatry* 32: 695-704.

Greenacre, P. 1963. Problems of acting out in the transference relationship. *Journal of the American Academy of Childhood Psychiatry* 2: 144-172.

Greenson, R. 1958. Screen defences, screen hunger, screen identity. *Journal of the American Psychoanalytic Association* 6: 242-262.

Grinker, R. 1955. Growth, inertia, shame. *International Journal of Psychoanalysis* 36: 242-253.

————. 1975. *Psychiatry in Broad Perspective.* New York: International Universities Press.

Grinker, R., Werble, B. and Drye, R. 1968. *The Borderline Syndrome.* New York: Basic Books.

Gunderson, J., and Singer, N. 1975. Defining borderline patients. *American Journal of Psychiatry* 132: 1-10.

Guntrip, H. 1968. *Schizoid Phenomena, Object Relations and the Self.* New York: International Universities Press.

Hartmann, H. 1950. Comments on the psychoanalytic theory of the ego. *Psychoanalytic Study of the Child* 5: 74-96.

————. 1964. *Essays on Ego Psychology.* New York: International Universities Press.

Hartmann, H., and Lowenstein, R. 1962. Notes on the superego. *Psychoanalytic Study of the Child* 17: 42-81.

Havens, L. 1974. On the existential use of the self. *American Journal of Psychiatry* 13: 1-10.

Heidegger, M. 1953. *An Introduction to Metaphysics.* New York: Basic Books.

————. 1954. *What is Called Thinking?* New York: Harper and Row.

Heimann, P. (1966). Comment on Dr. Kernberg's paper. *International Journal of Psychoanalysis* 56: 137-146.

Heisenberg, W. 1971. *Physics and Beyond.* New York: Harper and Row.

Hoch, P., and Catell, J. 1959. The diagnosis of pseudoneurotic schizophrenia. *Psychiatric Quarterly* 33: 17-43.

Hoch, P., Catell, J., Strahl, M. and Pennes, H. 1962. The course and outcome of pseudoneurotic schizophrenia. *American Journal of Psychiatry* 119: 106-115.

Hoch, P., and Polatin, P. 1949. Pseudoneurotic forms of schizophrenia. *Psychiatric Quarterly* 23: 248-276.

Hollender, M. 1970. The need or wish to be held. *Archives of General Psychiatry* 22: 445-453.

————, Luborsky, L., and Harvey, R. 1970. Correlates of the desire to be held in women. *Psychosomatic Research* 14: 387-390.

————, Luborsky, L., and Scaramella, T. 1969. Body contact and sexual enticement. *Archives of General Psychiatry* 20: 188-191.

Holton, G. 1973. *Thematic Origins of Scientific Thought.* Cambridge, Mass.: Harvard University Press.

Husserl, E. 1965. *Phenomenology and the Crisis of Philosophy.* New York: Harper Torchbooks.

Jacobson, E. 1964. *The Self and the Object World.* New York: International Universities Press.

Jaspers, K. 1963. *General Psychopathology.* Chicago: University of Chicago Press.

Kahn, M. 1974. *The Privacy of the Self.* New York: International Universities Press.

Kernberg, O. 1966. Structural derivatives of object relationships. *International Journal of Psychoanalysis* 47: 236-253.

————. 1967. Borderline personality organization. *Journal of the American Psychoanalytic Association* 15: 641-685.

————. 1968. The treatment of patients with borderline personality organization. *International Journal of the Psychoanalysis* 49: 600-619.

————. 1970a. Factors in the psychoanalytic treatment of narcissistic personalities. *Journal of the American Psychoanalytic Association* 18: 24-50.

————. 1970b. A psychoanalytic classification of character pathology. *Journal of the American Psychoanalytic Association* 18: 800-822.

————. 1971. Prognostic considerations regarding borderline personality organization. *Journal of the American Psychoanalytic Association* 19: 595-635.

————. 1972a. Early ego integration and object relations. *Annals of the N.Y. Academy of Sciences* 193: 233-247.

————. 1972b. The Kleinian school. In *Tactics and Techniques in Psychoanalytic Therapy,* ed. P. Giovacchini. New York: Jason Aronson.

————. 1973. Psychoanalytic object relations theory. In *Annual of Psychoanalysis*, vol. 1, New York: Quadrangle Books.

————. 1974a. Contrasting viewpoints regarding the nature and psychoanalytic treatment of narcissistic personalities. *Journal of the American Psychoanalytic Association* 22: 255-267.

————. 1974b. Further contributions to the treatment of narcissistic personalities. *International Journal of Psychoanalysis* 55: 215-240.

————. 1975a. *Borderline Conditions and Pathological Narcissism.* New York: Jason Aronson.

————. 1975b. Further contributions reply to discussion. *International Journal of Psychoanalysis* 56: 245-248.

Kinzie, J., and Jurgensen, R. 1976. Modes of experience and psychiatric education. *American Journal of Psychotherapy* 30: 276-288.

Knight, R. 1953. Borderline states. In *Drives, Affects, Behavior,* ed. R. Lowenstein. New York: International Universities Press.

————. 1962a. Borderline states. In *Psychoanalytic Psychiatry and Psychology.* New York: International Universities Press.

————. 1962b. Management and psychotherapy of the borderline schizophrenic patient. In *Psychoanalytic Psychiatry and Psychology.* New York: International Universities Press.

Kohut, H. 1959. Introspection, empathy and psychoanalysis. *Journal of the American Psychoanalytic Association* 7: 459-483.

————. 1966. The forms and transformations of narcissism. *Journal of the American Psychoanalytic Association* 12: 243-272.

————. 1971. *The Analysis of the Self.* New York: International Universities Press.

————. 1972. Thoughts on narcissism and narcissistic rage. *The Psychoanalytic Study of the Child* 27: 360-400.

Kuhn, T. 1972. *The Structure of Scientific Revolutions.* Chicago: University of Chicago Press.

Langer, S. 1942. *Philosophy in a New Key.* New York: Mentor Books.

Lazare, A. 1971. The hysterical character in psychoanalytic theory. *Archives of General Psychiatry* 25: 131-137.

Leuba, J. 1949. Introduction à L'etude Clinique du Narcissisme. *Revue Francaise de Psychoanalyse T.* XIII, 4: 456.

Levi, A. 1963. *The Six Great Humanistic Essays of John Stuart Mill.* New York: Washington Square Press.

Little, M. 1966. Transference in borderline states. *International Journal of Psychoanalysis* 47: 476-485.

Loewenstein, R. 1972. Ego autonomy and psychoanalytic technique. *Psychoanalytic Quarterly* 41: 1-23.

Mack, J. 1975. *Borderline States in Psychiatry*. New York: Grune and Stratton.

Mahler, W. 1952. Child psychoses and schizophrenia. *Psychoanalytic Study of the Child* 7: 286-305.

———. 1963. Thoughts about development and individuation. *Psychoanalytic Study of the Child* 18: 307-324.

———. 1971. A study of the separation-individuation process. *Psychoanalytic Study of the Child* 26: 403-424.

———. 1974. Symbiosis and individuation. *Psychoanalytic Study of the Child* 29: 89-106.

———. 1975. *On Human Symbiosis and the Vicissitudes of Individuation*. New York: International Universities Press.

Mahler, M., et al., 1975. *Psychological Birth of the Human Infant*. New York: Basic Books.

Mahler, M., and Gosslinger, B. 1955. On symbiotic child psychoses. *Psychoanalytic Study of the Child* 10: 195-212.

Mahler, M., and LaPerrier, K. 1965. Mother-child interaction during separation-individuation. *Psychoanalytic Quarterly* 34: 483-498.

Maltsberger, J., and Buie, D. 1974. Countertransference hate in the treatment of suicidal patients. *Archives of Psychiatry* 30: 625-633.

Masterson, J. 1972. *The Treatment of the Borderline Adolescent*. New York: Wiley.

Masterson, J., and Rinsley, D. 1975. The borderline syndrome. *International Journal of Psychoanalysis* 56: 163-178.

Meissner, W. 1974. Correlative aspects of introjective and projective mechanisms. *American Journal of Psychiatry* 131: 176-180.

Meyer, L. 1974. Concerning the sciences, the arts, and the humanities. *Critical Inquiry* 1: 163.

Modell, A. 1963. Primitive object relationships and the predisposition to schizophrenia. *International Journal of Psychoanalysis* 44: 282-292.

———. 1968. *Object Love and Reality*. New York: International Universities Press.

———. 1975a. The ego and the id: Fifty years later. *International Journal of Psychoanalysis* 56: 57-68.

———. 1975b. A narcissistic defense against affects and the illusion of self-sufficiency. *International Journal of Psychoanalysis* 56: 137-146.

Murphy, W. 1973. Narcissistic problems in patients and therapists. *International Journal of Psychoanalytic Psychotherapy* 2: 113-124.

Murray, J. 1964. Narcissism and the ego ideal. *Journal of the American Psychoanalytic Association* 12: 477-511.

Nacht, S. 1963. The non-verbal relationship in psychoanalytic treatment. *International Journal of Psychoanalysis* 44: 328-333.

———. 1969. Reflections on the evolution of psychoanalytic knowledge. *Psychoanalysis* 50: 597.

Nagera, H. 1967. The concepts of structure and structuralization. *Psychoanalytic Study of the Child* 22: 77-102.

Nef, J. 1967. *The United States and Civilization.* Chicago: University of Chicago Press.

Odier, C. 1956. *Anxiety and Magic Thinking.* New York: International Universities Press.

Ornstein, P. 1973. On narcissism. *Bulletin of the Philadelphia Association for Psychoanalysis* 23: 327-329.

———. 1974a. Discussion of the paper by Otto Kernberg. *International Journal of Psychoanalysis* 55: 241-247.

———. 1974b. On narcissism: Beyond the introduction. *Annual of Psychoanalysis* 2: 127-149.

Piaget, J., and Inhelder, B. 1966. *The Psychology of the Child.* New York: Basic Books.

Pfeiffer, E. 1974. Borderline states. *Diseases of Nervous System* (May) 212-219.

Pruyser, P. 1974. What splits in "splitting?" A scrutiny of the concept of splitting in psychoanalysis and psychiatry. *Bulletin of the Menninger Clinic* 39: 1-46.

Pulaski, M. 1971. *Understanding Piaget.* New York: Harper and Row.

Rangell, L. 1955. Panel Report in the *Journal of the American Psychoanalytic Association* 3: 285-298.

Rapaport, D. 1944. The scientific methodology of psychoanalysis. *Collected Papers,* ed. M. Gill. New York: Basic Books (1967).

———. 1951. The autonomy of the ego. *Bulletin of the Menninger Clinic* 15: 113-123.

Riesman, D., Denney, R. and Glazer, N. 1955. *The Lonely Crowd.* New York: Doubleday.

Russell, B. 1967. *Autobiography,* vol. 1. Boston: Little, Brown.

Sadow, L. 1969. Ego axis in psychopathology. *Archives of General Psychiatry* 21: 15-24.

Saul, L. 1958. *The Technique and Practice of Psychoanalysis.* Philadelphia: Lippincott.

———. 1970. Inner sustainment. *Psychoanalytic Quarterly* 39: 215-222.

Schafer, R. 1968. *Aspects of Internalization.* New York: International Universities Press.

Schmideberg, M. (1955). The borderline patient. In *American Handbook of Psychiatry,* vol. 1, ed. S. Arieti. New York: Basic Books.

Spitz, R. (1965). *The First Year of Life.* New York: International Universities Press.

Stern, A. 1938. Psychoanalytic investigation of and therapy in a borderline group of neuroses. *Psychoanalytic Quarterly* 7: 467-489.

————. 1945. A psychoanalytic therapy in the borderline neuroses. *Psychoanalytic Quarterly* 14: 190-198.

————. 1948. Transference in the borderline neuroses. *Psychoanalytic Quarterly* 17: 527-528.

Stone, L. 1961. *The Psychoanalytic Situation.* New York: International Universities Press.

Strupp, H. 1973. *Psychotherapy, Clinical Research, and Theoretical Issues.* New York: Jason Aronson.

————. 1975. Psychoanalysis "focal psychotherapy" and the nature of the therapeutic influence. *Archives of Psychiatry* 32: 127-135.

Ticho, E. 1970. Differences between psychoanalysis and psychotherapy. *Bulletin of the Menninger Clinic* 34: 128-138.

Toffler, A. 1970. *Future Shock.* New York: Random House.

Toulmin, S. 1960. *Philosophy of Science.* New York: Harper Torchbooks.

Tower, L. 1956. Countertransference. *Journal of the American Psychoanalytic Association* 4: 224-255.

Waelder, R. 1960. *Basic Theory of Psychoanalysis.* New York: International Universities Press.

Wangh, M. 1974. Concluding remarks on technique and prognosis in the treatment of narcissism. *Journal of the American Psychoanalytic Association* 22: 307-309.

Weiner, N. 1973. The ego ideal and melancholia. *Bulletin of the Department of Mental Health Sciences, Hahnemann Medical College and Hospital* 2: 4-17.

Whitaker, C., and Malone, T. 1953. *The Roots of Psychotherapy.* Philadelphia: Blakiston.

Wilie, D. 1972. Negative countertransference, therapist discouragement. *International Journal of Psychoanalytic Psychotherapy* 1: 36-67.

Winnicott, D. 1951. Transitional object and transitional phenomena. *Collected Papers.* New York: Basic Books.

————. 1958. *Collected Papers.* New York: Basic Books.

————. 1965. *The Maturational Processes and the Facilitating Environment.* New York: International Universities Press.

————. 1968. *The Family and Individual Development.* London: Tavistock.

Wolberg, A. 1973. *The Borderline Patient*. New York: International Medical Book Corporation.

Zavitzianos, G. 1974. Transference, therapeutic alliance and the principle of multiple function of the ego. *Journal of the Philadelphia Association for Psychoanalysis* 1: 298-313.

Zetzel, E. 1971. A developmental approach to the borderline patient. *American Journal of Psychiatry* 128: 867-871.

Zetzel, E., and Meissner, W. 1973. *Basic Concepts of Psychoanalytic Psychiatry*. New York: Basic Books.

Zucker, O. 1963. Psychoanalytic assessment of ego weakness. *American Journal of Psychotherapy* 17: 275-285.

Index